PRO/CON VOLUME 4

ENVIRONMENT

Published 2002 by Grolier Educational
Sherman Turnpike
Danbury, Connecticut 06816

© 2002 Brown Partworks Limited

Library of Congress Cataloging-in-Publication Data

Pro/con
p. cm
Includes bibliographical references and index.
Contents: v. 1. The individual and society – v. 2. Government – v. 3. Economics – v.
4. Environment – v. 5. Science – v. 6. Media.
ISBN 0-7172-5638-3 (set : alk. paper) – ISBN 0-7172-5639-1 (vol. 1 : alk. paper) –
ISBN 0-7172-5640-5 (vol. 2 : alk. paper) – ISBN 0-7172-5641-3 (vol. 3 : alk. paper) –
ISBN 0-7172-5642-1 (vol. 4 : alk. paper) – ISBN 0-7172-5643-X (vol. 5 : alk. paper) –
ISBN 0-7172-5644-8 (vol. 6 : alk. paper)
1. Social problems. I. Grolier Educational (Firm)

HN17.5 P756 2002
361.1–dc21

2001053234

Printed and bound in Singapore

SET ISBN 0-7172-5638-3
VOLUME ISBN 0-7172-5642-1

For Brown Partworks Limited
Project Editors: Aruna Vasudevan, Fiona Plowman
Editors: Sally McFall, Matt Turner
Consultant Editors: John M. Byrne, Projects Director,
Center for a Sustainable Future, Shelburne, Vermont
Bradley F. Smith, Dean, Huxley College of the Environment,
Western Washington University
Keith A. Wheeler, Executive Director,
Center for a Sustainable Future, Shelburne, Vermont
Designer: Sarah Williams
Picture Researcher: Clare Newman
Set Index: Kay Ollerenshaw

Managing Editor: Tim Cooke
Design Manager: Lynne Ross
Production Manager: Matt Weyland

GENERAL PREFACE

"All that is necessary for evil to triumph is for good men to do nothing."
—Edmund Burke, 18th-century British political philosopher

Decisions

Life is full of choices and decisions. Some are more important than others. Some affect only your daily life—the route you take to school, for example, or what you prefer to eat for supper—while others are more abstract and concern questions of right and wrong rather than practicality. That does not mean that your choice of presidential candidate or your views on abortion are necessarily more important than your answers to purely personal questions. But it is likely that those wider questions are more complex and subtle and that you therefore will need to know more information about the subject before you can try to answer them. They are also likely to be questions about which you might have to justify your views to other people. In order to do that, you need to be able to make informed decisions, be able to analyze every fact at your disposal, and evaluate them in an unbiased manner.

What is *Pro/Con*?

Pro/Con is a collection of debates that presents conflicting views on some of the more complex and general issues facing Americans today. By bringing together extracts from a wide range of sources—mainstream newspapers and magazines, books, famous speeches, legal judgments, religious tracts, government surveys—the set reflects current informed attitudes toward dilemmas that range from the best way to feed the world's growing population to gay rights, and from the connection between political freedom and capitalism to the fate of Napster.

The people whose arguments make up the set are all acknowledged experts in their fields, and that makes the vast differences in their points of view even more remarkable. The arguments are presented in the form of debates for and against various propositions, such as "Does Global Warming Threaten Humankind?" or "Should the Media Be Subject to Censorship?" This question format reflects the way in which ideas often occur in daily life: in the classroom, on TV shows, in business meetings, or even in state or federal politics.

The contents

The subjects of the six volumes of the set—*Individual and Society, Government, Economics, Environment, Science*, and *Media*—are issues on which it is preferable that people's opinions are based on information rather than simply on personal bias.

Special boxes throughout *Pro/Con* comment on the debates as you are reading them, pointing out facts or analyzing arguments to help you think about what is being said.

Introductions and summaries also provide background information that might help you reach your own conclusions. There are also comments and tips about how to structure an argument that you can apply on an everyday basis to any debate or conversation, learning how to present your point of view as effectively and persuasively as possible.

VOLUME PREFACE
Environment

While most people generally agree in principle that it is important to look after the environment, there is disagreement and strong debate about how exactly that should be done. Although governments frame laws and regulations to protect the environment, they may in turn conflict with other interests such as voters' rights. The subject of the environment therefore brings with it dilemmas, and these issues form the content of this volume.

Environment on the agenda

Thirty years ago protecting the environment was not high on the agenda in the United States. Foul air, water, and soil were tolerated as an acceptable trade-off for the economic prosperity that polluting industries provided. Public awareness about threats to the environment grew largely through the work of environmental organizations like Greenpeace and initiatives like Earth Day, the day set aside each year to concentrate on environmental concerns. Gradually the political will developed to protect the environment through legislation.

As a result the quality of the environment improved, and fresh economic opportunities were created, for example, with new technologies for cleaning up factory emissions and major projects to build municipal wastewater treatment systems and solid waste disposal facilities. An entirely new sector of environmental lawyers, scientists, and officials appeared.

At the beginning of the 21st century the world faces a different set of environmental challenges. The experience of the past 30 years has shown that the environment is inextricably linked to our social and economic systems. Problems therefore need to be addressed in ways that are beneficial to all three areas. For example, air quality can be improved in urban neighborhoods by switching diesel bus engines over to burn propane or natural gas. This eliminates particles that are harmful to breathe, benefits lower-income people who use public transportation more than average and are most exposed to diesel bus exhaust, and creates new economic opportunities for the entrepreneurs introducing the necessary technology.

Deciding how to create such solutions is our biggest challenge, and we face it in a very different world from that which existed during the first Earth Day in 1970. The planet is now closely connected via communications technology like the Internet. World population has grown to around six billion and is predicted to double by the mid-21st century. It is imperative that we work as a global community to address environmental issues.

Pro/Con

The topics included in this volume address the environmental dilemmas citizens and policymakers face in the 21st century in terms of ethics, economics, and regulations. As well as presenting the for and against arguments in a fair context, the volume also highlights the severity of problems such as global warming and the importance of taking action to nurture a healthy environment for the future.

HOW TO USE THIS BOOK

Each volume of *Pro/Con* is divided into sections, each of which has an introduction that examines its theme. Within each section are a series of debates that present arguments for and against a proposition, such as whether or not the death penalty should be abolished. An introduction to each debate puts it into its wider context, and a summary and key map (see below) highlight the main points of the debate clearly and concisely. Each debate has marginal boxes that focus on particular points, give tips on how to present an

argument, or help question the writer's case. The summaries to the debates have supplementary material to help you do further research.

Boxes and other materials provide additional background information. There are also special materials on how to improve your debating and writing skills. At the end of each book is a glossary that provides brief explanations of key words in the volume. The index covers all six books, so it will help you trace topics throughout the set.

background information
Frequent text boxes provide background information on important concepts and key individuals or events.

summary boxes
Summary boxes are useful reminders of both sides of the argument.

further information
Further Reading lists for each debate direct you to related books, articles, and websites so you can do your own research.

other articles in the *Pro/Con* series
See also boxes list related debates throughout the *Pro/Con* series.

marginal boxes
Margin boxes highlight key points in the argument, give extra information, or help you question the author's meaning.

key map
Key maps provide a graphic representation of the central points of the debate.

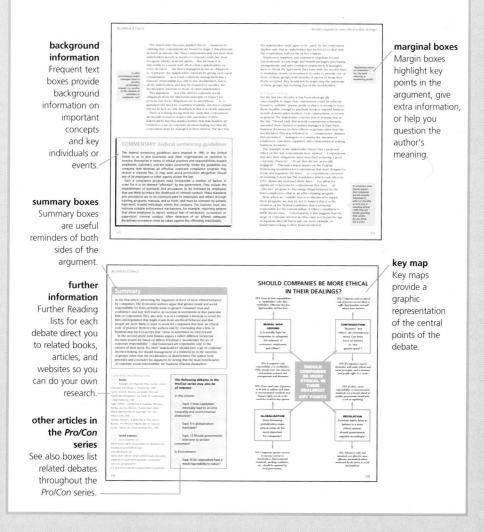

CONTENTS

ISSUES AND OPTIONS

People have always been concerned about their effect on the environment. The ancient Greeks, for example, complained about the effects of deforestation, which led to the erosion of hillsides, the silting of rivers, and the abandonment of ports. In the last 250 years anxiety has intensified. The industrial revolution (c.1760–1830) heralded the growth of industry, increased urbanization, and motorized transportation. The result was a rapid depletion of natural resources, such as oil, gas, and wood, and a growth in damaging pollutants, such as carbon monoxide and nitrogen oxides.

By the late 20th century it was apparent that the effects of pollution included a hole in the ozone layer, acid rain, and global warming. Human activity now threatens to destroy the very things that the increasing population needs to survive: clear air, clean water, natural resources, and adequate and healthy food supplies.

The articles in this section focus on some basic issues of environmental studies: global warming, overpopulation, famine and hunger, organic foods, and the wilderness. Similarly important issues are looked at in the other sections in this book.

Global warming

Global warming is caused by the release of greenhouse gases—from burning fossil fuels and various other human activities—into the atmosphere. The gases trap heat close to Earth, rather than letting it escape into space, resulting in a rise in global temperatures. The United States generates more greenhouse gases than any other country. The international community is trying to develop a protocol to decrease emissions (see box on Kyoto Protocol, page 90).

In Topic 1, *Does global warming threaten humankind?* Tom Jackson argues that an increasingly warm climate will result in diseases and other serious medical disorders. Tropical diseases such as malaria, and dengue and yellow fevers will spread farther north, while poverty and malnutrition will worsen in developing countries. Thomas Gale Moore, on the other hand, argues that global warming will result in better conditions for human health and prosperity.

Overpopulation and famine

In 1798 the English economist Thomas R. Malthus (1766–1834) wrote his *Essay on the Principles of Population*. He argued that unless population growth was checked, it would outstrip food resources and result in famine. Now that industrialization and advances in science and medicine (see *Science* volume) have led to lower infant mortality rates, the world population is booming. Around 250,000 babies are born each day,, and the United Nations Population Fund predicts that by the middle of the 21st century the world's population will be around nine billion people. Overpopulation could be disastrous for the planet, leading to increased urbanization, pollution, and a higher demand for food. In Topic 2, *Should the human population be stabilized?* Bill McKibben argues that the increasing population and subsequent use of energy and resources have had

value of their food, the dangers of pesticides, and the effects of what they eat on the environment. The popularity of organic food—produced without the use of artificial fertilizers or pesticides—is rising. A June 2000 survey showed that some 69 percent of Americans thought that an organic label meant a product was better for them and the environment. The Organic Consumers Association estimated that 10 million U.S. shoppers would buy

"Everybody can do something toward creating in his own environment ... happiness rather than misery."
—BERTRAND RUSSELL, PHILOSOPHER

catastrophic effects on the climate and that this must be controlled through population stabilization, among other things. Rod Andreason, however, examines the 1994 International Conference on Population and Development (IPCD) and attempts to show some of the hazards involved in population control.

Topic 3 asks *Are famine and hunger avoidable?* The Share International article argues that there is enough food to feed the entire world—the real problem is one of distribution. Lester Brown, however, asserts that famine and world hunger are inevitable and that governments across the world must address the issue before it leads to political and social instability.

Organic foods

While many of the world's population are concerned with how they are going to eat, a growing group is concerned with what they eat—the nutritional

around $8 billion worth of organic food in 2001. In Topic 4, *Is organic food better than other food?* Ronnie Cummins of the Organic Consumers Association argues that concern about pesticides, food poisoning, and the environment has led more Americans to buy organic products. Dennis Avery, in contrast, warns that organic food is no more nutritious than conventionally grown foodstuffs.

Wilderness

National parks were introduced in 1872 to protect wildlife and wilderness, but there has been increasing debate about whether the parks perform their designated function. John C. Miles describes how national parks conserve large tracts of land for native flora and fauna to exist. However, Nathan Page argues that that the balance of native animals has been upset in order to cater to visitors' tastes.

All of the topics in this section raise important issues for debate.

Topic 1
DOES GLOBAL WARMING THREATEN HUMANKIND?

YES
"IS GLOBAL WARMING HARMFUL TO HEALTH?"
TOM JACKSON

NO
"WARMER DAYS AND LONGER LIVES"
WWW.STANFORD.EDU/~MOORE/HISTORY_HEALTH.HTML
THOMAS GALE MOORE

INTRODUCTION

Humankind's influence on climate has grown with increasing population and industrial activity. Emissions of carbon dioxide and other gases from the burning of fossil fuel are accumulating in the atmosphere faster than they are being converted into other compounds. Many scientists believe that these gases contribute to a so-called greenhouse effect by allowing the Sun's energy to pass through to Earth to warm the surface, but then acting as an insulating layer that slows the loss of heat back to space. The insulating layer is becoming thicker as more carbon dioxide is emitted into Earth's atmosphere, and that is likely causing warmer climates overall. The resultant warming of Earth's climate is a matter of concern for, and debate among, the world's countries.

There is little scientific disagreement, and plenty of evidence, that Earth's climate has been warming up over the past 100 years. In the United States the average annual temperature has risen by almost 1 °F (0.6 °C), according to the United Nations Intergovernmental Panel on Climate Change (IPCC). What is more debatable is what the consequences of this warming trend might mean for humans—the melting of the polar ice caps and rising sea levels that flood coastal cities, faster growing crops and longer growing seasons, more frequent and more devastating flooding and hurricane events, alterations of habitats like coral reefs and cold-water fisheries, and many other possibilities with significant effects.

One consequence of great concern is how global warming could affect the health of the human race. What changes can we anticipate, and how do we prepare to meet them? As the climates of cooler northern areas grow warmer, the climatic barriers of tropical disease organisms could weaken to the extent that northerners become exposed to diseases such as malaria, cholera, and dengue fever. The northeastern United States has already experienced cases of the tropical West Nile virus for the first time ever. These organisms are carried by animals, plants, and by an increasingly mobile population. The human health risks of global warming are clearly significant.

"We humans are changing the global climate…. No nation can escape this danger. None can evade its responsibility to confront it, and we must all do our part."
—BILL CLINTON

Potential threats like those to human health are one aspect of global warming. But there are likely to be potential opportunities as well. The focus of much of the climate change research taking place is on anticipating the possible changes in order to be better prepared to adapt to them. For example, farmers may be able to alter their crop management practices and produce more food in areas where the growing season is lengthened. Energy costs for heating homes and offices, and the demand for fossil fuel, could fall in a warmer climate—although demand for air conditioning may perhaps offset this decline.

Taking a longer view of the relationship between human development and changes in climate brings a different perspective to the picture. From geological studies and archaeological evidence scientists know that Earth's climate has been variable and dynamic, fluctuating over tens of thousand of years from ice ages to periods of melting glaciers and warmer conditions. Human growth and survival during the ice ages were much more challenged than during thawing and warming periods. Many scientists point to the natural cycles of warming and cooling to explain the climate's current predicament, dismissing the idea that pollution is a major contributing factor.

In the first of the two articles Tom Jackson looks at the potential threats that global warming poses to human health. He argues that, as the temperature rises, so will the amount of disease. Malaria and other tropical diseases are likely to spread to newly warmed and heavily populated areas, including the southern United States. However, Jackson emphasizes that developing countries will suffer most, including those that were beginning to win the battle against disease. The predicted rise in droughts and flooding will worsen existing poverty and malnutrition, leading to epidemics of diseases such as tuberculosis, typhus, and dysentry.

The second article is a historical look at the development of humans over the millennia by Thomas Gale Moore, who argues that a warming climate will bring better conditions for human health and prosperity. Moore suggests that in the past warmer conditions have brought humans better nutrition and a longer life expectancy. Thus Moore argues the current period of global warming is actually beneficial to humankind and that there should be a positive change in human health as a result. The implication of this observation seems to be that humankind is on the right course and should devote its resources to more relevant issues. At the end of the article there is a key map that sums up the major points.

11

IS GLOBAL WARMING HARMFUL TO HEALTH?
Tom Jackson

Not all scientists agree on the basic issues of global warming. Jackson acknowledges this, but moves quickly on to his argument.

There is still much debate on the subject of global warming, but one fact is not disputed by the majority of scientists in the field: Earth's atmosphere has got warmer, and it will continue to do so. Many also argue that the rate of heating is increasing and predict that changes in the atmosphere will cause major upheaval around the globe, and sooner rather than later.

Many of the predicted results of temperature change are widely known. The most familiar predictions are that the pack ice around the poles will melt as the air and oceans heat up. This will cause sea levels to rise and huge areas of low-lying land, including cities and whole islands, will be covered by salt water. Many scientists have also suggested that the regions ideal for agriculture that girdle the globe will shift their position. Areas that were once mild and fertile will become arid and dusty, and places that were frozen for most of the year may become fertile grasslands. On top of all these changes, stormy weather across the world will become less predictable and more severe.

As global temperatures rise, disease rather than violent weather will pose by far the main threat to human health.

As pictures of glaciers tumbling into the sea and news of terrible floods and storms reach us in our homes, the predictions seem to be becoming a reality. Yet after the waters have receded and normality has returned, the real effects of climate change on human health will remain in the form of diseases and other serious medical disorders.

Toward a warmer world

Global warming can damage health in several ways. Some medical disorders are caused directly by heat and these become more common during heat waves. The atmosphere is not warming evenly and some parts of the world are experiencing more and stronger heat waves. Meteorologists have noticed that the largest increases in temperature have been recorded during the night in the normally mild regions at 50° latitude. With less night-time cooling bringing relief to people suffering from the heat, the number of deaths attributed to heat are set to double by 2020. Heat increases the amount of smog and ozone, which exacerbate asthma and other respiratory disorders. With asthma on the rise among children in the developed world, global warming is likely to make this problem worse. However, it is worth mentioning that less cold weather may result in fewer deaths due to cold, such as cold-induced heart attacks.

Opening the door to disease

As the climate of mild regions becomes warmer, the danger exists of a deadly disease, currently confined to hot, tropical areas, from spreading to newly warmed and heavily populated areas. This danger proved to be very real in 1999, when seven people in New York City died from West Nile virus, a disease that was new to North America.

Mosquitoes were the main carriers of the West Nile virus in New York. An abnormally high number of the insects survived the mild winter of 1998–1999.

   The increased mobility of people, especially those from developed countries, makes is very likely that the organisms that cause and spread tropical diseases will be introduced to new areas that match their ecological needs. Malaria will spread into southern parts of the United States and Europe, and the equally debilitating dengue and yellow fevers will find new victims across the world.

"We're motivated by survival. We're motivated by the threat of extinction."
—SAMOAN DELEGATE FOR THE ASSOCIATION OF SMALL ISLAND STATES

   However, developing countries will be most affected by the increases in disease. Climatic changes may tip the balance of disease control, and areas that have been cleared of certain types of disease will once again become infested with disease-causing agents. Poverty and their limited access to technology will make it much harder for developing countries to cope with these and the other changes caused by global warming.

Global warming will add to the burdens already faced by developing countries.

   Areas already prone to terrible droughts or flooding will find that their afflictions will probably worsen. The resulting increases in poverty and malnutrition of the population will directly damage health, making people more prone to disease and governments less able to deal with the consequences.

A Thai woman caught in a heavily flooded street. Her pet monkey sits on her head.

Although starvation and drowning are major killers during periods of drought or flood, the rise in diseases they cause are more deadly in the long term. Once an infectious disease takes root in a community it is likely to remain there.

The sorts of diseases that may become a problem are not necessarily the ones that are hard to control and treat, such as sleeping sickness or river blindness, but preventable illnesses that spring up during times of mass upheaval. Regular flooding and droughts are likely to displace whole communities on a regular basis. Similarly when the sea inundates coastal lands, entire cities of people will become homeless. People on the move and crowded into inadequate accommodation are prone to diseases such as hepatitis, tuberculosis, typhus, and dysentry. If the results of global warming are to be as bad as some are warning, then these diseases will surely claim many lives.

Jackson argues that easily treatable diseases such as dysentry will be the biggest killers.

Many parts of the world are already being affected by unusually violent weather patterns. This is because the warmed atmosphere can hold more water evaporated from the oceans. When rain does fall, it falls in larger quantities. The heat that evaporates the water from the oceans also beats down on the land. Areas far from water dry out more quickly, which results in larger pressure differences between the air masses over the land and sea. Large pressure differentials cause stronger winds and create more severe storms and powerful tornadoes. Changes in the paths of ocean currents being associated with warming will also take the bad weather to previously mild regions.

Averting catastrophe

Global warming is being caused, at least in part, by the carbon dioxide gas that is given out when we burn fossil fuels. Recently, many countries ratified the Kyoto Protocol, a commitment to reduce the amount of carbon dioxide they put into the air by 5.2 percent below their 1990 levels by 2010. The Intergovernmental Panel on Climate Change, run by the United Nations, has calculated that a reduction of at least 60 percent is required to stop the atmosphere from warming. About 4 percent of the world's population lives in the United States, a country that produces 25 percent of carbon dioxide emissions. While other big polluters, such as Europe, Japan, and India have opted to reduce their emissions, the United States government has ignored the Kyoto Protocol. While health risks will be worse for the poor, rich countries, including the United States, will also be affected also if nothing is done to solve the climate's problems.

Can you research the most important ways in which we contribute to the buildup of carbon dioxide and other greenhouse gases?

WARMER DAYS AND LONGER LIVES
Thomas Gale Moore

NO

History demonstrates that warmer is healthier. Since the end of the last Ice Age, the earth has enjoyed two periods that were warmer than the 20th century. Archaeological evidence shows that people lived longer, enjoyed better nutrition, and multiplied more rapidly than during epochs of cold.

That Ice Age ended about 12,000 to 10,000 years ago when the glaciers covering much of North America, Scandinavia, and northern Asia began to retreat to approximately their current positions. In North America the glacial covering lasted longer than in Eurasia because of topographical features that delayed the warming. Throughout history warming and cooling in different regions of the world have not correlated exactly because of the influence of such factors as oceans, mountains, and prevailing winds.

The author looks to the past for patterns in human geography that validate his ideas.

The last Ice Age is part of nearly 30 major climatic cycles that have taken place over the last 3.5 million years. It is natural for the planet to run warm and cool.

A long history of climatic fluctuation

As the earth warmed with the waning of the Ice Age, the sea level rose as much as 300 ft; hunters in Europe roamed through modern Norway; agriculture developed in the Middle East, the Far East, and the Americas. By 7,000 years ago and lasting for about four millennia, the earth was more clement than today, perhaps by 4 °F [2.2 °C], about the average of the various predictions for global warming from a doubling of CO_2. Although the climate cooled a bit after 3000 B.C., it stayed relatively warmer than the modern world until sometime after 1000 B.C., when chilly temperatures became more common. During the four thousand warmest years, Europe enjoyed mild winters and warm summers with a storm belt far to the north. Rainfall may have been 10 to 15 percent greater than now. Not only was the country less subject to severe storms, but the skies were less cloudy and the days sunnier.

From around 800 A.D. to 1200 or 1300, the globe warmed again considerably and civilization prospered. This warm era displays, although less distinctly, many of the same characteristics as the earlier period of clement weather. Virtually all of northern Europe, the British Isles, Scandinavia, Greenland, and Iceland were considerably warmer than at present. The Mediterranean, the Near East, and North Africa, including the Sahara, received more rainfall than they do today. During this period of the High Middle Ages, most of North America also enjoyed better weather. In the early centuries of the epoch, China experienced higher temperatures and a more clement climate. From Western Europe to China, East Asia, India, and the Americas, mankind flourished as never before.

Humans hostage to climate

This prosperous period collapsed at the end of the 13th century with the advent of the "Mini Ice Age," which, at its most frigid, produced temperatures in central England for January about 4.5 °F colder than today. Although the climate fluctuated, periods of cold damp weather lasted until the early part of the 19th century. During the chilliest decades, 5 to 15 percent less rain fell in Europe than does normally today; but, due to less evaporation because of the low temperatures, swampy conditions were more prevalent. As a result, in the 14th century the population explosion came to an abrupt halt; economic activity slowed; lives shortened as disease spread and diets deteriorated.

The author bases his argument on the effects of natural climate change, in contrast to human-influenced climatic warming.

Although the influence of climate on human activities has declined with the growth in wealth and resources, climate still has a significant effect on disease and health. A cold wet climate can confine people to close quarters, abetting contagion. In the past, a shift toward a poorer climate has led to hunger and famine, making disease more virulent. Before the industrial revolution and improved technology, a series of bad years could be devastating. If transportation were costly and slow, as was typical until very recently, even a regionalized drought or an excess of rain might lead to disaster, even though crops might be plentiful a short distance away.

The ability to heat, cool, and irrigate microenvironments allows modern humans to exploit almost every habitat on Earth.

The more, the merrier

For people in premodern times, perhaps the single best measure of their health and well-being is the growth rate of the population. Over history the number of humans has been expanding at ever more rapid rates. Around 25,000 years ago, the world's population may have numbered only about 3 million. Fifteen thousand years later, around 8000 B.C., the total had probably grown by one-third to 4 million. It took 5,000 more years to jump one more million; but, in the 1,000 years after 5000 B.C., it added another million. Except for a few periods of disaster, the number of men, women, and

The author claims that in the past a high population growth rate signified good human health. Is this valid today, when the world population is set to double over the next 40 years?

Chart 1: Life expectancy at various periods

Mesolithic People in Europe, Ice Age	32
Neolithic People in Anatolia, warm period	38*
Bronze Age in Austria, warm period	38*
Classical Greece, cooler	35
Classical Rome, cooler	32
England 1276 A.D., warm period	48*
England 1376–1400, Mini Ice Age	38

*shows longest life expectancies in warmest periods

Chart 2: Average height of Icelandic males

Period (A.D.)	Mean height, inches (cm)
874–110, medieval warmth	68 (170)
1650–1800, Mini Ice Age	66 (165)*
1952–1954, modern world	70 (175)

*fall in stature indicates lack of food during Mini Ice Age

Source: Lamb, Hubert H., Climatic history and the future. *Volume 2.*
Princeton: Princeton University Press, 1985.

children has mounted with increasing rapidity. Only in the last few decades of the 20th century has the escalation slowed. Certainly there have been good times when man did better and poor times when people suffered—although in most cases these were regional problems. However, in propitious periods—that is, when the climate was warm—the population swelled faster than during less clement eras.

Warmth and long life

Another measure of the well-being of humans is their life span. The life of the hunter-gatherer was less rosy than some have contended. Life was short—skeletal remains from before 8000 B.C. show that the average age of death for men was

The Mini Ice Age of the 14th century may have created suitable conditions for the spread of the Black Death, a plague bacillus carried by rats that killed one-third of Europe's population alone, as well as millions in Asia.

about 33 and that for women, 28. Death for men was often violent while many women must have died in childbirth.

Chart 1 (opposite) shows that the warmest periods—the Neolithic and Bronze Ages and England in the 13th century—enjoyed the longest life spans of the entire record. The rise in life expectancies during the latter warm period easily explains the population explosion that took place during the High Middle Ages. In contrast, the shortening of lives from the late 13th to the late 14th centuries with the advent of much cooler weather is particularly notable.

Good childhood nutrition is reflected in taller adults. As Chart 2 (opposite) indicates, Icelanders must have suffered from lack of food during the Mini Ice Age: their average stature fell by 2 inches (5 cm). Only in the modern world, with greatly improved food supplies and medicines, has their height risen to levels exceeding those enjoyed in the Medieval period.

In summary, the evidence supports overwhelmingly the proposition that, during warm periods, humans have prospered. They multiplied more rapidly; they lived longer; and they were healthier. If the IPCC [Intergovernmental Panel on Climate Change] is right and the globe does warm, history suggests that human health is likely to improve.

Summary

Tom Jackson points out how most scientists now agree that the world is warming, and doing so at an increasingly high rate. This phenomenon will result in more unpredictable and violent weather, with storms and floods striking at random. Rising global temperatures will have a direct effect on human health by creating lethal heat waves and killer smog that causes asthma and other respiratory complaints. Diseases that were once confined to the tropics will spread to temperate regions of the globe. Developing countries that were beginning to win the fight against disease will find the tables turned once more, as widespread poverty and starvation enable easily treatable diseases to become deadly epidemics.

A much more optimistic note is sounded by Moore, who does not refute that the world is warming and seems to welcome the fact. He points out how the world climate has been fluctuating naturally for millions of years, and that the most recent swings toward warmth have actually benefited humans. This claim is supported by archaeological evidence that indicates that people lived longer lives and achieved a greater mean stature during warm periods, and suffered corresponding shortages—in height and in life expectancy—in such natural phenomena as the Mini Ice Age that settled on Europe during the 14th century. In addition, increases in world population correlate to periods of warmth.

FURTHER INFORMATION:

Useful websites:

www.nacc.usgcrp.gov
The National Assessment Synthesis reports. Overview and Foundation documents.
www.cnn.com/SPECIALS/1997/global.warming/
"Our Changing Climate: A Special Report on the Global Warming Debate."
www.unfccc.de/index.html
UN Framework Convention on Climate Change.
www.ipcc.ch/index.html
Intergovernmental Panel on Climate Change.
www.seastar.vasc.org/erc/
NASA Langley Educator Resource Center.
www.sedac.ciesin.org/mva/iamcc.tg/articles/articles.html
Socioeconomic Data and Applications Center (SEDAC)
Thematic Guide to Integrated Assessment Modeling.
www.cit.cornell.edu/other_rcc.html
The Regional Climate Center.
www.wri.org/wri/climate/
World Resources Institute.

The following debates in the Pro/Con series may also be of interest:

In this volume:
Topic 7: Can a pay-to-pollute system significantly reduce air pollution?

Global Warming,
pages 70–71

How to Write an Essay,
pages 186–187

In *Government:*
Research Skills,
pages 58–59

DOES GLOBAL WARMING THREATEN HUMANKIND?

YES: The warming of temperate zones will enable tropical diseases, such as malaria, to extend their range

DISEASE

Will global warming significantly threaten human health?

NO: The archaeological record shows that humans have always been taller and healthier during warm periods

YES: Low-lying coastal plains in Bangladesh and other countries will be swamped. Some island chains may disappear.

SEA LEVELS

Scientists predict that sea levels will rise sharply: Should we be worried?

NO: Many scientific models are exaggerated; there will only be a modest rise in sea level

DOES GLOBAL WARMING THREATEN HUMANKIND?

KEY POINTS

YES: Warming accelerates the water cycle, leading to more extreme, variable weather

CLIMATE

Will global warming destabilize the world's climate?

NO: It will add little to the effect of the planet's naturally occurring temperature cycles

YES: Crop patterns will be destabilized, leading to famine, political unrest, and disease

AGRICULTURE

Will global warming threaten agricultural production?

NO: Past evidence shows that humans have always managed to work around food problems

Topic 2
SHOULD THE HUMAN POPULATION BE STABILIZED?

YES
"A SPECIAL MOMENT IN HISTORY"
THE ATLANTIC MONTHLY, MAY 1998
BILL MCKIBBEN

NO
"THE FALLACIES AND HAZARDS OF POPULATION 'CONTROL'"
THE INTERNATIONAL CONFERENCE ON POPULATION DEVELOPMENT
ROD N. ANDREASON

INTRODUCTION

The human population has been growing at an ever-accelerating rate, and there have never been so many people. Learning how to farm about 10,000 years ago empowered humans to provide an adequate supply of food and develop complex social systems. They have helped make *Homo sapiens* the immensely powerful species that it is today, able to live and prosper and adapt to almost any environment.

Humans have gone through an industrial revolution and a public health revolution that have enriched their quality of life and kept them alive and well longer than ever before. Though not true for all, on average, people have never had it so good as they do today.

The world's population has doubled since the 1950s and is set to double again by the mid-21st century. The growth rate is now slowing, however, and it is quite possible that a child

born today may actually live to see a decline in the world's population during the next century from a peak of somewhere around 10 billion (compared with the current level of six billion).

Why is population growth slowing? The simple answer is that women are having fewer children. Most are choosing to do so, though some are being coerced by government policy, as in China. Most population analysts attribute the trend toward smaller families to increasing education and personal wealth. Studies show that birth rates fall as women become more educated and as opportunities for economic development become more widely available.

Whatever the future brings in terms of human population numbers, an important consideration is how much of Earth's resources each person will consume, whether there will be enough capacity to provide it, and whether

Earth can continue to soak up the polluting by-products of industrial activities. Another way to ask this question is: How many people could Earth carry at a comfortable standard of living?

"How many people is the Earth able to sustain? The question is incomplete as it stands. One must modify the question by asking further: At what level of technology? And modify it still further by asking: At what level of human dignity?"

—ISAAC ASIMOV, U.S. NOVELIST

Many studies have tried to answer this difficult question, and the responses have been surprisingly varied. In his book *How Many People Can the Earth Support?* Joel Cohen made the most thorough comparison of all these studies to date. He found that the median value for all studies lay between 7.7 billion and 12 billion. The United Nations projections for population growth predict that humans will level out at around nine billion by the 2050s. Perhaps we are somehow naturally arriving at a stable pattern of growth in population. It is even conceivable that there will eventually be a negative rate of growth.

In Bill McKibben's article "A Special Moment in History" the author takes a look at the combined effect of human activity on Earth's atmosphere in terms of global warming and catastrophic changes in climate patterns. He argues that the combination of our large numbers and our consumption of energy and resources has reached a point at which we are altering our climate on a global scale. Furthermore, we may have only a few decades in which to figure out how to avoid catastrophes that will affect billions of people.

In effect, McKibben is saying that while we should consider population stabilization as part of the solution, we must figure out how to change individual lifestyle and consumption patterns so that we drastically reduce our effect on the atmosphere.

In this respect his argument echoes that of Rod Andreason, who takes a critical look at the 1994 International Conference on Population and Development (ICPD). Andreason attempts to show some of the fallacies and hazards involved in population control. The aim of his critique is to challenge the 1994 ICPD and advocates of population reduction to find better ways of improving the quality of life for all people rather than simple population reduction.

The message here is that it is not true that humans can improve their outlook simply by reducing numbers. In fact, he argues that people may create a more lonely and vulnerable society by doing so. Or that with a reduced population a bigger burden is placed on younger people, who will have to support greater numbers of older people.

As you read the articles, consider whether the future would be brighter if we could somehow control the level of the world's population.

A SPECIAL MOMENT IN HISTORY
Bill McKibben

YES

The "doubling" to which the author refers is the projected rise in the world's population by the year 2050, after which the rate of increase is expected to slow.

✓ When we think about overpopulation, we usually think first of the developing world, because that's where 90 percent of new human beings will be added during this final doubling. We fool ourselves when we think of Third World population growth as producing an imbalance. The white world simply went through its population boom a century earlier. If UN calculations are correct and Asians and Africans will make up just under 80 percent of humanity by 2050, they will simply have returned, in the words of [Harvard social scientist] Amartya Sen, "to being proportionately almost exactly as numerous as they were before the European industrial revolution."

A Malagasi is a native of the island of Madagascar.

And of course Asians and Africans, and Latin Americans, are much "smaller" human beings: the consumption balloons that float above their heads are tiny in comparison with ours. For example, an American uses 70 times as much energy as a Bangladeshi, 50 times as much as a Malagasi, 20 times as much as a Costa Rican. Since we live longer, the effect of each of us is further multiplied. In a year an American uses 300 times as much energy as a Malian; over a lifetime he will use 500 times as much.

Environmentally friendly technology?

I've spent much of my career writing about the need for cleverer technologies and humbler aspirations. Environmental damage can be expressed as the product of Population × Affluence × Technology. Surely the easiest solution would be to live more simply and more efficiently, and not worry too much about the number of people.

McKibben explains that he has changed his mind on the subject of population control. Does this give his argument more or less authority?

But I've come to believe that those changes in technology and in lifestyle are not going to occur easily and speedily. They'll be begun but not finished in the few decades that really matter. Remember that the pollution we're talking about is not precisely pollution but rather the inevitable result when things go the way we think they should. A gallon of gas weighs about eight pounds. When it's burned in a car, about five-and-a-half pounds of carbon, in the form of CO_2, come spewing out the back. It doesn't matter if the car is a 1958 Chevy or a 1998 Saab. And no filter can reduce that flow—it's an inevitable by-product of fossil-fuel combustion, which is why it has been piling up in the atmosphere ever since the Industrial Revolution. We're stuck with making real changes in how we live. We're stuck with dramatically reducing the amount of fossil fuel we use.

"When future generations evaluate the record of our time, one of the most important factors in their judgment will be the way in which we responded to population growth."

—RICHARD M. NIXON, 1969

But when it comes time to do our part, we don't. After all, Clinton warned of the dangers of climate change in 1993, on his first Earth Day in office. In fact, he solemnly promised to make sure that America produced no more greenhouse gases in 2000 than it had in 1990. But he didn't keep his word. The United States [emitted] an amazing 15 percent more carbon dioxide in 2000 than it did in 1990. What's important to understand is why we broke our word. We did so because Clinton understood that if we were to keep it, we would need to raise the price of fossil fuel. If gasoline cost $2.50 a gallon, we'd drive smaller cars, we'd drive electric cars, we'd take buses—and we'd elect a new president.

Perhaps our salvation lies in the other part of the equation—in the new technologies and efficiencies that could make even our wasteful lives benign, and table the issue of our population. We are, for instance, converting our economy from its old industrial base to a new model based on service and information. Surely that should save some energy, should reduce the clouds of carbon dioxide. Writing software seems no more likely to damage the atmosphere than writing poetry.

Forget for a moment the hardware requirements of that new economy—for instance, the production of a six-inch silicon wafer may require nearly 3,000 gallons of water. But do keep in mind that a hospital or an insurance company requires a substantial physical base. Even the highest-tech office is built with steel and cement, pipes and wires. People working in services will buy … more software, sure, but also more sport utility vehicles.

Do you think that U.S. consumers have an obligation to try to reduce their consumption of resources? Or is it everyone's right to live as they wish?

Even apparently hi-tech, low-energy industries use up valuable resources.

Two starving boys cling to each other outside a feeding center in the village of Acumcum, in the Bahr El Ghazal Province of southern Sudan. August 9, 1998.

The President's Council on Sustainable Development, in a little-read report issued in the winter of 1996, concluded that "Efficiency in the use of all resources would have to increase by more than 50 percent over the next four or five decades just to keep pace with population growth." Three million new Americans annually means many more cars, houses, refrigerators. Even if everyone consumes only what he consumed the year before, each year's tally of births and immigrants will swell American consumption by one percent.

In doing the math about how we're going to get out of this fix, we'd better factor in some unstoppable momentum from people on the rest of the planet who want the very basics of what we call a decent life. Even if we airlift solar collectors into China and India, as we should, those nations will still burn more and more coal and oil.

Is it fair to deny other peoples a "decent life" in order to protect the environment?

The numbers are so daunting, they're almost unimaginable. Say, just for argument's sake, that we decided to cut world fossil-fuel use by 60 percent—the amount that the UN panel says would stabilize world climate. And then say that we shared the remaining fossil fuel equally. Each human being would get to produce 1.69 metric tons of carbon dioxide annually—which would allow you to drive an average American car nine miles a day. By the time the population increased to 8.5 billion, in about 2025, you'd be down to six miles a day. If you carpooled, you'd have about three pounds of CO_2 left in your daily ration—enough to run a highly efficient refrigerator.

Imagine how your family would manage on this daily mileage.

The time for action

The next 50 years are a special time. They will decide how strong and healthy the planet will be for centuries to come. Between now and 2050 we'll see the zenith, or very nearly, of human population. With luck we'll never see any greater production of carbon dioxide or toxic chemicals. We'll never see more species extinction or soil erosion. Greenpeace recently announced a campaign to phase out fossil fuels entirely by mid-century, which sounds utterly quixotic but could—if everything went just right—happen.

So it's the task of those of us alive right now to deal with this special phase, to squeeze us through these next 50 years. That's not fair—any more than it was fair that earlier generations had to deal with the Second World War or the Civil War or the Revolution or the Depression or slavery. It's just reality. We need in these 50 years to be working simultaneously on all parts of the equation—on our ways of life, on our technologies, and on our population.

McKibben's argument—that more people will inevitably use more resources—leads him finally to propose "working ... on our population."

THE FALLACIES AND HAZARDS OF POPULATION "CONTROL"
Rod N. Andreason

NO

The International Conference on Population and Development (ICPD) has many admirable goals: It strives to reduce maternal mortality rates; it aims to enhance the lives of low-income residents of both residential and urban areas; and it seeks to eradicate poverty, perhaps its most important objective. Unfortunately, however, the theme of "population development" for many participants in the Conference is merely a subtle euphemism for population "reduction" or "control." Delegates to the conference assumed that people were "a problem rather than a resource." With so many challenges facing populations worldwide, our task should be to eliminate problems, not people.

Coercion is the common tool

Worse yet, the common result of fear-induced population reduction activism has been massive, state-run coercion. While Ehrlich may feel that "repression has been seen in a relatively few instances," the record is replete with both blatant and subtle uses of government power to force parents to limit or completely avoid having children. Blatant uses of force have caused the most obvious human rights abuses. China's population control programs based around its "one-child" policy have received the most focus in this area. Not all information on Chinese enforcement is available, but several methods are well documented, including threats of force, required contraception or abortion, and mass sterilization campaigns. There have also been denials of social benefits, demotions at work, fines, and psychological pressures not to have children, as family and coworkers are asked to influence women to use IUDs, be sterilized, or get abortions.

Current population trends pose new dangers. Evidence put forth by the United Nation's own World Population Prospects, 1996 Revision, and updated by the 1998 Revision, suggests that the world's population will peak in our lifetimes, and then commence an indefinite decline. As one writer notes, birthrates have fallen so far, so low, around the

The UN Population Fund held the ICPD during September 5–13, 1994, in Cairo, Egypt.

A concise summary of your argument helps people remember it.

Paul Ehrlich warned of the dangers of overpopulation in his 1968 book The Population Bomb.

The Chinese government tried to limit all families to have only one child. What methods might it have used without resorting to force and coercion?

world that avoiding depopulation may be the next major concern. Why should drops in world birth rates concern people? Baby busts, like baby booms, are geometric. Based on the current drops in birthrates worldwide, the next generation would be 30 percent smaller than ours. While it is true that for a few more years, "absolute increments" will increase the world population, current trends show that depopulation will begin by the year 2040, and world population will shrink by at least 25 percent with each successive generation.

The threat of underpopulation is equal to that of overpopulation, Andreason says.

The possibility of depopulation should concern us. Losing population voluntarily—for example, before war, famine, disease, and other causes take their toll—works against the maintenance (and even survival) of a species. Moreover, it brings with it a host of new problems for populations of the future.

Dramatically ageing populations

One of the most obvious problems caused by steep birthrate declines will be a dramatic population ageing. "Ageing populations will strain medical systems in many developing countries, which are still struggling to protect the health of younger age groups." The Programme of Action itself recognizes "record increases in proportion and number of elderly persons."

Can you see evidence in the United States that the population is getting older?

The median age of the world's population in 1995 was estimated at 25 years. According to the UN's "low variant" model, the median age 50 years from now could be over 42. Japan's median age would be 53; Germany's 55, and Italy's 58. This trend will weaken the workforce supporting populations of the future. In 2050, it is likely that over half of a nation's workers will be over 50.

There will be little money to support this "grayby boom." "First, [a]s the ratio of employees to retirees falls, a universal pay-as-you-go retirement system has only three options for preventing bankruptcy: reduce pension benefits; raise taxes; or restrict eligibility."

Second, the cost of health care will place a large burden on governments and their already overtaxed workforce. The practical costs will become extremely difficult to bear, especially for developing nations who attempt to provide Western-style health care. But population ageing will be a worldwide phenomenon, resulting in an international bidding war for scarce labor resources. As has happened throughout the world's history, people will migrate to the nations with the most favorable living and working

Andreason points out that in an aged population the workforce may be too small to raise the funds needed for the care of its retired citizens.

COMMENTARY: The right to reproduce

It is natural for people to want to have children: Procreation is crucial to the survival of the species, and strong populations are essential for strong countries. Demographic studies reveal that after wars or famine populations naturally bounce back to restore numbers. (This phenomenon was in part responsible for the postwar baby boom in the United States.)

Over time fertility among women has shown dramatic fluctuations; it is currently in decline in many parts of the developed world. Child-bearing has also been shaped by prevailing cultural conditions, such as religious constraint. For example, the Hutterites of North America place a value on high fertility and disdain any birth control, and among many cultures a taboo against extramarital sex reduces numbers of unplanned pregnancies.

In some countries the right to reproduce has been restricted by initiatives to curb soaring human numbers. In the People's Republic of China, where the population exceeds 1.2 billion, the government has often put intolerable pressure on couples to conform to its one-child family program. In Indonesia villagers are requested to apply intense peer pressure to neighbors who are considering having another child. During the 1970s the Indian government conducted a strenuous program of sterilization. Additionally, people may take disturbing steps of their own. Many Chinese couples have shown a preference for having a son rather than a daughter so that he can carry on the family name and also provide income by working. In some situations newborn Chinese daughters have been deliberately neglected or even killed.

Meeting in Cairo in 1994, the International Conference on Population and Development (ICPD) explicitly rejected coercion in population-planning programs, concluding that coercive programs have led to serious human rights violations. In countries where population stabilization is encouraged, the more acceptable options presented to couples include voluntary sterilization or contraception. Progress here has been slowed by general ignorance, but the United Nations has worked to educate women in particular, showing them that they can make an informed choice about birth control. Another important factor is the religious opposition to contraception espoused by various groups.

What, however, does the future hold? Among the arguments in this topic is the uncertainty about whether the planet can sustain the expected doubling of the world's population during the 21st century. The human race is in uncharted territory: There is no precedent to follow. It is partly this uncertainty that provokes countries to introduce population control programs for fear of mass starvation or civil unrest. Should we accept that our assumed right to reproduce may one day be taken away from us for the common good of humankind, or would this be an unacceptable degradation of our quality of life?

conditions. Third, the number of children being born that
will support that group is in relative decline.

The disintegration of the family

Population reduction seriously detracts from families in at
least three ways. First, it directly seeks to reduce the family
itself. While giving lip service to allowing families the right
to choose the number and spacing of their children, it
aggressively persuades them to reduce or eliminate the
number of children they will have.

In the guise of "offering choices," the Programme
encourages contraceptive use whenever possible. In other
words, "informed choice" is only a tool for the underlying
agenda of reducing birthrates.

More importantly, population reduction programs have
increasingly caused people to have only one child in the
family. The trend is worrisome indeed. Families of children
without brothers, sisters, aunts, and uncles will create a
sadder, lonelier society. In the year 2050 (according to its
present birthrate), nearly three-fifths of all Italian children
will have no siblings, cousins, aunts, or uncles! Less than five
percent of Italian children will have both siblings and
cousins. It is incredible to imagine a society in which the
"only biological relatives for many people—perhaps most
people—will be their ancestors."

Second, population reduction programs seek to replace
traditionally private family matters with governmental
intervention and decision making. Choices for when to
marry, how many children to have, and when to stop
bearing children would increasingly be the province of
administrative bureaucrats. Third, population reduction
programs increasingly are trying to take the most important
element of the family out of the equation—the mother—in
the guise of providing women with "more fulfilling"
opportunities of work and education.

Eliminate problems before people

In responding to the significant dangers of depopulation
and antinatalist policies in general, we must avoid
causing a pendulum shift to the other extreme. Instead,
we should simply stop promoting population reduction,
point out its damaging effects, then set about the task
of solving the world's real problems.

Focusing on people's problems will never be simple.
But it will be no more difficult, and much more rewarding,
than trying to eliminate the people themselves.

In defending the family, Andreason has moved on from practical issues (health care) to one that provokes an emotional response from us.

Is this emotional argument as effective as when Andreason uses facts and figures to support his case? Do you believe that people are growing more lonely because families are smaller?

Summary

Bill McKibben, in support of population control, goes instantly on the attack, pointing out that Americans use far more energy per capita than any other nation. Despite advances in technology producing cleaner auto engines and so-called paperless offices, the United States still pumps out more than its fair share of greenhouse gases and other pollutants. When, as anticipated, African and Asian populations soar over the next few decades, and as their standard of living gradually improves, there is no good reason why they will not become more profligate consumers in the American mold. However, the atmosphere will not be able to cope with the extra burden of carbon dioxide, nor will the oceans bounce back from the demands made on their fragile ecosystems. The time to cut consumption and to address overpopulation is now.

Rod Andreason does not deny that the world faces grave ecological harm from human wastefulness and overuse of fossil fuels. But the answer, he says, does not come from population control. That policy has already led to human rights abuses in China, Indonesia, India, and elsewhere. In fact, the threat of overpopulation may soon be matched by that of underpopulation, as a declining birthrate and improved medicine lead to an aging population. Such a scenario would break economies as they tried to provide Western-style health care. Andreason warns that population reduction would lead to emotional upset as smaller families lead to lonelier people, and the right to reproduce is removed from parental control to a government bureaucracy. Rather than eliminate people, he says, address the world's real problems.

FURTHER INFORMATION:

Books:

Ehrlich, Paul R., *The Population Bomb*. New York: Ballantine Books, 1968.

Cohen, Joel E., *How Many People Can the Earth Support?* New York: W. W. Norton & Co., 1996.

Brown, Lester R., Gary Gardner, and Brian Halweil, *Beyond Malthus: Nineteen Dimensions of the Population Challenge*. New York: W. W. Norton & Co., 1999.

Useful websites:

www.fao.org/sd/pe3_en.htm
The Sustainable Development Department of the Food and Agriculture Organization of the United Nations.
www.ucsusa.org/environment/pop.resources.html
Union of Concerned Scientists.
www.iisd.ca/linkages/cairo.html
UN International Conference on Population and Development.

The following debates in the Pro/Con series may also be of interest:

In this volume:

Part 1: Issues and Options

Topic 1 Does global warming threaten humankind?

Topic 3 Are famine and hunger avoidable?

How to Write an Essay, pages 58–59

SHOULD THE HUMAN POPULATION BE STABILIZED?

YES: Given their per capita consumption versus that of Africans or Asians, Americans can ill afford even a modest population rise

YES: If we cannot curb our destructive lifestyle, we must consider population stabilization

EARTH'S RESOURCES
Does excessive use of resources in the United States necessitate population control?

CONTROL
Are control or reduction viable answers to overpopulation?

NO: Americans simply need to address their lifestyles

NO: Where any form of coercion is used, population control is a violation of human rights

SHOULD THE HUMAN POPULATION BE STABILIZED?

KEY POINTS

YES: The earth may not be able to cope with the soaring human population

YES: The planet can barely accommodate six billion people; how will it cope with twice the number?

LOOKING AHEAD
Should we be concerned about projections for the future global population?

NO: The global population is set to decline in the middle of the next century (although that in itself may present problems)

NO: Ninety percent of the rise is expected in Africa and Asia, where per capita consumption is currently well within acceptable limits

33

Topic 3

ARE FAMINE AND HUNGER AVOIDABLE?

YES
"TWELVE MYTHS ABOUT HUNGER"
SHARE INTERNATIONAL, JANUARY/FEBRUARY, 1999

NO
"FACING REALITY AT THE WORLD FOOD SUMMIT"
WORLDWATCH INSTITUTE
LESTER BROWN

INTRODUCTION

In 2000 the world's population reached six billion, and by 2050, the United Nations estimates, it will probably near nine billion—or even 12, say some estimates. The majority of that growth will occur in developing countries. More than 800 million people still regularly receive inadequate food to meet their nutritional and physical needs. Less than every four seconds someone in the world dies of hunger, with three-quarters of the victims being children.

Some people argue that these figures indicate an improvement because they represent a decrease compared to the 960 million people estimated to go hungry in the world in the 1960s. But at the same time, the world's available cultivable land per person is declining. With the increasing population comes a mounting loss of arable land. The amount of land available for farming has declined steadily since 1960 and will decrease by over half again in the next 50 years.

In 1798 Thomas Malthus wrote "An Essay on the Principles of Population." Malthus hypothesized that population tends to grow exponentially (on a nonlinear path) while food supplies grow only arithmetically (on a linear path), which has always caused stress associated with overpopulation in human societies.

We have consistently ignored the potential dangers of overpopulation or countered with arguments that "technology" would solve the problem. The so-called Green Revolution since the 1960s, in which new, improved hybrids of crops have been engineered, farming practices mechanized, fields irrigated, and chemical treatment used, fell some way short of the miracle it was once prophesied to achieve. Somehow those hunger statistics are still with us.

Often there is a confusion of definitions when dealing with issues of famine, food security, hunger, and malnutrition. Food security and famine and hunger are different concepts, although they deal with the same basic need of life—food.

Food security indicates the reliable availability of food, while famine and hunger are the result of food insecurity and refer to the effects of the nonavailability of food. In 1986 the World Bank defined food security as the "access by all people at all times to

---

" More than one in seven people—13 percent of the global population— still do not have enough to eat, despite technological progress increasing food production."
—UN FOOD AND AGRICULTURE

ORGANIZATION, 2000

---

enough food for an active and healthy life." Additionally, that food supply was to be sustainable.

Famine is an absolute lack of food affecting a large population for a long time period. Famine is a disaster of food insecurity. Hunger is not famine. It is similar to undernourishment and is related to poverty. In many developing and developed countries there are always varying numbers of hungry and undernourished people. People become weakened as a result of not having had adequate food for days. When hunger persists for a longer period, covering a large number of the population and resulting in mass migration and death, it then becomes famine.

Trends and correlations of where and who are susceptible to famine focus on south Asia, particularly India and Bangladesh, followed by sub-Saharan Africa. The incidence of hunger and malnutrition is highest in Africa and south Asia and considerably lower in east Asia and Latin America and the Caribbean. While the incidence of hunger and malnutrition in south Asia has decreased, the absolute number of cases in south Asia and sub-Saharan Africa has increased.

There is a high correlation between food insecurity and climate. Hunger and malnutrition tend to be least prevalent in wet ecological zones and most prevalent in arid ecological zones. Urban food insecurity and malnutrition will become an increasingly important problem in the future as rates of urbanization increase while problems with urban sanitation, diet quality, and food safety grow. As a consequence of armed conflicts and discrimination, large numbers of the poor migrate to more peaceful areas in their own country or into neighboring countries to secure adequate food. There are now an estimated 50 million displaced people who face problems of increased food insecurity and specific nutritional problems.

In the following articles the arguments for and against the notion that famine and hunger are avoidable are outlined. "Twelve Myths about Hunger" argues that there are enough food and distribution mechanisms in the world to feed the entire population. The World Watch Institute report asserts that even given the technological advances toward food security and improved agricultural production and distribution systems there will still be famine and hunger in the world.

TWELVE MYTHS ABOUT HUNGER
Share International

This article presents 12 common explanations for world hunger and presents specific arguments against each. This is a highly effective way of building an overall argument.

Today nearly 800 million people around the world experience hunger. But no one needs to go hungry. There is enough food for all. One of the greatest obstacles to ending hunger is the way we think about it.

Myth 1: Not enough food to go round

Reality: Abundance, not scarcity, best describes the world's food supply. Enough wheat, rice, and other grains are produced to provide every human being with 3,500 calories per day. Enough food is available to provide at least 4.3 pounds of food per person a day worldwide: 2½ pounds of grain, beans, and nuts, about a pound of fruits and vegetables, and nearly another pound of meat, milk, and eggs. The problem is that many people are too poor to buy readily available food. Even most "hungry countries" have enough food for all their people right now.

Myth 2: Nature's to blame for famine

Reality: It is too easy to blame nature. Human-made forces are making people increasingly vulnerable to nature's vagaries. Food is always available for those who can afford it—starvation during hard times hits only the poorest. Natural events rarely explain deaths; they are simply the final push over the brink. Human institutions and policies determine who eats and who starves during hard times. The real culprits are an economy that fails to offer everyone opportunities, and a society that rates economic efficiency above compassion.

Myth 3: Too many people

Reality: Birth rates are falling rapidly worldwide as remaining regions of the Third World begin the demographic transition—when birth rates drop in response to a decline in death rates. Although rapid population growth remains a serious concern in many countries, nowhere does population density explain hunger.

How might these factors help lessen population growth and hunger?

Rapid population growth and hunger are endemic to societies where land ownership, jobs, education, health care, and old-age security are beyond the reach of most people.

Myth 4: The environment v. more food?

Reality: We should be alarmed that an environmental crisis is undercutting our food-production resources, but a trade-off between our environment and the world's need for food is not inevitable. Indeed, environmentally sound agricultural alternatives can be more productive than environmentally destructive ones.

Myth 5: The Green Revolution is the answer

Reality: The production advances of the Green Revolution are no myth. Thanks to the new seeds, millions of tons more grain a year are being harvested. But focusing narrowly on increasing production cannot alleviate hunger because it fails to alter the tightly concentrated distribution of economic power that determines who can buy the additional food. That is why in several of the biggest Green Revolution successes, grain production, and in some cases exports, have climbed while hunger has persisted and the long-term productive capacity of the soil has been degraded.

Launched in the 1960s, the Green Revolution aimed to improve agricultural production around the world. The new materials and technologies it introduced are too costly for many farmers, and the chemical treatments can be polluting.

Myth 6: We need large farms

Reality: Large landowners who control most of the best land often leave much of it idle. Unjust farming systems leave farmland in the hands of the most inefficient producers. By contrast, small farmers typically achieve at least four to five times greater output per acre, in part because they work their land more intensively and use integrated, and often more sustainable, production systems. Many millions of tenant farmers in the Third World have little incentive to invest in land improvements, to rotate crops, or to leave land fallow for the sake of long-term soil fertility.

Myth 7: The free market can end hunger

Reality: Unfortunately, such a "market-is-good, government-is-bad" formula can never help address the causes of hunger. Such a dogmatic stance misleads us that a society can opt for one or the other, when in fact every economy on earth combines the market and government in allocating resources and distributing goods. The market's marvelous efficiencies can only work to eliminate hunger, however, when purchasing power is widely dispersed.

Myth 8: Free trade is the answer

Reality: The trade promotion formula has proved an abject failure at alleviating hunger. In most Third World countries exports have boomed while hunger has continued unabated

Some experts argue that making it easy for countries to trade overseas will encourage them to import food.

COMMENTARY: Foreign food aid

Programs to feed countries suffering from hunger or famine are funded and operated by governments and nongovernmental organizations (NGOs) in the United States and elsewhere in the developed world.

Among the largest international aid organizations are those controlled by the United Nations. They include the Food and Agriculture Organization (FAO), an agency specializing in agriculture, forestry, fisheries, and rural development. FAO encourages long-term, sustainable development rather than short-term solutions, which tend to be environmentally destructive. Also run by the UN is the World Food Programme (WFP). The primary beneficiaries of WFP aid are those caught up in humanitarian crises in sub-Saharan Africa and North Africa, south and east Asia, and the Middle East. They increasingly are found among war-torn populations and other victims of human, rather than natural, disasters. In many WFP programs food is distributed to schools, hospitals, maternity support, and initiatives that promote self-reliance rather than continuing dependence on foreign aid.

The U.S. Department of Agriculture (USDA) provides foreign food aid through three channels: Food for Peace, the Agricultural Act (1949), and the Food for Progress Program. In some instances USDA aid is paid for by the needy government, but in emergency situations a donation of agricultural commodities is made. The Department of Agriculture collaborates with WFP in, for example, the Global Food for Education Initiative. In this program USDA funds are channeled through the WFP to procure food and use it as a "lure" to attract the hungry to schools or immunization programs, thereby improving literacy standards and health respectively. A similar strategy is used to attract the hungry to work on environmental projects, such as forest planting or irrigation programs.

Withdrawing aid

Food aid is not simply a matter of passing one nation's surplus over to another nation's deficit. Goodwill and good intentions alone do not ensure that the needy are fed. In many parts of Africa, the Middle East, and central Asia war, civil unrest, and corruption stand in the way of aid programs to the extent that the food ends up in the wrong hands or simply lies rotting in stockpiles through logistical problems or bureaucratic bungling. A donor nation or NGO may exercise the right to withhold aid on political or ethical grounds. For example, in January 2001 the International Monetary Fund and the World Bank refused to hand over to Kenya aid worth more than $20m because the government there had failed to tackle corruption.

At the same time, however, donors have begun to recognize that nations crippled by famine and poverty simply cannot pay back their aid debts. Canada declared a moratorium on debt collection from heavily indebted poor countries, taking no more payments from Ethiopia after January 2001.

or actually worsened. Where most people have been made too poor to buy the food grown on their own country's soil, those who control productive resources will, not surprisingly, orient their production to more lucrative markets abroad. Export-crop production squeezes out basic food production.

Coffee, cocoa, tobacco, and exotic fruits are examples of export crops that are grown in developing countries, often at the expense of staple food crops.

Myth 9: Too hungry to fight for their rights
Reality: Bombarded with images of poor people as weak and hungry, we lose sight of the obvious: For those with few resources, mere survival requires tremendous effort. If the poor were truly passive, few of them could even survive. People will feed themselves, if allowed to do so. It is not our job to "set things right" for others. Our responsibility is to remove the obstacles in their paths.

Myth 10: More U.S. aid will help the hungry
Reality: Most U.S. aid works directly against the hungry. Foreign aid can only reinforce, not change, the status quo. Emergency or humanitarian aid, which makes up only 5 percent of the total, often ends up enriching American grain companies while failing to reach the hungry, and it can dangerously undercut local food production in the recipient country. It would be better if there was a foreign aid budget for unconditional debt relief, as it is the foreign debt burden that forces most Third World countries to cut back on basic health, education, and antipoverty programs.

Paying the interest on foreign loans often cripples developing nations. Should developed nations write off such debts?

Myth 11: We benefit from their poverty
Reality: The biggest threat to the well-being of the vast majority of Americans is not the advancement but the continued deprivation of the hungry. In a global economy, what American workers have achieved in employment, wage levels, and working conditions can be protected only when working people in every country are freed from economic desperation. The growing numbers of "working poor" are those who have part- or full-time low-wage jobs yet cannot afford adequate nutrition or housing for their families.

Myth 12: Curtail freedom to end hunger
Reality: There is no theoretical or practical reason why freedom, taken to mean civil liberties, should be incompatible with ending hunger. We see no correlation between hunger and civil liberties. A definition of freedom more consistent with our nation's dominant founding vision holds that economic security for all is the guarantor of our liberty. Such an understanding of freedom is essential to ending hunger.

FACING REALITY AT THE WORLD FOOD SUMMIT
Lester R. Brown

NO

One outcome of the 1974 summit was the foundation of the World Food Council. Based in Rome, the council meets annually to discuss strategies for food policy.

In mid-November 1996 heads of state and ministers of agriculture gathered in Rome for the opening of the World Food Summit. It was the first such gathering since the first world food conference held 22 years ago, also in Rome. At that gathering in November 1974, U.S. Secretary of State Henry Kissinger promised that by 1984 no man, woman, or child would go to bed hungry. Although an expert in real politic, Kissinger had little understanding of what was needed to eradicate hunger or how to implement a meaningful plan to do so. We have to hope that this gathering will be more successful.

Many things have changed since 1974. At that time, there were scarcely 4 billion people in the world. Today there are more than 6 billion. During the seventies, the world fish catch was expanding. It no longer is. During the seventies, the world grain harvest was expanding rapidly. In recent years, it has expanded slowly. From 1950 to 1990, the oceanic fish catch climbed from 19 million tons to 89 million tons, boosting seafood consumption per person as a whole from 8 kilograms [16 lb.] per person to 17 kilograms [37 lb.] per person. It was an era of phenomenal progress in boosting seafood consumption. But since 1990, there has been no growth in the catch. With all 17 oceanic fisheries being fished at or beyond capacity, there is little prospect for future growth in the oceanic fish catch. For the first time in history, the world's farmers can no longer count on fishermen to help them expand the world food supply.

Grouping facts and figures in a paragraph is a powerful way to support your argument without continually interrupting its flow.

Meeting demand for grain

From 1950 to 1990, the world grain harvest climbed from 631 million tons to 1,780 million tons, expanding by 182 percent. From 1990 to 1996, it increased to 1,830 millions, a gain of 3 percent. The contrast between these two periods is startling. For 4 decades, the world's farmers expanded the grain harvest at nearly 3 percent a year, but during the nineties they have expanded it by only 3 percent in 6 years. Even if farmers can somehow pick up the pace, growth in the harvest promises to fall far short of earlier decades and far short of growing demand. Although growth in the grain harvest is slowing, the world continues to add nearly 90 million people per year. If these additional 90 million cannot be fed from an expanded harvest, then they will be fed by reducing consumption among those already here.

This is the core of Brown's argument—that more people will inevitably need more food.

Farmers now are coping not only with population growth but an unprecedented growth in affluence in Asia. Asia today, including the region from Pakistan east through Japan, contains over 3.1 billion people. Excluding Japan, the regional economy has grown by nearly 8 percent, enabling vast numbers of people to move up the food chain, consuming more grain-intensive livestock products—pork, poultry, eggs, and beef. There is no precedent for the rate of economic expansion or the scale of the growth.

Nowhere has this been more evident than in China. From 1991 to 1995, the Chinese economy expanded by 57 percent, raising income per person by roughly half. Much of this boost in income went to diversify diets, consuming more livestock products. This explosive growth in the demand for grain, combined with a loss of cropland to rapid industrialization, converted China from a net exporter in 1994 to the world's second largest grain importer in 1995, trailing only Japan.

In 1995 livestock consumed about 37 percent of the world's grain crop. To produce 1 lb. of beef requires 11 lb. of grain.

There are several reasons for the loss of momentum in the growth in the world grain harvest. For one thing, there is little fertile new land waiting to be plowed. There are some gains in cultivated area from reclamation projects, but overall, gains are small. They are likely to be offset by losses to non-farm uses, to industrial expansion, to residential development, and to the construction of roads, highways, and parking lots to accommodate automobiles.

Draining the world dry

Water scarcity, too, is constraining growth in the harvest. Water tables are falling in major food-producing regions: the southern Great Plains of the United States; much of northern India, including the Punjab, the breadbasket of India; and much of northern China. As aquifers are depleted, irrigation cutbacks are inevitable. Irrigated area is already shrinking in leading agricultural states, such as California, Texas, Kansas, Oklahoma, and Colorado, and in some provinces of northern China.

"Aquifers" are underground layers of rock that hold water.

In addition, the growing demand for water in cities is being satisfied by pulling irrigation water away from farmers. In cities as different as Los Angeles and Beijing, taking irrigation water from agriculture is satisfying growing water demand.

Consider the ways in which you use water at home or school. Are any of them wasteful?

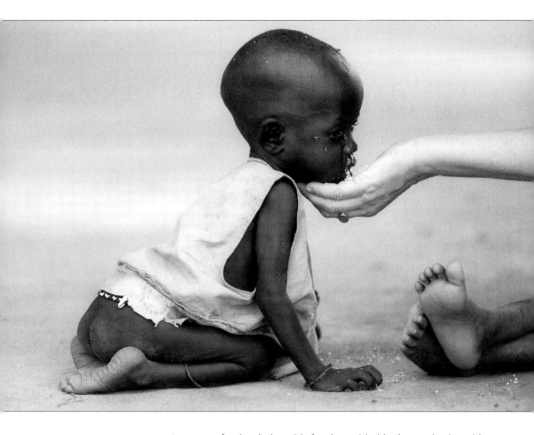

A woman feeds a baby with food provided by humanitarian aid workers in the village of Akon, in the Bahr El Ghazal province of Sudan, in October 1998.

In many countries, the amount of fertilizer being used is pressing against the physiological capacity of existing crop varieties to use additional fertilizer. As a result, fertilizer use has leveled off or declined in North America, Western Europe, the former Soviet Union, and Japan.

The author refers to the initial successes of the Green Revolution in the latter half of the 20th century.

In much of the world, the old formula of combining more and more fertilizer with ever higher-yielding varieties that was so successful for nearly half a century is no longer working very well. And there is no new formula to take its place. This is not only a challenge to farmers; it is a challenge to our late 20th-century civilization.

How political leaders respond to this potentially destabilizing situation in the next few years will tell us a great deal about the kind of world the next generation will be living in.

Hunger is the road to political instability

With these emerging constraints on efforts to expand food production, it comes as no surprise that there has been so little growth in the harvest during the nineties. This slowdown, combined with a continuing strong growth in demand, helps explain why world grain stocks have dropped, and why carryover stocks of grain are at the lowest level on record. It also helps explain why both wheat and corn prices are climbing to all-time highs.

Cereals exported as food aid by the United States dropped from 7.5 million tons in 1990–1991 to 3.2 million tons in 1994–1995.

Rising grain prices may be the first economic indicator signaling trouble in the relationship between ourselves and the natural systems and resources on which we depend. It may be telling us that we are on demographic and economic paths that are not environmentally sustainable. The message may be that it is time to change direction.

Those most immediately affected by food scarcity are the 1.2 billion people who, according to the World Bank, live on $1 per day. Of this, at least 70 cents is spent on food. If food prices double, heads of households will simply not be able to buy enough food to sustain their families. They will hold their governments responsible for rises in food prices, taking to the streets. The result could be political instability.

If you had to live on a low income, what would be the most important foodstuffs you would buy?

The bottom line of this analysis is that the world's fishermen and farmers can no longer assume the principal responsibility for achieving an acceptable balance between food and people. If national leaders fail to recognize the new constraints on efforts to expand food production and the associated need to dramatically step up efforts to stabilize world population, then food scarcity could lead to political instability and social disintegration in many countries, diminishing the economic prospect everywhere.

Summary

The notion that hunger and famine are caused by an exploding population only paints part of the picture of the world food situation. "Twelve Myths about Hunger" outlines that, in a simple calculation of numbers of people divided by the amount of total food production at the minimum daily requirements to sustain life, there is plenty of food to feed our population projections. What is lacking is the political infrastructure and motivation to distribute the food to poor and hungry people. It is precisely because hunger is more avoidable than it used to be that its continued prevalence is all the more intolerable. Lester Brown argues that population growth is the cause of famine and hunger. Already a large number of people cannot afford to buy the minimum amount of food necessary to sustain themselves. To make matters worse, prices will rise dramatically as more and more farmland goes out of production and our environment is stressed by expanding populations. If we are to avoid famine and hunger in the future, we are going to have to find solutions to the problem of food production and also ensure that it is priced so people around the world have access and can afford to buy it.

FURTHER INFORMATION:

Books:

Cohen, Joel E., *How Many People Can the Earth Support?* New York: W. W. Norton & Co., 1996.

Boucher, Douglas M., *The Paradox of Plenty: Hunger in a Bountiful World.* Oakland: Food First Books, 1998.

Evans, Lloyd. T., *Feeding the Ten Billion: Plants and Population Growth.* Cambridge, U.K.: Cambridge University Press, 1998.

Useful websites:

www.usaid.gov/

U.S. Agency for International Development, a government-funded aid agency.

www.ucc.ie/famine/

International Famine Center in Cork, Ireland. Collects and disseminates up-to-date news items on famine-related issues around the world.

www.fao.org/

The Food and Agriculture Organization. A United Nations agency tasked with improving food security and agricultural practices worldwide.

www.wfp.org/

The World Food Programme is the food aid organization of the United Nations.

The following debates in the Pro/Con series may also be of interest:

In this volume:

Topic 1 Does global warming threaten humankind?

Topic 2 Should the human population be stabilized?

Topic 4 Is organic food better than other food?

Topic 12 Is genetically modified food safe enough to feed the world's population?

Genetic Modification, pages 160–161

ARE FAMINE AND HUNGER AVOIDABLE?

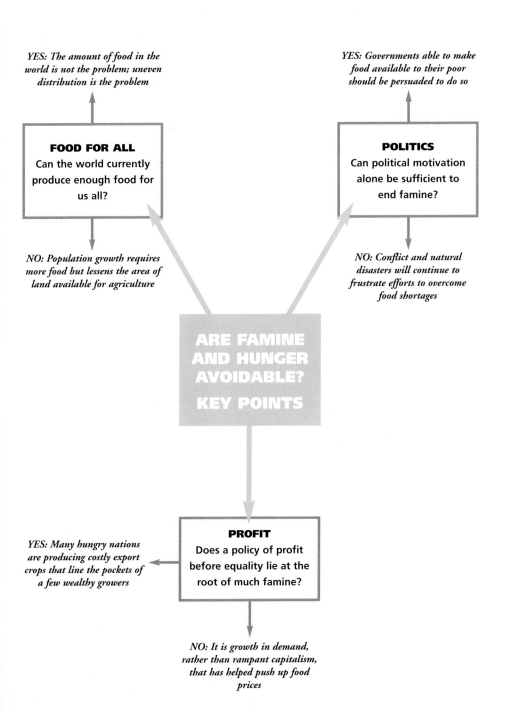

YES: The amount of food in the world is not the problem; uneven distribution is the problem

FOOD FOR ALL
Can the world currently produce enough food for us all?

NO: Population growth requires more food but lessens the area of land available for agriculture

YES: Governments able to make food available to their poor should be persuaded to do so

POLITICS
Can political motivation alone be sufficient to end famine?

NO: Conflict and natural disasters will continue to frustrate efforts to overcome food shortages

**ARE FAMINE AND HUNGER AVOIDABLE?
KEY POINTS**

YES: Many hungry nations are producing costly export crops that line the pockets of a few wealthy growers

PROFIT
Does a policy of profit before equality lie at the root of much famine?

NO: It is growth in demand, rather than rampant capitalism, that has helped push up food prices

45

Topic 4
IS ORGANIC FOOD BETTER THAN OTHER FOOD?

YES
"WHY AMERICANS ARE TURNING TO ORGANIC FOODS"
DULUTH (MN) NEWS TRIBUNE, JULY 3, 2000
RONNIE CUMMINS

NO
"THE FOLLY OF ORGANIC FARMING"
CHEMISTRY AND INDUSTRY, ISSUE 24, 1997
DENNIS AVERY

INTRODUCTION

There seems to be a trend throughout the developed world for people to become more concerned not just with what they eat in terms of its fat content or nutritional value, but also with where it comes from and how it is produced. Consumers in many countries are turning away from the products of agribusiness, the large commercial concerns that grow crops or raise livestock on a vast scale. They associate such farming with intensive production methods, such as the use of pesticides and other potentially harmful chemicals or the confinement of animals in inhumane living conditions.

Instead, there is ample evidence that consumers are turning increasingly toward organically grown food—defined as food produced without the use of artificial fertilizers, pesticides, growth hormones, and feed additives. Growing consumer demand has, for example, boosted the number of U.S. farmers using organic methods by 17 percent per year while other agricultural sectors are losing farmers.

Consumers who buy organic food do so for a number of reasons. Some are concerned about the ethical issues involved in intensive stock rearing. Others cite the potential damage to the environment from artificial chemicals. One of the most frequently heard arguments is that organic food, because of the lack of chemicals, is safer for people to eat. Some people argue that organically produced food simply tastes better than other food.

Such arguments seem straightforward enough, but there is fierce debate about the claims for organic food—in part, at least, because of the value of the retail food sector and the promise of high profits. Both the pro-organic lobby and their opponents, which include some scientists and the powerful forces of agribusiness, are well organized and skilled at achieving publicity for their particular point of view.

Supporters of the organic movement argue that artificial chemicals carry a greater risk of causing disease such as cancer. Opponents argue that, on a molecular level, such products simply work in the same way as chemicals in the natural world. Food is, in any case, some argue, only one potential source of disease; people should be more worried about air pollution or about the fat content of their food, not how it was grown. Organic consumers believe that genetic modification of plants or animals will disrupt the balance of nature; opponents argue that such has occurred in nature through crossfertilization of plants and animals for millennia. Opponents also argue that organic farmers, who have to work the land harder to raise the same amount of food, actually do more harm to the environment than farmers using chemical fertilizers.

> *"Those wishing to exploit the land for their own private benefit never cease their political efforts. Those who would protect the natural world cannot afford to do less."*
>
> —R.F. DASMANN,
> AUTHOR OF *WILDLIFE BIOLOGY*

Opposition to the organic movement also argues that the industry has grown so large that "green" companies driven by the need to make profits are no longer as trustworthy as they might

have been when the movement was younger and more idealistic. Some organic practices are not wholly free of artificial substances, for example, and consumers are unable to rely on truthful product labeling to know what food is organic and what not.

U.S. consumers rely for information on organic food on the Department of Agriculture (USDA). The USDA has established food production standards and practices for organic farming and a certification process for food that can be sold with an "organic" label. But the USDA is careful to state that such labeling applies only to the methods used in food production—without the use of irradiation, sewage sludge, or genetic engineering, for example—and does not reflect any judgment on the quality or safety of the food itself.

The following two articles outline the main issues in the organic food debate. Ronnie Cummins, national director of the Organic Consumers Association, argues that food safety issues make organic food a safer option. He states that most normally produced food is tainted by toxic-pesticide residues, antibiotic drugs in food, food poisoning, irradiation, and the threat to the environment from industrialized agricultural pollution. Taking all those factors into consideration, organic food offers a far safer and healthier alternative to conventionally produced food.

In "The Folly of Organic Farming" Dr. Dennis Avery, an outspoken critic of organic farming, argues that there are no advantages in growing and eating organic food. He claims that organic crops produce low yields, cause soil erosion, sap the soil of nutrients, are a danger to wildlife, and that pesticide levels are not a health risk.

WHY AMERICANS ARE TURNING TO ORGANIC FOODS
Ronnie Cummins

See
www.purefood.org
for more
information on
organic foods.

YES

Organic foods are the fastest growing and most profitable segment of American agriculture, according to government statistics. A February 1997 poll by the genetic engineering corporation Novartis found that 54 percent of U.S. consumers would prefer to see organic agriculture become the predominant form of food production—as opposed to conventional, chemical-intensive farming or agricultural biotechnology.

Environmentally friendly

A June 2000 survey carried out by the National Center for Public Policy, a conservative think tank, indicated that 68 to 69 percent of the U.S. public believe that the organic label on food products means that they are safer and better for the environment. This is the main reason why 10 million organic consumers will buy eight billion dollars worth of organic food this year in the United States. In Europe trends indicate that 30 percent of all farming may be organic by the year 2010. More and more health and environmentally conscious Americans are turning to organic food. And for good reason:

Concern over toxic pesticide residues

For further
information about
pesticides and
their effect on
children, see
www.epa.gov/pestic
ides/food/pest.htm.

A March 1999 study by Consumer Reports found that organic foods had little or no pesticide residues compared to conventional produce. A 1999 study by the Environmental Working Group found that millions of U.S. children eating non-organic fruits and vegetables were ingesting dangerous amounts of a variety of pesticide neurotoxins and carcinogens.

Concern over antibiotic drug residues

Organic farming prohibits the use of antibiotics in animal feed. Recent scientific research has confirmed the fact that antibiotics, routinely fed to factory farm animals to make them grow faster, are creating dangerous antibiotic-resistant pathogens which are infecting Americans who eat these animal products.

Concern over food poisoning

[With] deadly e-Coli 0157:H7, campylobacter, salmonella, listeria, and other food-borne diseases, the Centers for Disease Control admit that there are at least 76 million cases of food poisoning every year in the United States. While there are no documented cases of organic meat or poultry setting off food poisoning epidemics, filthy slaughterhouses, contaminated feed, and diseased animals are commonplace in industrial agriculture. According to government statistics, most non-organic beef cattle are contaminated with e-Coli 0157:H7; over 90 percent of chickens are tainted with campylobacter, and 30 percent of poultry are infected with salmonella.

In 1999 the USDA announced certified labeling of organic meat, poultry, and meat products.

Concern over food irradiation

Organic certification prohibits irradiation, sewage sludge, and genetic engineering. A 1997 poll by CBS found 77 percent of Americans opposed to food irradiation, while a recent survey by the Angus Reid polling group found the majority of U.S. consumers opposed to genetically engineered foods. Consumers are especially incensed that industry and

The Organic Consumers Association is running a campaign against irradiation. They want labeling of irradiated foods to continue to preserve consumer choice.

A farmer's market, showing some of the range of organically grown foods that are currently available.

Summary of results from ten animal studies: Comparisons of organic with conventional feed

Reproduction

FEMALES: Higher ovum production in rabbits (6 versus 3 eggs per dam) and chickens (192 versus 150 eggs per hen).

MALES: Testes in better condition in mice; sperm motility greater in bulls.

YOUNG: Fewer perinatal deaths and other deaths prior to weaning in rabbits (mortality rate of 27 percent versus 51 percent), in mice (mortality rate of 9 percent versus 17 percent) and rats.

OVERALL: Fertility rate of rabbits remained constant over three generations in organically fed rabbits and declined in rabbits fed conventionally produced feed.

Weight maintenance and growth

- Lower percentage weight loss (22.4 percent versus 37.4 percent) and longer survival (50 versus 33 days) in birds with polyneuritis.

- Better weight maintenance in lactating female rats.

- Higher percentage weight gain in young rats (77 percent versus 51.4 percent) and in chickens.

- Better weight gain after coccidial illness and fewer incidents of illness in chickens.

the FDA refuse to require labeling of genetically engineered food. Numerous polls over the past 15 years have found that 80–95 percent of Americans want labels on gene-altered foods, mainly so that they can avoid buying them.

Would you prefer to know exactly what is in the food you are eating?

Concern over the environment

Studies indicate that the industrialization and globalization of agriculture are a leading contributor to greenhouse gases and climate destabilization. Other research shows an increasing percentage of municipal water supplies are contaminated by pesticide residues, chemical fertilizers, and sewage runoff from factory farms and feedlots.

It's no wonder consumers are turning to organic foods while biotechnology and agri-chemical special interests are starting to panic.

Danger to wildlife

But don't pesticides kill birds and other wildlife? Regrettably, there are still some accidents and misapplications, both from farming and home use of pesticides. We must continue trying to find still-safer pest controls and to extend further integrated pest management. However, the world's recent losses of wildlife to modern farming have been trivial compared with the billions of birds and other wild creatures whose homes have been saved from the plow by higher yields.

THE FOLLY OF ORGANIC FARMING
Dennis Avery

NO

Movie star Paul Newman has just added a line of organic foods to his Newman's Own food company (which he runs as a charity sideline). He did it at the behest of his daughter, Nell, who's a biologist, a Californian, and passionate about the environment.

European governments are subsidizing organic farming because it uses fewer man-made chemicals than mainstream agriculture.

A danger to the environment?

The Chicago Tribune says organic food is now becoming mainstream. "No longer does organic mean apples with worm holes or scrawny carrots ignored at the end of the produce aisle. Marketers and manufacturers are blending the environmental appeal of traditional organic agriculture with a gourmet image. An armada of new organic goods is sailing into mainstream markets." This might be enough to make organic foods a significant danger to the environment.

To date, organic food hasn't been much of a problem. It has met only about 1 percent of the food demand in the United States and other affluent countries. Most organic production has been of fruits and vegetables, which get fairly high yields per acre, even on organic farms. If the organic fad goes mainstream, however, the world will be faced with the true environmental cost of organic production—low yields.

Lower yields

Organic farmers get only about half as much output per acre of farmland as modern mainstream farmers. That means they would need twice as much farmland to produce the food supply we use today. We would have to clear another 5 million or 6 million square miles of wildlife habitat for crops—or the total land equivalent of the United States and Mexico. Most of those wildlands would be cleared to grow nitrogen-fixing crops. Nitrogen is the key nutrient for crops. Mainstream farmers apply nitrogen captured from the atmosphere by an industrial process. But organic farmers claim chemical nitrogen is "bad", and insist on using organic

Critics of organic farming, like Dennis Avery, claim that lower yields lead to plowing out weeds, which causes soil erosion. The solution of mainstream farmers is to use chemical herbicides to control weeds, rather than plowing to remove them.

nitrogen. Thus, the average organic farm has one-third of its land planted to "green manure crops" such as clover, instead of producing grains, oilseeds, or vegetables.

Soil erosion

More organic farming would also mean more soil erosion—the biggest single threat to the sustainability of the human race. Erosion would increase both because organic farmers get lower yields, and because they refuse to use the chemical herbicides that mainstream farmers are now using to control weeds in "conservation tillage" systems. By using herbicides to control weeds instead of plowing, conservation tillage cuts soil erosion by 65–95 percent. It is being used now on hundreds of millions of acres of farmland all around the world. (It also encourages more earthworms and subsoil bacteria; these hate being plowed.) Rather than use herbicides, the organic farmers still insist on "steel solutions" such as plowing, hoeing, and mechanical cultivation.

For more information on conservation tillage, see the Core 4: Conservation for Agriculture's Future website at ctic.purdue.edu/ Core4/CT/CT.html.

"Humans simply cannot exist in the natural world without exerting some impact. Nevertheless, while we cannot hope to have no impact, we can hope to have less impact."

—JON WITMAN,

PROFESSOR OF ECOLOGY AND EVOLUTIONARY

BIOLOGY

Replacement minerals

Trace minerals are minerals used by organisms that exist in the soil in minute quantities.

Organic farmers claim that chemicals wear out the soil, or poison it. Just the opposite is true. When plants grow, they take nitrogen, phosphate, potash, and 26 other trace minerals out of the soil. Mainstream farmers replace precisely what the crops have used up. Organic farmers try to replace the nutrients indirectly. Sometimes it works, sometimes not. They seem to have forgotten that millions of America's organic farmers went West in the 19th century—because they had worn out their farms in the East. (Mainly, they had used up the nitrogen and phosphate in their soils.)

Most consumers are also astounded to find that organic farmers generally use more pounds of pesticide, applied more often, than "chemically-supported" farmers. The "natural" pesticides that organic farmers use are also worse for the soil. Such elemental chemicals as sulfur and copper don't break down in the soil, and aren't readily taken up by the plants. Cornell University recently concluded that the sulfur used in organic farming was the most environmentally harmful substance widely used in farming.

Nutrient levels

But aren't organic foods more nutritious? An international conference at Tufts University recently got reports from a dozen countries comparing the nutrient levels of organic and mainstream crops. Most of the comparison tests were done by organic enthusiasts—and they couldn't find any significant nutritional differences. (The variety of carrot made more difference than the farming system.)

The U.S. National Research Council (NRC) recently made its most comprehensive examination of pesticide residues and cancer. It concluded that natural carcinogens in our fruits and vegetables represent a far greater cancer risk than the low levels of pesticide residues found in our foods—and that neither is present at high enough levels to constitute a health risk. The report comes as close as real scientists ever will to saying "don't worry." Instead, the NRC urges people to eat more fruit and vegetables—because eating five a day can cut total cancer risks by half, no matter how they were grown!

Danger to wildlife

But don't pesticides kill birds and other wildlife? Regrettably, there are still some accidents and misapplications, both from farming and home use of pesticides. We must continue trying to find still-safer pest controls and to extend further integrated pest management. However, the world's recent losses of wildlife to modern farming have been trivial compared with the billions of birds and other wild creatures whose homes have been saved from the plow by higher yields.

Does this conclusion by Cornell academics surprise you? Do you think enough information is available on the chemicals used in farming?

This issue is discussed further in an FDA publication: The Future Role of Pesticides in U.S. Agriculture (2000), which is free online on the National Academy Press website at www.nap.edu/books/0309065267/html/.

Summary

The question of whether organic food is better than other food is difficult to answer definitively. Ronnie Cummins is concerned about pesticide residues in food that may have a detrimental effect on millions of children, while Dennis Avery maintains that the levels of pesticide residues are not high enough to constitute a health risk.

Mainstream farming practices are dubious, according to Ronnie Cummins. He claims to have statistics to prove that bad practice in meat production causes millions of cases of food poisoning each year. Dennis Avery counters with the statement that far from preserving the quality of the soil, organic farmers wear it out or poison it by adding organic chemicals that don't break down in the soil.

According to the "no" lobby, organic farming is bad for the environment. Their argument is that it produces lower yields, which means lower profits. The argument seems to be based on what would happen if there was only organic farming; it does not allow for the possibility that both mainstream and organic farming could coexist. Organic farming is more labor intensive, hence employs more people. It takes longer to produce organic food, but it is distributed locally rather than traveling thousands of miles.

Ronnie Cummins is also concerned about food irradiation, toxic sewage sludge spread on farmland, and antibiotic drug residues in food that affect the health of consumers. He says that water supplies are contaminated with sewage runoffs, as well as pesticides and fertilizers, and that modern agriculture contributes to greenhouse gases and climate problems.

The taste of food is not mentioned by either side, but that may well be a consideration for the consumer.

FURTHER INFORMATION:

Books:

Brown, Lynda, *Organic Living: Simple Solutions for a Better Life (Organic)*. London: DK Publishing, 2001.
Clover, Charles, and HRH The Prince of Wales, *Highgrove: An Experiment in Organic Gardening and Farming*. New York: Simon & Schuster, 1993.

Useful websites:

www.ofrf.org
Website for the Organic Farming Research Foundation.
www.ers. usda.gov/briefing/Organic
ERS (Economic Research Service) U.S. Department of Agriculture website.
www.epa.com
Gives information on pesticide residues in food.

www.attra.org/attra-pub/perma.html
Describes permaculture.
www.hdra.org.uk
Researches and promotes organic farming and food.

The following debates in the Pro/Con series may also be of interest:

In this volume:

Topic 12 Is genetically modified food safe enough to feed the world's population?

IS ORGANIC FOOD BETTER THAN OTHER FOOD?

YES: Organic methods mean lower greenhouse gases, no contamination due to pesticide residues, no sewage runoff, and no fouling of water supplies

YES: In the case of exposure to pesticides, hormones, and antibiotics, particularly in regard to children's health, it is better to be safe than sorry

ENVIRONMENT
Do organic crops limit the damage to the environment?

HEALTH
Should we eat organic food for the sake of our health?

NO: Organic farming methods cause soil erosion and mineral deficiencies in the land

NO: There is no concrete proof that organic food is healthier for us than other food

IS ORGANIC FOOD BETTER THAN OTHER FOOD?

KEY POINTS

YES: Because of the advantages to the environment, general health, and animal welfare

YES: Organic food has, on average, a higher nutrient content

HIGH PRICE OF ORGANIC FOOD
Is it worth paying extra for organic food?

NO: The better taste of organic food cannot justify the extra cost

NO: Because nonorganic fruit and vegetables can be washed and peeled, then safely eaten

Topic 5

DO NATIONAL PARKS PRESERVE WILDERNESS?

YES

"NATIONAL PARKS AND WILDERNESS"

JOHN C. MILES

NO

"LIMITS OF NATIONAL PARK PROTECTION OF WILDERNESS"

NATHAN PAGE

INTRODUCTION

The start of wilderness destruction in America came with the earliest settlers. Clearing land for homes and agriculture and cutting down trees for timber began the destruction of native forests, prairies, wetlands, and other ecosystems that are now threatened. Today, once expansive natural habitats exist only in minute fragments. Animals that were once able to roam across the entire country are now restricted to small islands of their natural habitat.

In 1964 Congress enacted the Wilderness Act. The purpose of this act is to "assure that an increasing population accompanied by expanding settlement and growing mechanization does not occupy and modify all area … leaving no lands designated for preservation and protection in their natural condition." In other words, the law preserves wilderness sites for future generations.

This preservation is becoming increasingly important as more and more native habitats are threatened. Every day hundreds of species go extinct worldwide because of human activities. Wilderness areas are becoming ever more important since they offer the only refuge for some species. Thus, protecting the remaining areas has become even more vital. Areas designated as wilderness do not permit commercial enterprises or the building of permanent roads. They are devoted to conservation and to scientific, educational, scenic, and recreational purposes.

The Wilderness Act was a refinement of the national park system: Not all national parks are wildernesses. National parks came into being in a similar way. In 1832 George Catlin returned from the Dakotas worried about the effect that the westward movement was having on Indian civilization, wildlife, and wilderness. He wrote that they might be preserved "by some great protecting policy of the government … in a magnificent park." His idea came into being in 1864, when the government donated Yosemite Valley to California to preserve as a state park. In 1872 Yellowstone was reserved as a national park, which was protected by the Department of the Interior. By 1916 the Department of the Interior had 14 parks and 21 national monuments to manage.

Since there was no one to oversee these parks, President Woodrow Wilson approved the creation of the National Parks Service. Originally the parks were established to preserve areas that contained natural phenomena such as the geysers at Yellowstone, areas of historic significance, and places with awe-inspiring scenery like the Grand Canyon. Today national parks have expanded to include glaciers, mountains, and forests; there are 379 national parks across the United States. Every year millions of people visit national parks to see wildlife, escape the confines of the city, and learn about nature.

"The finest qualities of our nature, like the bloom on fruits, can be preserved only by the most delicate handling."

—HENRY DAVID THOREAU, PHILOSOPHER AND NATURALIST

It may seem odd to question whether or not national parks protect wilderness. At first glance it seems clear that the parks must inevitably protect areas by preserving them from destruction. They can be used for educating the public about wilderness, teaching them things they can do to save fragile habitats. National parks raise money through admission fees and donations that can be used to acquire more lands.

On the other hand, national parks attract many people to them, disrupting the unspoiled environment they are intended to protect. More than 10,000 people a day visit Yosemite Valley at popular times, for example. Roads, parking lots, hotels, restaurants, even cycle paths and campgrounds can potentially have detrimental effects on wildlife and their habitats. Visitors can affect wildlife by leaving litter, taking flash photographs, or making noise. Natural processes such as wildfires, insects, disease, and predator–prey relationships are altered when park workers interfere with natural events.

Today national parks are doing their part to protect natural habitats. They have instigated programs to remove nonnative plants. Researchers have been studying ways to clean up aquatic contaminants. Air quality is monitored to insure that human activities are not creating pollution. A new program has been established to ensure that roads in national parks "lie lightly on the land."

Parks such as Yosemite are actively reducing the number of parking lots they provide or offering alternatives to private automobiles as ways to visit. National parks also teach the public ways in which they can protect native habitats and the environment—lessons they can put to use in their own neighborhoods.

The following articles examine whether national parks can really protect wilderness. If you have visited a national park, think about the number of ways in which you were affecting the environment, and try to come up with ways in which that effect might have been reduced.

NATIONAL PARKS AND WILDERNESS
John C. Miles

Wilderness is a slippery concept. When people speak of wilderness they may mean many things: a natural landscape entirely without people or their works; a natural landscape where people spend time and build trails … but do not live; a huge tract of land in either of these conditions; a place where nature is wild and thereby threatening, as in occupied by grizzly bears and mountain lions and without the amenities associated with the "civilized" life.

The author sets out by defining what is meant by "wilderness." Loose terms, when used in acts of law like the Wilderness Act are easy to misinterpret.

Defining wilderness

John Muir, one of the earliest and most effective advocates of preserving wilderness, defined it as a place where natural processes continue to function unimpaired. Aldo Leopold, an influential forester and wilderness advocate, described wilderness as "a continuous stretch of country preserved in its natural state, open to lawful hunting and fishing, devoid of roads, artificial trails, cottages, or other works of man." And Bob Marshall, an influential wilderness advocate within the United States Forest Service in the 1930s once wrote that "I shall use the word wilderness to denote a region which contains no permanent inhabitants, possesses no possibility of conveyance by any mechanical means, and is sufficiently spacious that a person crossing it must have the experience of sleeping out." Common to these definitions are the qualities of naturalness and absence of human habitation.

If you follow Marshall's criteria, have you ever visited a wilderness?

In 1964 the United States Congress weighed into the argument over what constituted wilderness with a definition contained in the Wilderness Act of 1964. Section 2 of this act, which established a National Wilderness Preservation System in the United States, specified that: "A wilderness, in contrast with those areas where man and his own works dominate the landscape, is hereby recognized as an area where the earth and its community of life are untrammeled by man, where man himself is a visitor who does not remain."

Miles again defines a loose term used in an act of law.

The word "trammel," when used as a verb, means to restrain and confine. As used in the Wilderness Act, "untrammeled" specifies that natural communities in wilderness will not be constrained by human activity. They will be free to exist as they did before humans entered the landscape.

What is a national park?

The question I am exploring in this essay is whether national parks in the United States protect wilderness. With wilderness defined, the next task is to define national park. That should be easy, since everyone knows what a national park is, but care must be taken because there are many kinds of national park units in the United States' national park system. There are, in fact, no less than twenty categories of areas within the national park system, including national park, national monument, national historic site, national recreation area, and sixteen more. We must be specific about what we mean by "national park."

A national park is a tract of public land, designated by the United States Congress as a national park which, according to the National Park Index, contains "a variety of resources and encompasses large land or water areas to help provide adequate protection of resources." A national park is defined by the range of resources it contains—a greater range of resources than in other types of units—and by its scale, which is large and thus contributes to protection of the resources. When we think of national parks we think of Yellowstone with its geysers, mountains, elk, bison, grizzly bears, and now wolves. Or, perhaps we think of Glacier with its bears, glaciers, lakes, and mountains. National parks are big, beautiful, natural areas where these resources are protected from damage or destruction.

Many national parks exist to protect sites such as famous battlefields rather than areas of wilderness.

Imperfect protection

National parks do protect wilderness, though perhaps not perfectly. One can argue that there are roads and hotels and other developments in all national parks, so the wilderness is not protected. Or [one] might argue that wildlife that once lived in an area that is now a national park has been exterminated, so the wilderness is incomplete, therefore not protected. I will grant that complete protection of wilderness has not been achieved in national parks. National parks are not completely natural. Their ecological communities are not all intact. Some national parks are better than others in these regards, but on the whole the wild qualities of significant parts of the national parks are being protected.

Every park is different. I should be more specific. Consider, for instance, the North Cascades National Park Complex (it is called "Complex" because two national recreation areas, one with a town and the other with three dams and a reservoir, abut the park). The complex includes

Miles concedes that only partial protection is possible, but argues that this does not mean that national parks have failed.

North Cascades National Park, in Washington, was established in 1968.

684,243 acres, of which 634,243 acres are designated by Congress as the Stephen Mather Wilderness, named for the founding director of the U.S. National Park Service. Thus 93 percent of the complex is legally established wilderness. What this means is that in this 93 percent no roads can be built, no hotels or buildings of any kind constructed. No permanent human habitations of any sort will be allowed. Motors cannot penetrate the wilderness, except the occasional helicopter used for rescue or essential activity. Visitation to the wilderness is restricted to those who can hike or, in restricted areas, ride a horse into it. The community of living things in this wilderness is believed to be nearly intact, though threatened. It may be a refuge for a few grizzlies, fishers, and wolves, species that are very rare in the region. Around the park complex in the United States and Canada are over two million acres of wilderness in national forests and provincial parks.

The fisher or pekan, Martes pennanti, resembles a large pine marten. It preys on birds and small mammals.

The North Cascades National Park Complex is not without development, though it is obviously primarily a wilderness park. A road bisects it, passing through the Ross Lake National Recreation Area. Tourists can travel up Lake Chelan to the village of Stehekin where they can stay overnight, set out on a back- or horse-packing trip or, after a short foray, set out back down the lake on one of several commercial boats. The park can be visited, but tourists in their cars and RVs really only touch the fringes of this mountainous region. This is a park where if people really want to experience the essence of it, they must do so under their own power. The National Park Service carefully controls the numbers of people who can enter the park backcountry, where they can camp, and monitors the impact they are having upon the park resources. If visitors are creating a problem, measures to solve the problem can be taken.

Minimizing tourist intrusion

Yosemite was reserved as a state park in 1868 and made a national park in 1890.

Or, consider Yosemite National Park, one of the first parks in the system. In this 759,000-acre park, nearly 93 percent is designated wilderness. Yosemite is one of the most visited parks in the system, hosting nearly 3.5 million visitors in 1999. Most of these visitors do not experience wilderness, and do not wish to. They visit Yosemite Valley with its massive granite walls, truly monumental scenery, or tour the Mariposa Big Tree Groves and marvel at the grandeur of giant sequoias. The other 93 percent of the park certainly hosts visitors, but the National Park Service strives, as at

North Cascades, to control and manage backcountry use so as to minimize damage to the physical wilderness or to the wilderness experience.

Numbers like these certainly do not tell the whole story. Consider, for instance, that in Alaska there are 32.5 million acres of national parks, a little over 80 percent of which are designated wilderness (that's 26.5 million acres). So, the National Park Service strives to keep 80 percent of these lands "untrammeled," yet nearly all of the Alaska parks, whether officially designated as wilderness, meet most of the criteria defining wilderness. On the other hand, three of the largest and most popular national parks in the "lower 48," Grand Canyon, Yellowstone, and Glacier national parks, have not been designated by Congress as wilderness, yet significant portions of them are truly wild and are managed by the Park Service to keep them that way. Visitation in these parks, as in the Valley at Yosemite, is concentrated in a relatively small portion of the area.

Some of the largest national parks are in remote locations. Do you think that government should maintain wilderness areas even if they are not highly visited?

A contradictory mission

The National Park Service Act passed by Congress in 1916 specified that the National Park Service, which was created by the Act, would "provide for the enjoyment of" the national parks but "in such manner and by such means as will leave them unimpaired for the enjoyment of future generations." The Park Service has struggled since its inception with the contradictory nature of this mission. How does it make the parks accessible to ever-growing numbers of people while not impairing the qualities of these special places that led to their designation in the first place as national parks? Since its inception the Park Service has tried to develop the parks as unobtrusively as possible so as to meet the first part of its mission without compromising the second. It has been successful to a remarkable degree. Perhaps the best testimony to this is that after the Wilderness Act was passed in 1964, the Park Service was asked to inventory its lands for possible inclusion in the National Wilderness Preservation System. That inventory revealed that despite more than a half-century of pressure to develop the parks, there were still significant portions of most parks that remained wild. Many of them have since been added to the official wilderness system.

In what ways are the aims of the NPS contradictory?

What pressures might there be for the development of wilderness areas?

The national park system in the United States contains more than 44 million acres of congressionally designated wilderness. This land enjoys the highest level of protection of any part of the American landscape. The national parks do indeed protect wilderness.

LIMITS OF NATIONAL PARK PROTECTION OF WILDERNESS
Nathan Page

NO

Page's introduction provides a precise summary of the history and purpose of the National Park Service.

The National Park Service in the United States was established by Congress in 1916. This action was taken because of a need to improve administration and management of the thirteen national parks that Congress had earlier designated. The legislation was intended to state clearly the purpose of national parks and the goals the Park Service would seek to achieve in its administration of them. The Act stated that the Park Service would manage the parks to conform to the purpose Congress stipulated for them, "which purpose is to conserve the scenery and the natural and historic objects and the wild life therein and to provide for the enjoyment of the same in such manner and by such means as will leave them unimpaired for the enjoyment of future generations." The goals stated in the Act were conservation of the parks' resources and public enjoyment of them.

Conflict between conservation and commerce

This language sowed the seed of difficulty for the Park Service, for it built a contradiction into its mandate. That contradiction is that protecting scenery and wildlife and other resources and developing parks so that visitors can "enjoy" them have often proven to be conflicting actions. For instance, the greatest need of visitors is for access to parklands, and providing that access has involved the building of roads. Roads have concentrated the visitors, led to other development (the visitors need places to eat and sleep), and have often altered the scenery and disturbed the wildlife. Since the beginning of the debate about how national parks should be managed to meet Congress' mandate, defenders of wilderness have argued that to build a road into a wild place is to reduce or eliminate its wildness. Since most national parks have roads in them, their wilderness has not been as thoroughly protected as it might have been.

Do Americans have a right to expect to be able to drive to all parts of the country?

Throughout the history of the national park system, Park Service leaders have argued that they are protecting the wilderness. In 1929 Park Service Director Horace Albright responded to criticism that wilderness was not being protected in national parks by pointing out that less than 10 percent of the parks had been penetrated by roads and other works of humans. The rest of the parks, he argued, were therefore wilderness.

A few years later, in 1933, a team of the Park Service's own biologists released a report which described how national parks were hard pressed to protect wildlife because none of them had been established as "independent biological units" with protection of wildlife in mind. Park boundaries had been drawn with scenery or unique natural attractions in mind (like geysers at Yellowstone, an unusual volcanic lake at Crater Lake, or a monumentally scenic valley at Yosemite). The habitat needs of the wild creatures comprising the natural communities of these areas had not been considered. Furthermore, the Park Service had even actively eradicated certain "bad animals," usually predators like wolves, coyotes, and mountain lions, so that the "good animals" like elk and bison which people enjoyed watching, and which were hunted by these predators, could thrive. The result was anything but natural, wild parks. By 1933 some animals like wolves had been entirely eradicated from national parks, while others were in serious trouble.

The boundaries of national parks are based on human factors, not on considerations such as the ranges of animals within them.

Page argues that visitor demands led to disruption of wildlife communities early in the parks' history.

A return to nature?

Decades passed during which the National Park Service fielded a steady drumbeat of criticism about its park management practices. It ceased its predator control practices, and struggled to define what "wilderness" was and how it could cater to tourists while at the same time maintaining nature "unimpaired."

In 1963 a group of independent biologists, commissioned by the Park Service to assess its resource management, drew some of the same conclusions [as did] the earlier scientists, this time with a more sophisticated ecological perspective. If the national parks were managed to be wild and unimpaired, each park should be managed so that "a vignette of primitive America" would be reestablished comparable to conditions of that landscape at the time of first European contact. This would mean that animals no longer present in parks where they had been (as wolves at Yellowstone) should be restored to them, that natural wildfire (as caused by lightning) should be allowed to burn, thereby acting as the ecological agent it had been for eons, and where natural communities had been altered they should be restored as much as possible.

Wolves were reintroduced into Yellowstone in 1995.

Moose (Alces alces) thrive in some American national parks, especially those where the intrusion caused by access roads has been kept to a minimum.

The Park Service tried to do this, but ran into many difficulties, not the least of which was that the public, whose "enjoyment" of park resources the Service was also bound to serve, did not always want wolves and grizzly bears in their parks and could not accept the naturalness of landscapes scorched by wildfire. The Park Service's efforts to restore fire as an ecological process in national parks was, for instance, severely criticized in 1988 at Yellowstone as fires roared through that park.

Congress passed the Wilderness Act in 1964 and instructed the Park Service to identify the parts of the park system that remained wild and recommend what parts of the system Congress should designate as part of the National Wilderness Preservation System. The Park Service did as instructed, and many wilderness areas were designated, totaling over 44 million acres in 2001.

The Service has been striving to restore wildness where it has been reduced, and to maintain it where it exists, but its challenges to do so are many. There is constant pressure from commercial interests to gain access to resources "locked up" in wilderness. Most parks, even the newest ones, were not delineated with any biological unit in mind, so maintaining natural conditions for wildlife is difficult. Bison, for instance, wander outside Yellowstone during hard winters and are killed by hunters or agricultural officials worried about livestock disease. Development outside the boundaries of national parks proceeds rapidly. The skies over the Grand Canyon are at times a haze of air pollution generated by power plants in the region. The air space over many parks buzzes and roars with sight-seeing aircraft. Trees are logged right to park boundaries, and "gateway communities" of people capitalizing on the economic opportunities provided by the popularity of national parks are growing along those boundaries. Not the least of the challenges is the sheer numbers of people coming for their share of the "enjoyment" of the parks, a number approaching 300 million visitors annually as the 21st century begins.

The Park Service manages to maintain a significant portion of the national park system in a relatively wild condition. But the national parks are not "unimpaired" as the 1916 law says they should be, and their wilderness is not, in many places, "untrammeled" to the extent intended by the Wilderness Act. The whole responsibility for this cannot be laid upon the Service. Maintenance in a natural state of any part of a world of six going on ten billion technologically powerful human beings may be impossible. Only time will tell.

What factors might make it unrealistic to try to restore wilderness today? Do you think many Americans actually want to experience "real" wilderness?

Bison can transmit brucellosis and tuberculosis to domestic cattle.

Page concludes that in a strict interpretation the Park Service not only fails in its duties, but possibly has no chance of succeeding.

Summary

The article "National Parks and Wilderness" describes how national parks preserve wilderness. Wilderness can be defined in many ways. Most of the definitions, however, insist that wilderness is natural, and humans do not live in it. National parks are defined as tracts of public land that are large enough to preserve a variety of resources. While national parks are not completely natural, they do protect wilderness by preserving large areas of natural habitat. The main areas of human effect lie on the fringes of national parks; the majority of the area is wild, with no human habitation and very little human influence. In most national parks less than 10 percent of the area is openly accessible by visitors. The remaining 90 percent or more is being protected as required by the Wilderness Act.

The article "Limits of National Park Protection of Wilderness" states that national parks go only so far in preserving the wildness of the land, given the extent to which tourists are permitted to intrude. Furthermore, the balance of native animals has been distorted for the benefit of humans; in many parks the big cats and wolves are gone, eradicated to create a sanitized "wilderness." Today efforts are under way to redress that imbalance. In its defense the National Park Service states the difficulty of meeting the challenge set by the 1916 Act: both to provide recreation and enjoyment, and to preserve the wilderness for future generations. In the mechanized, industrialized United States of today that challenge is greater than ever.

FURTHER INFORMATION:

Books:

Davis, Richard C. (editor), *Encyclopedia of American Forest and Conservation History* (2 volumes). New York: Macmillan 1983.

Richard King Mellon Foundation (sponsor), *National Parks for a New Generation: Visions, Realities, Prospects.* Washington, D.C.: The Conservation Foundation, 1985.

Sax, Joseph L., *Mountains without Handrails*. Ann Arbor, MI: The University of Michigan Press, 1980.

Useful websites:

www.nps.gov
Website of the National Park Service.
www.epa.gov/globalwarming/impacts/parks/
A site run by the Environmental Protection Agency concerned with conservation of U.S. national parks.
www.wilderness.net/nwps/default.cfm
National Wilderness Preservation Wildlife.
www.blm.gov/nhp/Preservation/wilderness

Bureau of Land Management.
www.wilderness.org/
Wilderness Society site.
www.enn.com
Environmental News Network.

The following debates in the Pro/Con series may also be of interest:

In this volume:

Topic 5 Is sustainable development possible?

Topic 7 Can a "pay-to-pollute" system significantly reduce air pollution?

DO NATIONAL PARKS PRESERVE WILDERNESS?

YES: The most popular parts of national parks draw the big crowds away from the more pristine wilderness areas

YES: Though they are not perfect, parks are the last refuges for flagship species like bears, big cats, and wolves

TOURISM
Should national parks encourage visitors?

WILDLIFE
Are national parks suitably managed for the protection of wildlife?

NO: The Park Service has long struggled with the contradictory demands of pleasing tourists and preserving wilderness

NO: Few parks are big enough to accommodate wide-ranging predators and herbivores; many boundaries cut across animal migration routes or ranges

DO NATIONAL PARKS PRESERVE WILDERNESS?
KEY POINTS

YES: The Park Service is constantly updating its strategies for following ecologically sound procedure

YES: In our increasingly urbanized world people place a high value on wilderness

PEOPLE PRESSURE
Can we continue to preserve wild spaces in the United States?

NO: Increasing pressure on land abutting national parks is seriously degrading park air and water quality

NO: Government concessions to ecologically destructive commercial enterprises reveal a cynical policy of "profit before preservation"

GLOBAL WARMING

Global warming is caused by the release of excess greenhouse gases from burning fossil fuels, burning vegetation to clear lands, and various other human activities. These gases, which include carbon dioxide, methane, and nitrous oxide, have the effect of trapping the sun's heat in the atmosphere, reflecting it back toward Earth rather than allowing it to escape into space. The result is that global temperatures are higher than they would be normally. Most climate experts estimate that global average temperatures will rise by 0.5 °F (0.3 °C) per decade if current emission trends continue. This would mean that temperatures would rise by 1.8 °F (1 °C) by 2025 and 5.4 °F (3 °C) before the end of this century.

A changing climate

Before the industrial revolution in the early 19th century climate change was a natural phenomenon. Very few gases were released into the atmosphere by human activity. However, the industrial revolution brought rapid change and development, initially in Europe and then in the rest of the world, through more machine-intensive industry and agricultural practices. Today rapid population growth, increasing urbanization, fossil-fuel burning, and deforestation have all affected the mixture of gases in our atmosphere, and that has led to changes in the global climate.

The rate of change

Global average temperatures have already increased an estimated 0.5–1.0 °F (0.3–0.6 °C) since the late 19th century. The 10 warmest years of the 20th century all occurred between 1985 and 2000—and 1998 was the warmest year. Over the same period worldwide sea levels have risen by 3 to 9 in. (7.5–23 cm), a phenomenon with two main causes. The world's oceans have heated up, leading to an expansion of ocean water, while higher average air temperatures have significantly reduced the amount of floating ice in the Arctic Ocean.

The cost of global warming

Average global precipitation (rainfall) will increase as the climate warms and the rate of evaporation increases. Severe rainstorms are likely to become more frequent, and the sea level along most of the U.S. coast will rise by an estimated 2 feet (0.6 m). Over the next few hundred years rising sea levels may flood hundreds of islands, possibly devastating Tuvalu and Kiribati in the Pacific and the Maldives in the Indian Ocean. Low-lying farmland and cities occupied by hundreds of millions of people might also be inundated. Meanwhile vast tracts of the Amazon and other rain forests will disappear because the trees and vegetation will be unable to adapt fast enough to the sudden changes in the

GREENHOUSE GASES

Some greenhouse gases occur naturally in the atmosphere; others result from human activities. Estimates of greenhouse gas emissions are usually measured in units of million of metric tons of carbon equivalents (MMTCE), which weigh each gas by its Global Warming Potential or GWP.

Powerful gases not naturally produced include:

Hydrofluorocarbons (HFCs)	All of these gases
Perfluorcarbons (PFCs)	are a by-product of
Sulfur hexafluoride (SF6)	industrial processes

Powerful gases produced naturally include:

Carbon dioxide	Released when fossil fuels such as oil, natural gas, and coal, wood, wood products, and solid waste are burned.
Nitrous oxide	Released during combustion of solid waste and fossil fuels and agricultural and industrial waste and fossil fuels. It absorbs 270 times more heat per molecule than carbon dioxide.
Methane	Emitted during production/transportation of coal and natural gas. It traps over 21 times more heat per molecule than carbon dioxide.

world's climate. Entire coral reefs—among the richest of all marine habitats—will suffocate and die because coral is susceptible to even slight changes in water temperature.

Global warming and the United States

According to the Environmental Protection Agency (EPA), the United States emits around 6.6 tns. (about 15,000 1bs. carbon equivalent) of greenhouse gases (see above) per person per year. Emissions per person increased between 1990 and 1997, rising by around 3.4 percent per person. This mostly originated from burning fossil fuels to run cars and generate electricity, and generating methane from waste products in landfills, gas pipelines, coal, industrial chemicals, and raising livestock.

The United States generates more greenhouse gases per person than any other country in the world. Despite that fact, in 2001 George W. Bush's administration refused to ratify the Kyoto Protocol, aimed at reducing the world's greenhouse gas emissions (see page 90). That decision has brought heavy criticism from environmental pressure groups and other nations ready to ratify the agreement, who believe that the United States is not acting in the world's best interests.

PART 2
ECONOMIC FORCES

Economic growth, especially since the mid-19th century, has frequently had a detrimental effect on the environment. Environmentalists are concerned about the protection and preservation of the world's natural resources, but this can come at a cost. Nonrenewable resources, such as oil and coal, need to be balanced against renewable energy sources, such as wind and solar power.

In today's society money is a driving motivational factor. People are sometimes unwilling to invest money in the environment because they do not see a monetary return. However, this is short-sighted since they overlook the fact that nature provides many services for free. The production of oxygen, filtering of pollutants, and reduction of carbon dioxide are just a few of the valuable processes that nature performs. As the value of the services that nature provides become more widely accepted, the economics behind decisions involving the environment will become more important.

Cost-benefit analysis

One way in which environmentalists decide on the best course of action is through cost-benefit analysis, which calculates all the benefits of an activity (both in the short and long term) and then subtracts all of the costs of the activity, leaving a monetary value that can be compared to the value of alternative activities.

The problem with relating cost analysis to environmental matters is that it is very difficult to assign a monetary value to the benefits or costs of, for example, having clean air. It would, of course, be possible to estimate the medical costs of people with breathing disorders, but that would not take into account all the plants and animals affected by polluted air. It would also not allow for what effect smog hovering over a city would have. Thus sometimes another model is used to determine the effects of a planned activity.

Impact assessment

An environmental impact assessment is used to predict the repercussions of a planned activity (usually development) on the environment. The assessment analyzes what effects construction will have, as well as what effects the actual structure will have. Air pollution, land degradation, and water contamination are all examined. Quality of life impacts such as noise pollution, visual intrusion, and loss of scenic beauty are also looked at. When all of the effects are assessed, the project can be analyzed to see if the benefits outweigh the costs. The decision-maker then decides if it is in the best interest of the public to go ahead with the project. Sometimes he or she decides that it is worth proceeding and tries to offset some of the costs of production by charging them to the consumer. This subject is examined in Topic 6, *Should corporations pay the full environmental costs of producing their goods?* Introducing a "pay-to-pollute" system to reduce fossil-fuel emissions and help prevent global warming is looked at in Topic 7, *Can a "pay-to-pollute" system significantly reduce air pollution?*

detrimental effects might not become apparent for many years. There may be serious consequences, but assigning a cost to them is extremely challenging.

Assessing environmental value

As environmental functions and processes become better understood and appreciated, their value will be easier to assess. When the actual value of the environment is determined,

---

"Over the long haul of life on this planet, it is the ecologists, and not the bookkeepers of the business, who are the ultimate accountants."

—STEWART L. UDALL, U.S. SECRETARY OF THE INTERIOR

Types of environmental costs

When calculating costs associated with the environment, there are many types to consider. The first are internalized or direct costs. They are the easiest to discern and involve costs associated with performing environmental impact assessments, preventative actions like installation of safety valves, mitigation, reclamation, and compensation. A reclamation cost is the cost of returning a site to its former state. Compensation costs are those incurred for damage to the environment that cannot be fixed.

Externalized or indirect costs are also important. They are harder to determine and include costs associated with degradation of the environment, global climate change, and depletion of natural resources. It is hard to calculate what effect global climate change (see *Global Warming*, pages 70–71) or the depletion of natural resources will have on future generations, since

it will be harder to destroy natural habitats and degrade the ecosystem. New laws and regulations will make it more costly to do work that will negatively affect the environment.

Businesses cannot afford to waste money on expensive mitigations or site reclamations, so they will begin incorporating practices that do not damage the environment. Environmentally friendly practices might have higher direct costs; but because they prevent accumulation of indirect costs, they will be much cheaper overall.

Since it is inevitable that nonrenewable resources will eventually run out, society and industry have had to investigate using alternative methods of power. Topic 8, *Can wind and solar resources meet our energy needs?* and Topic 9, *Will hydrogen replace oil as our primary energy source?* examine these issues.

Topic 6

SHOULD CORPORATIONS PAY THE FULL ENVIRONMENTAL COSTS OF PRODUCING THEIR GOODS?

YES
"JUSTICE AND FINANCIAL MARKET ALLOCATION OF THE SOCIAL COSTS OF BUSINESS"
JOURNAL OF BUSINESS ETHICS, VOLUME 29, ISSUE 1/2, JANUARY 2001
SANDRA L. CHRISTENSEN AND BRIAN GRINDER

NO
"A CONSUMER'S GUIDE TO ENVIRONMENTAL MYTHS AND REALITIES"
REASON FOUNDATION, POLICY REPORT NO. 165, SEPTEMBER 1991
LYNN SCARLETT

INTRODUCTION

When we look to see where the biggest effects on the environment come from, it is pretty evident that people are number one. Humankind has gone from being a small part of the Earth's ecosystem, with effects that were well buffered and minimal, to being a huge part of the system, with impacts that are large and frequent. Many of these effects are related to increased industrial activity and increased demands on natural resources. The link between the environment and economy is very close.

The main institution of the present economic and environmental era is the corporation. The top 1,000 companies in the United States account for over 60 percent of its gross national product. The top 400 companies employ nearly 25 percent of the U.S. population. Because they are such an important part of our economy, and because so many people work for them, people have come to believe that the success of corporations is inextricably linked to the success of humanity.

The key measure by which most companies evaluate success is economic profit. However, as concerns for the environment and for social justice have taken root, so has scrutiny of the ecological and human health effects that corporations create as a result of doing their business. The first response to this concern was the passage of air and water pollution laws to protect the environment and laws to protect the health and safety of workers and other people exposed to harmful wastes and dangerous jobs. They improved the quality of air and water and reduced the risk of getting hurt or sick from exposure to harmful substances and from other practices in the workplace.

There is a growing movement, within both the environmental and the corporate community, to expand the notion of profit and costs beyond purely economic terms. These broader definitions see environmental impact as a negative cost and the improvement of the environment as a form of profit that increases not economic but natural and social capital. Natural and social capital have become part of the language of business. Can a company operate in a way that it makes a financial profit, but also increases the ability of ecosystems to produce the natural resources and services that humanity relies on? And can it create a net gain in the health and well-being of people who work for it and who live in the communities where it operates?

Take for example, the Interface company, whose founder and chief executive officer Ray Anderson has transformed its vision and mandate from simply making money by selling the best carpeting to becoming the first truly sustainable corporation. In fact, Anderson wants to go beyond sustainable to become a "restorative" corporation—one that develops technologies and practices that emulate the natural system and in the process helps improve the environment (rather than just doing no harm).

Since 1994 Anderson has changed how Interface operates. By the end of the year 2000 his company eliminated over $165 million in waste from its products and processes. It has also reduced by 26 percent the amount of waste that has to somehow go back into the environment. The goal is zero waste. Recently Interface introduced the first commercial carpeting that is entirely biodegradable and recyclable. It is made from corn.

There are other good examples of companies that are making a positive difference in protecting the environment and helping improve people's lives. Possible ways to encourage companies to accelerate their movement toward more socially and environmentally responsible ways of doing business include legislation and financial incentives or fines. The profit motive might prompt more responsible actions. If a company is making a profit on goods produced from rain forest clearing, should it not pay for the loss of biodiversity in the forest or the loss of food and shelter sources of the people who live in and around the rain forest? Or if their product causes harm to people, like cigarette smokers, should they not pay for the loss of health and life? Such questions may seem straightforward, but they raise complex issues. Should a company take into account the social and environmental costs of its operations and pass them on to its customers, for example? Prices of many goods would probably rise. Yet consumers are not responsible for companies' business practices and have no direct say in how they produce their goods and services; so, why should the consumers pay the cost?

In the articles that follow, Sandra Christensen and Brian Grinder argue that shareholders should bear the cost since it is they who profit when the company does. Lynn Scarlett looks at solid waste management and argues that the imposition of incentives or disincentives through government intervention is a poor way to address problems. She believes that the free-market system is the best mechanism we have for finding solutions to our environmental problems.

JUSTICE AND FINANCIAL MARKET ALLOCATION OF THE SOCIAL COSTS OF BUSINESS
Sandra L. Christensen and Brian Grinder

Developed in the 18th century, "neoclassical economic theory" argues that the most efficient economy is not regulated by government, but responds only to the laws of supply (the resources available) and demand (what consumers want and what they are prepared to pay).

Standard neoclassical economic theory asserts that the price mechanism works to bring together willing buyers and willing sellers to complete an exchange which is mutually beneficial, while at the same time achieving an optimum allocation of scarce resources in a society. A transaction, as described, between two willing participants each acting for their own benefit is voluntary, and therefore just. However, few economists would argue that such a "perfect" transaction exemplifies the modern market system.

There are, most agree, market failures, and these failures include transactions that are characterized by externalities (effects of an activity are felt by parties not participating in the exchange), and by information asymmetries (parties to the transaction have dissimilar knowledge of the transaction or of its effects). When either of these two characteristics are present, social costs may result, the transaction is no longer entirely voluntary, and it may result in injustice.

Externalities and information asymmetries

For more information on the effects of Texaco's toxic wastewater, see the article "Legal Wrangling Won't Restore the Rain Forest" in Business Week, October 11, 1997.

Externalities place burdens on parties that do not benefit from the exchange transaction in question. An example is environmental pollution. When Texaco left Ecuador after pumping out 1.2 billion barrels of oil, the company left behind toxic wastewater. The wastewater is an externality because when Texaco contracts with its customers to sell the refined product gasoline from the oil, the residents of Ecuador are not parties to the transaction. They are, however, bearing a burden from the transaction in increased health costs and harm to their living environment. These costs are not borne by the private individuals who entered into the contract, but instead are costs generated by the transaction that have been transferred to other individuals, or to society.

Information asymmetries also generate social costs. Consider the tobacco industry, for example. For most of the history of tobacco use, the transaction between smokers and tobacco suppliers was considered mutually beneficial. However, in recent decades, it has become apparent that, not only are there externalities attached to the transaction, but also, buyers of tobacco products were not provided with the full information necessary to make a rational choice as to use of the product. There was information available to the tobacco industry as to the safety of the product that was intentionally withheld from buyers. As evidenced by the recent cases brought by state governments against the tobacco manufacturers for recovery of health care costs (which have resulted in large settlements by the manufacturers), this information imbalance has shifted significant costs from the private contracting parties (smokers and tobacco firms) to society.

An example of one such court case was brought against British American Tobacco and its subsidiary Brown & Williamson on June 16, 1998 by the government of Minnesota.

Social costs and injustice

The tobacco manufacturers' decision to not inform their customers of the dangers of the product in order to maintain or increase their own well being was unjust and resulted in injustice. By the same reasoning, Texaco's failure to look to the third-party effects of their actions in Ecuador was unjust and resulted in injustice. In both cases, the firms' decisions had the effect of a disproportionate distribution of benefits and burdens among the parties with stakes in the transaction (stakeholders).

Having given examples of social costs, the author uses this paragraph as a transition to move on to the next stage of her argument.

Once it is shown, however, that social costs have been accrued and injustice has been done, the question of the allocation of responsibility to achieve a just distribution of benefits and burdens of the already-completed exchange must be addressed.

Allocation of responsibility

In fact, many societies have decided that society should, through government, take action to ensure that those who benefit, pay. The problem is one of compensation, and that is a distributional problem, to be decided by politics.

The degree to which governments should intervene in an economy is a central economic debate. It is also a moral issue because it addresses such problems as unfairness of wealth distribution. What arguments can you make for and against intervention?

While some philosophers would disagree that governments have the moral right to intervene in the decisions and results of the free market, other philosophers, such as J. Rawls, have put forward convincing arguments as to why it is both moral and necessary to do so. Economists, too, have argued that under conditions where the market has failed (such as externalities and information asymmetry) the government has a role to play in correcting the situation.

In American society, the moral principle that there should be a direct relation between consumption and production

These tires have been dumped in a pond near a tire factory. Who pays the price for this sort of damage to the environment?

(without government intervention) is strongly supported, but it is also the case that, with appropriate justification, governments are expected to intervene to promote a just society.

Justice and the stockowner

If it is unjust that those who have not benefited from an exchange are forced to bear burdens as a result of the exchange, and the society has determined that it is a proper role of government to attempt to correct the maldistribution of burdens and benefits, the next question is, by what means? However, justice requires that benefits and burdens be appropriately distributed among all affected parties—all stakeholders. However just it might seem to be to ask the customers of the product to pay the full price of the externality, the customer is not, in fact, the only stakeholder to benefit from the exchange contract. Another party to the contract, the stockowner, also benefits from the transaction. Indeed, some economists have argued that the sole responsibility of the management of the business firm is to benefit stockowners by increasing their wealth.

Some might argue that, because stockowners do not control the assets of a business organization, but only have rights to profits, they ought not be made to share in the burdens of the decisions made on their behalf by managers and directors. But, when benefits are accepted, obligations of fairness are created. Stockowners do benefit as a result of their rights to income, and so must fulfill their obligations of fairness. The burdens of justice should not fall solely on the customers (or employees) of a business, but must be shared by stockowners.

It is clear that society has a basis for policy interventions to ensure that the stockowner obligation to fairly share the burden of social costs is met. This is especially true when social costs might otherwise fall solely on consumers when taken into the firm, or on society if left external to the firm.

The authors make a broad assertion of principle, then explains it in more detail. Moving from the general to the specific is an effective way to build an argument.

A CONSUMER'S GUIDE TO ENVIRONMENTAL MYTHS AND REALITIES
Lynn Scarlett

NO

EPA is the abbreviation for the Environmental Protection Agency. It was established in 1970 as an independent agency to safeguard the natural environment and to protect human health.

Consumer response to market incentives

More than two-thirds of U.S. households face no economic cost for disposing of greater volumes of solid waste. If they paid the full cost of disposing of their garbage, people would have an incentive to alter their buying habits, recycle, compost and buy items in less bulky packaging.... An EPA study found that a 10 percent increase in the cost of garbage disposal resulted in a one to two percent reduction in household waste. While the 10 percent increase leads to only small reductions in waste, current underpricing of garbage service by at least 20 to 30 percent, coupled with escalating landfill costs, suggest that full-cost pricing to consumers would lead to more substantial decreases in waste generation.

The idea of charging households based on the amount and type of waste they dispose of is not new...When waste-handling was done by private scrap dealers and haulers, companies typically charged households different fees, based on categories of hard-to-handle materials. Today, a number of cities are rediscovering the virtues of the price system.

Case studies are useful sources of factual evidence, but opponents of an argument might have contradictory case studies of their own.

Case study: Seattle

Since 1981 Seattle has charged residents based on the volume of garbage they generate. One consequence is that more than 85 percent of Seattle's residents participate in a recycling program and the city recycles between 18 percent and 35 percent of its municipal solid waste. As one study reported:

• In response to economic incentives, Seattle residents have reduced the average number of garbage cans from 3.5 down to just over one can per week, with households recycling, composting and compacting and actually generating less waste through revised purchasing habits. In Seattle, where people are billed for the amount of garbage they generate, over 22 percent of solid waste has been diverted from the landfill.

• About 24 percent of the garbage was being recycled before the introduction of any city-sponsored recycling program.

Should corporations pay the full environmental costs of producing their goods?

Landowner and city response to market incentives

A key challenge is to overcome the NIMBY syndrome and find places that will accept landfills. Entrepreneurs have discovered that one approach that works is to pay a benefit fee to any community agreeing to host a facility. The fee is compensation for perceived or actual negative impacts of that facility. In return for host fees, NIMBY is converted into YIMBY—FAP: Yes, In My Back Yard—For A Price.

"NIMBY" is the acronym for "not in my backyard." What other acronyms can you think of that are used to describe political or social types?

Case study: Charles County, Virginia

In exchange for a host benefit fee of at least $1.1 million per year, Charles City County, Virginia, accepted a regional landfill. Thanks to the landfill, the county cut property taxes by 20 percent, even though spending on schools went up. As a local administrator remarked, "We're good capitalists; we realized there was money in garbage."

Would you support a landfill near your home if it meant taxes could be cut?

Privatization and innovation

In many places in the United States, garbage disposal is a function of city governments. Traditionally, a city-owned and city-operated sanitation service picked up the garbage and delivered it to a city-owned solid waste facility. Even today, with the rapid spread of privatization, private contractors often have little flexibility under contracts written by city governments. As a result solid waste disposal is (1) more costly than it needs to be, (2) less safe than it could be, and (3) less amenable to innovation.

Lowering costs

Several studies of privatization of collection, disposal, and recycling services have shown that competitive contracting can achieve significant savings—as high as 30 percent. In large part, these savings have been achieved through innovation and increases in productivity as private service providers reduce costs to remain competitive.

Increasing safety

In addition, private landfill operators have better environmental records than do public operators:
- Experience shows that private operators have been more willing than their public counterparts to install liners, leachate collection systems, and groundwater monitoring equipment.
- Studies dating from the mid-1980s show that privately owned landfills have been designed with leachate collection systems more frequently than have publicly owned facilities.

In a "leachate collection system" harmful elements are drawn out of the soil to keep it clean.

- Privately owned landfills also are more likely to conduct groundwater monitoring (30 percent versus about 15 percent for county- and city-owned), and surface water monitoring (31 percent versus 24 percent for county and 13 percent for city).

Encouraging innovation

Typically, public sector programs also are less responsive to opportunities to innovate and change. And, city-mandated recycling programs may prevent the development of more effective private sector programs. One reason may be that public officials rarely know the real costs of the services they provide. For example, in a 1971 study of refuse collection in New York City, E.S. Savas found "that the full cost [of service] was 48 percent greater than the cost indicated in the city's budget."

Case study: recycling

Cities and states that mandate specific kinds of curbside recycling may be inhibiting development of more cost-effective recycling technology, for example recycling through centralized, automated separation or recycling using co-collection, or "Blue Bag" systems, where recyclables are all collected in one bag. Typically, household separation is very incomplete, with individual recyclers excluding large portions of waste that are in principle recyclable. For example:

- A curbside program for a small town of around 23,000 people may collect 15 to 20 tns. of recyclables in a year.
- Centralized separation by a waste hauler may extract from the solid waste stream twice that amount from the same small city in only a week.

Case study: composting

As people in agriculture have known for centuries, composting is nature's way of recycling. The process takes organic materials and turns them into a product that can be used in agriculture and plant nurseries, on parks and golf courses, by landscapers and gardeners, even on Christmas tree farms. Can composting also help solve the solid waste disposal problem? Some [people] think so.

Since about 60 percent of solid waste is organic (yard waste, paper, and food waste), as much as 60 percent of America's solid waste could in theory be composted if the economics are right.

Using composting to dispose of solid waste is not a new idea. In Europe, it has been done for almost two decades. But in recent years, some U.S. facilities have developed cutting-edge technology that is drawing the attention of the rest of the world. For example, a steady stream of foreign visitors makes its way each year to the Delaware Reclamation Plant in Pigeon Point, Delaware. The plant's integrated solid waste system composts, recycles, incinerates, and landfills trash—all at the same site.

For more information on the Delaware Reclamation Plant, see the Spring 1996 newsletter of the Northeast Recycling Council News website at nerc.org/newsletter/1996/spring96.html #DE.

Avoiding future myths

Millions of schoolchildren and unwary adults have been told that there are simple rules by which they can judge the environmental correctness of products. In fact, there are no simple, reliable rules. Since every simple rule is based on only one environmental concern, following the rules may cause more harm than good overall.

The most comprehensive studies of consumer products are life-cycle, or cradle-to-grave, studies. These studies attempt to look at all of the environmental aspects of a product's production, use, and disposal. Because they are expensive, only a handful of products have been analyzed. Once completed, most life-cycle studies are still incomplete. For example, the typical method counts the total volume of air or water pollutants without consideration for whether some pollutants are worse than others.

For more information on life-cycle studies, see www.acnatsci.org/erd/ea/big–picture.html.

Fortunately, environmentally conscious consumers have a much more reliable guide—market prices. For most products, market prices already reflect the cost of valuable resources used in their production, as well as the cost of controlling air and water pollution and making efficient use of energy. Market prices allow us to compare the cost of resources used to produce a product with other values we hold.

Scarlett argues that prices—including those of recycling or waste disposal— free the consumer to contribute to the environmental or social costs of what they consume.

The biggest problems in the solid waste stream occur in areas where there are no market prices, either as a result of government actions or where costs of environmental impacts have not been included in solid waste collection and disposal pricing.

Summary

The authors of the two previous articles would probably agree that the environmental and social effects of business activity need to be addressed. The difference is more in how to go about accomplishing it. There are a growing number of companies that have accepted the challenge to do well financially by doing good socially and environmentally. And it is to those companies that we may want to look for the leadership and the best practices for achieving these multiple bottom lines.

In the first article Sandra Christensen and Brian Grinder clearly believe that the responsibility for carrying the costs of environmental effects should lie not with the consumer but with the corporations and their stockowners, who are in the position to make a profit from such business activities. It is therefore only fair that it is they who should pay the costs for damages done to the environment and to people affected, and she advocates that the government intervene to make sure that justice is done.

Lynn Scarlett, however, believes that the consumer has to pay something toward the costs of environmental and social effects. She argues that when consumers cooperate in taking on some of this responsibility, it has been shown, using the example of waste disposal in the United States and analyzing case studies, to provide various benefits, including increased awareness and more efficient, creative solutions to environmental problems.

FURTHER INFORMATION:

 Books:

Dunning, J.H. (editor), *Governments, Globalization, and International Business.* New York: Oxford University Press, 1999.

Gautier, D., *Morals by Agreement.* Oxford, UK: Clarendon Press, 1986.

Nozick, R., *Anarchy, State, and Utopia.* New York: Basic Books, 1992.

Articles:

Christman, J., "Distributive Justice and the Complex Structure of Ownership." *Philosophy and Public Affairs* 32, 1994.

Friedman, M., "The Social Responsibility of Business is to Increase Its Profits." *New York Times Magazine,* September 13, 1970.

Milde, M., "Under Pressure: Distributive Ideals in the Market." *Alternatives 21.*

Phillips, R.A., "Stakeholder Theory and a Principle of Fairness." *Business Ethics Quarterly 7,* 1997.

 Useful websites:

www.epa.org
The Environmental Protection Agency.
www.socialfunds.com
Social Funds. Shows how the biggest companies are trying to make strides toward doing well and making money.

The following debates in the Pro/Con series may also be of interest:

In this volume:

 Topic 10 Do corporations have a moral responsibility to nature?

Topic 16 Should corporations be socially responsible?

SHOULD CORPORATIONS PAY THE FULL ENVIRONMENTAL COSTS OF PRODUCING THEIR GOODS?

YES: By protecting the environment, they are safeguarding the natural resources of their products and the health of their employees

YES: Money is the only language that corporations understand, and financial incentives are the only reason for a corporation to change its practices

COMPANY PROFITS
Can a corporation make a profit and still cover the costs of protecting the environment?

INCENTIVES
Would financial incentives encourage companies to meet their responsibilities in protecting the environment?

NO: Corporations will see their profits dwindle if they try to address environmental problems

SHOULD CORPORATIONS PAY THE FULL ENVIRONMENTAL COSTS OF PRODUCING THEIR GOODS?

KEY POINTS

NO: This would only pass the buck on to the consumer, since it is the government that will have to protect the environment, and the taxpayer who will have to pay for it in the end

YES: The stockholders of a company should be the ones to pay for such costs because they are the ones who have invested in and will profit from the product

YES: It would be unfair to pass on such costs to consumers who have no say in how a corporation operates

DAMAGE
Should corporations have to pay all costs for any damage done by their product to people or the environment?

NO: If consumers want to use certain products, they should be prepared to pay full costs

NO: This will only cause corporations to be more worried about their profit margin and cause them to raise consumer prices

Topic 7

CAN A "PAY-TO-POLLUTE" SYSTEM SIGNIFICANTLY REDUCE AIR POLLUTION?

YES

"GREENHOUSE GAS REDUCTION HAS BECOME A SELLER'S MARKET"

E MAGAZINE, VOL. 12, ISSUE 1, JANUARY/FEBRUARY 2001

DENNIS BLANK

NO

"SMOKE AND MIRRORS: WILL GLOBAL POLLUTION TRADING
SAVE THE CLIMATE OR PROMOTE INJUSTICE AND FRAUD?"

TRANSNATIONAL RESOURCE & ACTION CENTER, OCTOBER 1998

MICHAEL BELLIVEAU

INTRODUCTION

Topic 1 in this volume deals with the issue of global warming (*Does global warming threaten humankind?*). If the scientific evidence that the earth's climate is warming because we are overloading the atmosphere with carbon dioxide and other gases that trap heat is accepted, the next question is what can we do about it?

Efforts so far fall into two major areas: the reduction of carbon sources, and strategies for adapting to the consequences of global warming. Mitigation for the United States means reducing the amount of carbon dioxide and other gas emissions to 7 percent below their 1990 levels by 2012. This level was set by the 1997 Kyoto Protocol (see page 90). According to it, each country has to ratify the protocol and develop its plan for achieving the reduction in emissions.

The best mechanisms for achieving the 7 percent reduction lie in using state-of-the-art technology that removes more pollution and in the use of more efficient, cleaner fuels. Companies that invest in these mechanisms will generate smaller quantities of greenhouse gases. But such investment costs money, and for many pollution generators it costs less to ignore any suggested changes—to simply keep going with existing technology and fuels regardless of the effects on the environment. One answer to this dilemma is pollution credits, in which companies are effectively required to pay for the pollution they create. A system that combined the overall goal of declining emissions with a financial market for buying and selling pollution credits could encourage companies to adopt cleanup policies.

The basic idea works well in reducing acid rain pollutants in the United States. The government set a cap to reduce the amount of acid-rain-causing pollutants that it would allow in the air, starting in 1995 and declining each year after. Then it issued tradable certificates to 110 of the nation's dirtiest power plants that matched their share of the cap. Companies that cut emissions below their cap had extra certificates to sell. Companies that did not meet their quota had to buy certificates from the cleaner companies. Companies can save certificates from year to year, but federal clean air standards still limit how much pollution can be released.

According to the Environmental Protection Agency, between 1994 and 1997 this program was responsible for a 30 percent reduction in the amount of sulfur dioxide pollution nationally.

"If actions are not taken to reduce the projected increase in greenhouse gas emissions, the Earth's climate is likely to change at a rate unprecedented in the last 10,000 years with adverse consequences for society. The welfare of this and future generations is in your hands."

—ROBERT T. WATSON, CHAIRMAN, INTERGOVERNMENTAL PANEL ON CLIMATE CHANGE

Applying this approach to reduce global greenhouse gases would give each industrial nation an "emissions budget" that would reflect its proportion of the global limit. Industrial nations that reduced emissions below 1990 levels would have credits to sell, and countries that failed to do so would have to buy them. Companies could buy better technology to meet their emissions quotas, or they could spend money on cleanup projects in other countries to obtain credits.

It is difficult to predict the chances of success for the U.S. program on acid rain since there is no single governmental authority or established financial system for certifying and regulating credit deals. Establishing a globally accepted trading system is a more ambitious task. While a "pay-to-pollute" scheme may make financial sense, will it result in reduced emissions? And can it be done in such a way that it improves the disproportionate health and economic effects on poor communities that live near harmful pollution sources?

The following extracts examine the advantages and disadvantages of a pay-to-pollute system. Michael Belliveau's article looks at the reasons why such a system may not work. Belliveau argues that we cannot rely on the market and regulatory reform to reduce global pollution and cut the health risks to people living in poor communities or countries next to emissions sources.

On the other hand, in the first article Dennis Blank examines how investors and financial institutions are responding to the potential new market that greenhouse-gas emissions credits are creating. Optimism for this approach appears to be building momentum, and an early market is starting to materialize—even in the absence of the U.S. ratification of the Kyoto Protocol in 2001 by President George W. Bush's administration and the fact that this may jeopardize the protocol.

GREENHOUSE GAS REDUCTION HAS BECOME A SELLER'S MARKET
Dennis Blank

YES

Can clean money be exchanged for dirty air? That's the premise of an emerging trade in carbon credits, which hold out the tantalizing promise of allowing industries to insulate themselves from greenhouse gas regulations by voluntarily agreeing to pay for "global cooling."

Emissions trading, the selling of federally recognized "right to pollute" credits from one industry to another, is well-established. But a specific market for carbon dioxide (CO_2) reduction is a product of the 1998 Kyoto Accords on Global Warming, which calls for reducing worldwide CO_2 emissions to below 1990 levels.

See box on Kyoto Protocol on page 90.

Carbon trading

[S]ome coal-burning utilities lack the technology to reduce emissions to Kyoto levels on their own, [and] they are banking on greenhouse gas trades with farmers, who can "sequester" carbon (absorb it through the land) using such methods as no-till cultivation. That's sent a host of carbon brokers to Iowa, Nebraska, and Illinois in search of credit deals. These carbon trades, though engineered by reputable brokerages, are totally unregulated and there are no guarantees that any government will officially recognize the credits. That hasn't prevented several major players in Canada, Australia, New Zealand, United Kingdom and the European Union from signing contracts.

Since this piece was written, the U.S. government declined to ratify the protocol. See page 90.

Emissions and the global community

Unlike the U.S., which still hasn't ratified the Protocol, Canada has agreed to reduce emissions to six percent below 1990 levels by 2008, at a rate of 100 million metric tons per year. That deadline lights a fire under Canadian greenhouse-gas producers such as GEMCo, a Vancouver-based consortium of 10 major Canadian utilities, which recently purchased options on 1.4 million acres of Iowa farmland. The deal was handled by Cantor Fitzgerald Environmental Brokerage Services in New York and the money funneled through IGF of Des Moines, the nation's largest crop insurer.

An acre of farmland can sequester an estimated one ton of carbon. GEMCo will pay an average of $1.50 a ton to obtain 2.8 million metric tons of greenhouse gas reduction credits. The deal could eventually exceed $5 million, according to GEMCo, because the credits become more valuable the longer they are held until the year 2008, the deadline in the Protocol. "North American farmlands have the potential to offset a very significant portion of greenhouse gas emissions from this highly industrial continent," says Aldyen Donnelly, president of GEMCo.

Late last year, Australia set up the first official futures exchange in carbon credit trades and is expected to do an annual $5 billion (U.S.) in transactions. "Trading in carbon credits is a new market for the new 21st century," said Bob Smith, CEO of States Forest of New South Wales.

The situation in the United States

In the [United States,] regulators are so far keeping hands off the issue because there is no official American involvement in the Kyoto Protocol. "It is a real awkward situation," says one high Environmental Protection Agency (EPA) official, who prefers anonymity. "They risk a lot. There are assumptions that that these deals will be honored."

Look at www.newscientist. com to see U.S. policy on gas emissions.

The Washington-based Edison Electric Institute, which represents U.S. utilities, claims that the Kyoto Protocol is "severely flawed." It points out that the Protocol, which is still being adjusted in worldwide forums, has not yet met the demands of a U.S. Senate resolution insisting that developing nations meet the same six to eight percent CO_2 reduction by 2008 standard as industrial countries. "The futility of the Kyoto approach is made evident by the fact that the largest developing nation, China, is expected to surpass the U.S. as the single-largest source of greenhouse gas emissions by 2015," says the Institute, adding that the American taxpayer could be forced to pay hundreds of billions [of dollars] annually.

In testimony submitted to Congress in 1998, the New York-based Environmental Defense reported that a "business as usual" strategy could mean that the U.S. would emit 30 percent more greenhouse gas emissions in 2008 than it did in 1990. Carbon credit programs provide many opportunities, the group said: Livestock farmers could drastically reduce methane emissions, the second-largest category of greenhouse gas; farmers in New England and the Southeast could gain credits from managing forest parcels; and agricultural water rights in the Northwest could be traded

COMMENTARY: Kyoto Protocol

Background

In 1992 most major nations signed the United Nations Framework Convention on Climate Change (UNFCCC), following concerns that there had been a substantial growth in "greenhouse gases," such as carbon dioxide and methane, in the atmosphere. The United States was one of the first nations to ratify this treaty, which included a voluntary pledge by major industrialized countries that they would significantly reduce their greenhouse gas emissions to 1990 levels by the year 2000. It became apparent very quickly that large nations such as Japan and the United States would not meet the stipulated levels. Consequently, there were further negotiations on a protocol to establish legally binding reductions on greenhouse-gas emissions for "developed countries." In the pre-Kyoto discussions there were disagreements on three main issues: First, on what the amount of reductions in greenhouse gases should be and on what gases should be included; second, on whether developing countries should be included; and third, on whether emissions trading (see pages 86–87) should be allowed.

COP–3

From December 1 to 11, 1997, the major industrial nations of the world met at the United Nations Climate Change Conference in Kyoto, Japan. After long and sometimes acrimonious negotiations at COP–3, (the Third Conference of the Parties to the UN Framework Convention on Climate Change) they committed to legally binding restrictions on emissions of six greenhouse gases. The overall targets agreed by 2008–2012 were a 7 percent cut from 1990 levels for the United States, an 8 percent cut for the European Union, and a 6 percent cut for Japan and Canada. Australia was allowed an 8 percent increase, while Russia had a target of 0 percent (i.e., 1990 levels). It opened for signature in March 1998 for one year and then after that was open for ratification.

The United States

From the beginning the United States made it clear that it would not ratify the protocol unless major developing countries, such as India and China, agreed to significantly reduce and control future emissions. It also required a valid framework for emissions trading. Although the United States sent delegates to the COP–4 meeting in Buenos Aires in November 1998, and to subsequent COP meetings, in May 2001 President George W. Bush's government refused to ratify the Kyoto Protocol, citing the cost to U.S. consumers as its reason. Critics, however, blamed the influence of his corporate sponsors, such as Exxon. In 2001 the United States was responsible for 25 percent of the world's carbon dioxide emissions.

to leave more water in rivers, [therefore] generating more hydroelectric power and reducing loads on fossil fuel plants. Traders are still advocating these deals as the best "market-based solution" to reduce worldwide air pollution. "What is missing right now are the rules and regulations, and that is why there is uncertainty," says Gary Hart, president of the Emissions Trading Association.

Reductions and the law

The agreements are definitely a gamble. "Until governmental rules define matters otherwise, greenhouse gas emissions are a figment of parties' contracts," says Mark Perlis, a Washington, D.C. attorney specializing in environmental law. "Would-be seller's of reductions or credits have no vested entitlement to any benefit under existing law." Perlis points out there is no U.S. law that even so much as defines greenhouse gas credits.

Should the government become involved in regulating the trade in credits? Look at www.cnn.com or www.washington. post.com to see if you can find any U.S. policy on regularizing gas credit prices.

The uncertainty results in a very volatile market. Australian traders are paying prices that range widely from $10 to 5,200 a ton. "The numbers are all over the board," Hart says. "It is very uncertain right now."

"The GEMCo transaction demonstrates the potential of the marketplace to provide low-cost solutions to address the greenhouse effect," says Carlton Bartels, managing director at Cantor, the firm that brokered the deal. "The agricultural sector has a tremendous capacity for removing carbon dioxide from the atmosphere and abating the emission of its own greenhouse gases."

Carbon emission reduction credits

Once a farmer has his land audited, he or she can choose to cash in the carbon emission reduction credits (CERCs) or hold on to them in a procedure similar to a futures call option. Prices escalate as the schedule draws closer to the 2008 deadline. Greg Lewis, president of CQuest, a Des Moines brokerage that deals in CERCs, said that for each dollar that a utility spends, 55 cents goes to the farmer and the other 45 cents goes for commissions, fees and salaries for brokers, land auditors and engineers who actually visit the farms and verify the CERCs. Buying and selling CERCS has tremendous potential, Lewis says. "I could probably sell 100 million CERCs to the utility market. The atmosphere is [a] big bowl of soup to which everyone can add or subtract greenhouses gases." The next step is to set up an Internet auction system for CERCs. That may increase the volume of trades, with excellent prospects for reducing worldwide CO_2 emissions, but it probably won't satisfy all the concerns of investors.

SMOKE AND MIRRORS
Michael Belliveau

NO

Based on the now extensive U.S. experience with trading in emission reduction credits several problems will plague global trading in carbon dioxide. Together these troubles add up to continued global warming.

If the Kyoto Protocol winds up relying on emissions trading as a key tool to reduce greenhouse gas emissions, it will only prolong overconsumption in the North and lock in a place a fossil fuel dependent economy in the South. Here are the deadly sins that condemn pollution trading to certain failure.

Listing your arguments numerically may help you present a clear and well-constructed argument.

Look at www.geocities.com/ Athens/Forum/4821/, and see who are the worst recent offenders.

1. Rewards the worst polluters

Pollution trading programs entitle the polluter to an emissions rate based on their historic levels of pollution. Once emission levels are set, polluting countries or companies can emit to those levels, sell unused portions of their entitlement or bank their balance for future use or financial speculation. The worst polluters earn the highest pollution entitlements.

In developing countries, the Kyoto Protocol creates a perverse incentive to increase emissions in the near term. No specific emission reductions are required yet for these nations. Under a pollution trading scheme, higher emissions mean a greater entitlement to pollute and more potential to bank valuable credits.

2. Promotes fraud

Any policy strategy must ensure that emission reductions are verifiable and enforceable. Here's where pollution trading is at a distinct disadvantage when compared to real regulation.

Compliance with technology-forcing mandates can be readily determined because polluting technologies are measurable and preventive solutions are verifiable. For example, suppose the U. S. required that within five years 50 percent of industrial fossil fuel use be slashed through conservation, solar energy, and hydrogen-powered fuel cells. Through reporting, emissions monitoring and on-site inspection, compliance with these goals can be verified.

By contrast, a pollution trading scheme depends on highly accurate accounting of emissions and reductions. Instead of monitoring polluting technologies and industries, emission reduction credits will be accrued from countless transactions around the globe that are brokered by far removed "middle men." Trading advocates decry independent verification before each trade as market interference. Even after-the-fact enforcement remains daunting. How many emissions were reduced? [H]ow accurate are the credits for future emissions reductions? And how can credits be objectively assigned to carbon "sinks" like tree planting or habitat preservation?

3. Undermines technology innovation

The technical capacity, human resources, and capital needed to develop new technologies to reduce carbon emissions are concentrated in industrialized countries, such as in the United States, Japan, and the European Community. Under the proposed trading provision, these countries will buy up cheap and sometimes bogus emission reduction credits for the next 10 to 15 years. This means that they will have little incentive to develop alternative energy sources or pollution reducing technology. The demand for new technology in both North and South will be slowed, as will the reduction of greenhouse gas emissions in the North, which is responsible for about three quarters of all global warming gasses.

> Does the author present any evidence that credits may be "bogus"?

4. Deepens environmental racism in the United States

One of the most potentially tragic aspects of the push for global trading in carbon dioxide is that it would exacerbate the disproportionate impact on low income communities of color in the United States, a country which plans to purchase carbon credits rather than adequately reduce its emissions.

> Look at www.eelinks.com, and see if you can find evidence to support this claim.

Carbon dioxide emissions cannot be separated from the other co-pollutants that result from the same sources—the production and combustion of petrochemicals and fossil fuels. Therefore, whenever a company forgoes reductions in carbon dioxide emissions because it purchased a credit, much more than carbon dioxide continues to flow from that company's stack. These include cancer-causing products of incomplete combustion such as polycyclic aromatic hydrocarbons (PAHs), unburned toxic hydrocarbons, and fine particulate matter linked to excessive death rates.

In the U.S., oil refineries and other industrial polluters are disproportionately located in poor communities of color. This means that in a country where 100 million people breathe polluted air every day, low income people of color will continue to be hardest hit.

5. Widens global economic injustice

The developing countries lose twice in the global market in greenhouse gas reduction credits. Pollution trading will encourage efforts to reduce carbon emissions in the South, where energy use is less efficient, in order to generate low-cost emission reduction credits for sale to the big polluters in the North. Competition among developing countries to produce the cheapest possible credits will tend to minimize the capital investments really needed to overhaul their energy wasteful economies. These capital starved nations need sustained investment in state of the art, clean energy technology. Instead, they will experience entrepreneurial "hit and run" projects aimed at bleeding off the cheapest reductions available.

The second problem strikes deeper and later. During the next phase in the long term struggle to reverse global warming, the South will be required to reduce carbon emissions just as the Kyoto Protocol mandates reductions in the North. By that time, however, the industrialized countries will have already used up easy emission reductions in the South through pollution trading. This leaves the developing countries in the lurch—deeply locked into a fossil fuel development path, reliant on what will quickly become obsolete technology and with few means to meet their own future obligations to reduce carbon.

Even though pollution is worse in developed countries, he argues that the credit system will affect poorer countries more.

6. Empowers the corporate elite

Many transnational corporations and the institutions that support them need firm control over a fossil-fuel reliant global economy to stay profitable. The pollution trading provisions of the Kyoto Protocol, unless altered, will aid that outcome. By creating a carbon reduction scheme that eliminates public participation and minimizes government intervention, climate change negotiators will allow the transnationals to control the pace and degree of real reductions in greenhouse gases. In the final analysis, the ultimate market incentive remains unchanged: profit. Those who gain from oil, coal, and other petrochemicals, have no motive to abandon their fossil-fuel dependent markets and technologies. Yet we need to rapidly phase out the fossil-fuel economy to minimize the destructive effects of climate change.

Do you think that economic considerations always work against environmental issues?

A just alternative to global pollution trading

Any strategic response to climate change must base itself on environmental and economic justice for workers and communities around the world. Such a just alternative should incorporate three features: technology-forcing mandates, progressive pollution taxes and just transition funding for the displaced and disadvantaged. These elements are briefly sketched below.

Technology-forcing mandates

MIT Professor Nick Ashford has demonstrated that firm regulatory mandates create incentives that force technological innovation to reduce industrial pollution. Such a regulatory approach drives market demand more effectively than an inherently flawed pollution trading system. Other market-based policies that are more effective than pollution trading can complement tough regulations to promote carbon reductions.

The author uses an academic to lend authority to his argument. This is a useful tool.

Progressive pollution taxes

Market disincentives, such as significant taxes on pollution, will directly discourage the use of polluting products and technologies. However, pollution taxes alone are regressive, falling disproportionately on those who can least afford increased costs of living. Shifting taxes away from wages and savings onto pollution sources coupled with other progressive tax reforms, force those who can most afford it to pay for carbon reductions. For example a much higher tax on gasoline would provide a strong incentive to drive less and increase fuel efficiency in cars. By creating disincentives to pollute up front and progressive tax relief at the back end, the costs of transitioning to a more sustainable economy would be borne by the wealthiest sector of society.

Just transition funding

Funding from a Tobin tax and progressive pollution taxes would enable a more rapid and just transition to clean energy alternatives and environmental restoration. It should be used to offset the economic impacts on workers displaced by this transition, as well as on lower income consumers and developing countries.

James Tobin (1918–) was awarded the Nobel Prize for Economics in 1981.

The same market forces that created and perpetuate the ecological and health disasters of the industrial era will not solve the climate change crisis. By negotiating the ground rules of global pollution trading transactions governments … will only concede the future to those who profit from delaying the transition to a sustainable economy. [A] global strategy to save the climate should be based on international solidarity together with environmental and economic justice.

Belliveau concludes with a concise summary of the core of his argument.

Summary

The two articles agree that while there are some successful precursors for a "pay-to-pollute" system, as shown by the United States acid-rain-pollutant trading system, developing a global trading system is a very different challenge. The success of a global carbon-credit trading system seems to depend a lot on trust. An international system for carbon trading would require transparent trading, strong regulations and monitoring to assure that emissions levels were being met, and severe sanctions that would act as a deterrent to cheating or falsification of reports. And the system would have to be able to demonstrate that it was in fact causing the agreed on reductions in greenhouse gases in the atmosphere. The players involved in such a system, and the taxpayers of the countries that would finance the startup of such a system, would have to feel that they could trust it. As Belliveau points out, the system would also have to work so that poorer, underdeveloped countries in the southern hemisphere did not end up selling off their carbon credits at the expense of their opportunities to finance investments in newer, cleaner, more efficient technology. In the meantime, some interesting examples of how such a system can lead to creative approaches and win-win outcomes have emerged. One example is New York State's Niagara Mohawk Power Corporation. It reduced its carbon dioxide emissions by 2.5 million tons. It exchanged those emission rights to an Arizona utility company for 20,000 tons of sulfur dioxide allowances the company had "saved." Then Niagara Mohawk donated those allowances to local environmental groups, which retired them. So, while the amount of carbon dioxide remained the same, there are 20,000 tons less sulfur dioxide in the air. And with the $125,000 of tax benefits Niagara Mohawk received for donating the sulfur credits they are helping residents of a Mexican fishing village acquire and install nonpolluting solar power.

FURTHER INFORMATION:

Articles:

Cone, Marla. "AQMD Tightens Rules of Car Scrapping Program," *Los Angeles Times*, July 11, 1998.
Cooper, Mark, "Smoke Screen," *New Times*, 3, no. 6 (1998).

Useful websites:

www.state.gov/www/global/oes/fs_kyoto_climate_980115.html
Factsheet on State Department site about Kyoto Protocol.
www.foe.co.uk/pubsinfo/infoteam.pressrel/2001/2001032
Friends of the Earth site on gas emissions.

The following debates in the Pro/Con series may also be of interest:

In this volume:

Topic 1 Does global warming threaten humankind?

Topic 10 Do corporations have a moral responsibility to nature?

CAN A "PAY-TO-POLLUTE" SYSTEM SIGNIFICANTLY REDUCE AIR POLLUTION?

YES: This system encourages developed nations to invest in "hit-and-run" projects aimed at bleeding the cheapest reductions possible from developing countries

YES: Companies can use credits to purchase better technology for their operations

RICH V. POOR
Would a "pay-to-pollute" system unfairly disadvantage poor countries?

TECHNOLOGY
Can emissions quotas promote the use of better technology?

NO: Poor countries will benefit from developing countries using better, cleaner technology and fewer pollutants

NO: There are lots of other things that companies can spend their coupons on that have fewer benefits for developing countries and for the environment

CAN A "PAY-TO-POLLUTE" SYSTEM SIGNIFICANTLY REDUCE AIR POLLUTION?

KEY POINTS

YES: In 2001 U.S. carbon dioxide emissions were 25 percent of the world's total; thus if the United States fails to reduce its emissions, the world can expect further global warming

KYOTO PROTOCOL
Has the U.S. refusal to ratify the Kyoto Protocol put emissions reductions in jeopardy?

NO: The United States argues that only one country has officially ratified the agreement, so there is nothing to jeopardize

Topic 8
CAN WIND AND SOLAR RESOURCES MEET OUR ENERGY NEEDS?

YES

"CAN THE WORLD MEET FUTURE ENERGY NEEDS USING WIND AND SOLAR ENERGY?"
J. RICHARD MAYER

NO

"RENEWABLE ENERGY—WHY RENEWABLE ENERGY IS NOT CHEAP AND NOT GREEN"
NATIONAL CENTER FOR POLICY ANALYSIS
ROBERT L. BRADLEY JR.

INTRODUCTION

The growing demand for energy is on a lot of people's minds. With the world population expected to nearly double by the middle of the 21st century and developing countries increasing their use of energy, the need for new sources of energy will be huge.

Currently, most of our energy comes from the burning of fossil fuels. Fossil fuels consist of coal, petroleum, and natural gas. They are readily available, easy to use, and inexpensive in terms of energy costs. Their environmental costs, however, are much higher. Burning fossil fuels releases pollutants such as carbon dioxide (CO_2), nitrogen oxides (NO_2), and sulfur dioxides (SO_2). The buildup of carbon dioxide in the lower atmosphere prevents heat from sunlight from escaping into space. This phenomenon is known as the greenhouse effect and results in global warming. Scientists have predicted that global warming will lead to more frequent droughts, storms, floods, and hurricanes. Changes in climate will result in habitat destruction and extinction, the spread of diseases, and sea level rise. All of these consequences will greatly affect life on earth.

To reduce global warming, scientists are now examining alternatives to fossil fuels. These alternatives, known as green energy, produce energy through renewable resources such as solar, wind, geothermal, hydroelectric, and biomass. Solar energy can be produced two ways. Direct sunlight can be used to heat water to generate steam, which turns turbines. Sunlight can also be used with photovoltaic cells, which convert sunlight energy directly into an electrical current.

Wind power is generated when the force of the wind turns turbines similar to windmills. Hydroelectric power is produced when water drives turbines. Large hydroelectric power production causes numerous environmental problems, especially with fish trying to reach upstream spawning areas that are blocked by dams. Geothermal energy uses steam from the earth to produce electricity. Biomass utilizes renewable organic matter such as trees, plants, and animal waste to produce steam that can be turned into electricity. All of these methods of energy production are in use. Altogether they constitute roughly eight percent of the total energy production in the United States. Scientists consider solar and wind power to be the best candidates for meeting increased energy needs.

> *"15,000 times more solar energy strikes the earth's surface each year than all the energy the world uses annually."*
> —J. RICHARD MAYER

Those opposed to green energy point out the pitfalls in its use—mainly that it is uneconomic and insufficient. Wind turbines take up large quantities of land and can kill birds if they are placed in migratory routes. They are also noisy and unsightly. Solar panels are expensive to manufacture and cannot supply enough energy to meet peak demands. Both rely on forces that are out of our control; if the sun does not shine and the wind does not blow, no energy can be produced.

Advocates of green energy insist that it is the only method of energy production that will fulfill our future needs, since the supply of fossil fuels is limited. Currently, solar and wind power make up less than eight percent of America's energy production. But this proportion could be greatly increased if people would support the use of alternative energy. The Department of Energy calculates that wind energy could power the entire country's energy needs many times over. Also, when wind and solar energy are produced on larger scales, their costs will come down, making them more competitive with fossil fuel energy.

In the future it might be common for people to power their homes using solar panels on their rooftops. Extra energy produced during the day could be stored in fuel cells that use hydrogen to produce energy when no sunlight is available. Skyscrapers in New York City are already experimenting with this technology. The Million Solar Roofs Initiative, started by President Clinton in 1997, is aiming to have solar panels on the tops of one million buildings by 2010. The following two articles discuss whether this is an achievable goal as well as other energy issues.

CAN THE WORLD MEET FUTURE ENERGY NEEDS USING WIND AND SOLAR ENERGY?
J. Richard Mayer

Mayer makes a dramatic start by outlining an energy crisis in California to identify the seriousness of the issue under discussion.

As I write this article, the state of California is experiencing "rolling blackouts." Power is being shut off on a rotating basis in several parts of the state as an energy crisis which began in 2000 deepens. The current crisis stems from unanticipated new demands for electric power by consumers and drought in the Pacific Northwest, which is limiting the export of hydroelectric power to California. More importantly, electric power deregulation in California has failed to stimulate new power plant construction. Statewide demand for electricity is growing about seven percent a year while energy production remains flat. The fear is that California's power supply problems may soon be experienced in other parts of the United States and indeed in other parts of the world.

Renewable energy

The current crisis is leading U.S. state and federal power planners to consider building new coal, natural-gas-fired, and even nuclear-power generating facilities. But the development of sustainable energy sources, including wind and solar power, is not being considered to the extent some experts think they should be. While many wind and solar facilities are operating in the United States and other nations, the compelling question is, "Can a significant fraction of future energy needs be met using renewable energy?"

Focus your argument by asking a pertinent question.

Currently, worldwide energy demands total about 10,700,000 MW (megawatts) of power. The demand is met using petroleum (39 percent), natural gas (24 percent), coal (23 percent), renewable sources including biomass and hydroelectric power (8 percent), and nuclear power (6 percent). Industrial nations use over half of this total—5,700,000 MW—while developing nations use about 5,000,000 MW. In the near future, however, power demands by developing nations, particularly in Asia, will increase more rapidly than in industrial countries.

Statistics are a useful tool to support an argument. But can you confuse your audience by overusing them?

The world's dependence on fossil fuels exacerbates air, soil, and water pollution, and global climate change caused mainly by rising levels of atmospheric carbon dioxide gas. But 15,000 times more solar energy strikes the earth's surface each year than all the energy the world uses annually. Available solar power provides 100 times more energy than all proven reserves of coal, oil, and natural gas could generate. Only 0.01 percent of available solar energy would have to be captured each year to meet all of the world's energy demands. A much smaller fraction could satisfy world electric power needs. The most practical and potentially cost-effective ways of doing this employ wind turbines and solar-cells.

Offering solutions to a problem will make a more convincing case for your argument.

Wind turbines

Yesterday's windmills have evolved into today's high-tech wind turbines. One of the earliest wind-turbine farms was built in the 1970s at Altamont Pass, 30 miles east of San Francisco, California. More than 5,000 wind machines were built generating 544 MW of electric power, but most of these machines were poorly designed and developed mechanical problems. The electricity they generated cost about 25¢/kWh; electricity from coal power costs about 6¢/kWh.

Today's high-tech wind turbines generate electricity at 2 or 3¢/kWh, making wind power competitive with any other electric power source. It is also environmentally benign; that is, wind power adds no pollutants to air, water, or soil. It is therefore ecologically sustainable. As a result, wind power is the fastest growing sector of the worldwide energy marketplace today.

Critics complain that wind farms are noisy. Should noise be seen as an important form of pollution?

Installed wind capacity increased from 2,000 MW in 1990 to 15,000 MW by mid-2000, an average rate of growth of 24 percent per year. Most of the new wind turbines have been installed in Western Europe, with Germany being the current leader—5,000 MW (one-third of world capacity). The United States is in second place with close to 3,000 MW; Denmark, a leader in wind turbine design and construction, is third with about 2,000 MW.

A recent study published by the German Wind Energy Institute and [the environmental campaigners] Greenpeace shows that Germany, Britain, the Netherlands, Belgium, and Denmark together have sufficient wind resources to generate more than three times the combined electric power needs of these five countries. A similar study concludes that there is more than enough wind power in the American midwest to meet all of the country's current electrical needs.

The author has shown wind power to be a viable and cost-effective energy source. Why do you think it has not been fully exploited by the government?

A wind farm, such as the one shown above in Denmark, consists of up to 100 wind turbines set up in areas that benefit from a regular prevalent wind. Wind farms have been built in the United States in California and Hawaii, among other states.

Solar power

The most important ways that sunlight can be captured and converted into electric power are thermal-solar power and photovoltaic (PV) power. Thermal-solar power uses mirrors to reflect solar energy to heat synthetic oils or molten salts which power steam-electric generators. PV power depends on solar cells that produce electricity when exposed to sunlight. A natural-gas-fired generator [can be] used to supplement power production when sunlight is obscured.

Almost 80 percent of the world's solar power is generated today in California's Mojave Desert by nine thermal-solar power plants. The 354 MW of power produced (enough power to meet the electricity requirements of 354,000 homes) are purchased by Southern California Edison, the region's leading electric power utility. This power is used mainly to meet "peaking load" demands for summer air-conditioning. The cost of producing electricity using the most recently built thermal-solar power plants is 8¢/kWh.

Japan initiated its government-subsidized residential rooftop PV program in 1997. Amoco/Enron, a world energy leader, is collaborating with Misawa Homes Co., Ltd., one of Japan's major home builders. The U.S. "Million Solar Roofs" program calls for the Department of Energy to install solar panels on one million public and private buildings, perhaps reducing the cost of PV power to 6¢/kWh. Germany announced its "100,000 Roofs Program" in 1999. Under this program, German citizens are encouraged to buy solar panels at zero percent interest with no payments for two years.

Efforts to invest in solar energy are taking place worldwide. What other measures could the United States take internationally to implement renewable energy?

Paying the costs

A world-wide transition from fossil-fuel-based economies to environmentally-sustainable energy strategies based largely on wind and solar power will be costly. But many argue that it must occur because fossil fuels constitute a non-renewable resource and while proven reserves are rising in some cases, they must eventually fall. Costs associated with extracting and burning fossil fuels, including hidden costs called externalities are rising. They include global climate change, urban air pollution, and degraded water quality.

Do you think that the financial costs of investing in solar and wind energy outweigh the environmental costs?

103

RENEWABLE ENERGY:
WHY RENEWABLE ENERGY IS NOT CHEAP
AND NOT GREEN
Robert L. Bradley, Jr.

NO

A centerpiece of the environmentalist agenda has long been the regulation of fossil fuel consumption. While antipollution controls are the accepted short-term solution to many of the environmental problems posed by fossil fuels, many believe that the long-term answer is the gradual replacement of fossil fuels with other, less environmentally threatening fuel sources. This philosophy can perhaps best be described as eco-energy planning: The belief that government intervention in the energy economy is necessary to maximize environmental protection and, in the end, America's economic vitality.

Not all renewable energy is viable

Renewable energy—power generated from the nearly infinite elements of nature such as sunshine, wind, the movement of water, the internal heat of the Earth, and the combustion of replenishable crops—is widely popular with the general public and governmental officials because it is thought to be an inexhaustible and environmentally benign source of power, particularly when compared to the supposedly finite and environmentally problematic alternative of reliance on fossil fuels and nuclear power. It is the centerpiece of eco-energy planning. Yet all renewable energy sources are not created equal. Some are more economically and environmentally viable than others. The list of those renewable fuels that were once promising but that are now being questioned on economic and/or environmental grounds is growing and threatens the entire "supply side" strategy of eco-energy planning.

Wind power is currently the environmentalists' "favorite" renewable-energy resource and is thought be the most likely energy to replace fossil fuel for generating electricity in the 21st century. Hydropower has lost favor with environmentalists because of the damage it has done to river habitats and freshwater fish populations. Solar power, at least when relied upon for central-station electricity generation, is not environmentally benign on a total fuel cycle basis and is highly uneconomic, land-intensive, and thus a fringe electric power source for the foreseeable future. Geothermal has turned out to be "depletable" with limited capacity, falling output and modest new investment. Biomass is also uneconomic and produces air-emissions comparable to and sometimes worse than fossil fuels.

Problems of wind power

Despite its revered status within the orthodox environmental community, wind power poses several major dilemmas. First, wind remains uneconomic despite heavy subsidies from ratepayers and taxpayers over the last two decades. Second, from an environmental viewpoint, wind farms are noisy, land-intensive, unsightly and hazardous to birds, including endangered species. With the National Audubon Society calling for a moratorium on new wind development in bird-sensitive areas, and an impending electric industry restructuring that could force all generation resources to compete on a marginal cost basis, wind power itself is a problematic choice for future electric generation without a new round of government subsidies and preferences.

The National Audubon Society aims to conserve and restore natural ecosystems.

Because of the precarious economics of acceptable renewable energies, eco-energy planners have turned to taxpayer and ratepayer subsidies for energy conservation as an alternative means to constrain the use of fossil fuels. Yet fundamental problems exist here as well. Multibillion-dollar taxpayer and ratepayer subsidies over two decades have resulted in severely diminished returns for future conservation investments. The potential price reduction from electric industry restructuring threatens to lengthen the payout period of energy conservation investments to worsen this problem.

Do you think that taxpayers should subsidize energy conservation? If not, who should pay?

Natural gas

A major but largely unrecognized development in the public policy debate over subsidized renewable generation and energy conservation has been the elevated role of natural gas in electric generation. Not only is natural gas significantly cleaner-burning and less expensive than a decade ago, it has increasingly become the fuel of choice for new generation capacity. The eco-energy planning agenda for electric generation—developed with coal and fuel oil in mind—must now be reconsidered. Such a reconsideration places into question some of the most important public-policy missions of government energy agencies, from the California Energy Commission (CEC) to the U.S. Department of Energy (DOE).

Eco-energy planning is a public-policy paradigm favoring taxpayer and ratepayer subsidies and governmental mandates for renewable generation and energy conservation in the electricity sector to promote "sustainable" energy development. With the end of energy shortages in the 1970s, the focus of federal energy policy shifted from price and allocation regulation to reducing fossil fuel consumption in order to address ozone formation, acid rain, and climate change. The key assumption of eco-energy planning is that state and federal air-emission standards alone are inadequate to address those public-policy issues.

The new (post-1980) mission of many state public utility commissions, the California Energy Commission, and the Department of Energy has been to intervene in the market with incentives for renewable energy generation and conservation, particularly in the electric generation sector. Those government interventions have included the following supply-side and demand-side alternatives:

Supply-side policies attract energy producers; demand-side policies aim to change the attitudes or behavior of energy consumers.

Supply side:

• Tax code preferences for renewable energy generation (federal and state).

• Ratepayer cross-subsidies for renewable energy development (state).

• Mandatory utility purchases of power generated by renewable energy sources at the utility's "avoided cost" (federal/state).

• Imputed environmental costs ("full environmental costing") to penalize fossil-fuel generation planning choices (state).

• Fuel-diversity premiums to penalize reliance on natural gas in power generation (state).

• Government payments for renewable energy research, development, and commercialization (federal and state).

• Early entry into open-access programs for renewable energy generation (state).

• "Green pricing" programs that are subsidized by the utilities' other electric sources (state).

Demand side:

• Taxpayer subsidies for energy-efficiency programs (federal and state).

• Ratepayer subsidies for energy efficiency, so-called demand-side management, or DSM (state).

- Minimum energy-efficiency building and appliance standards (federal and state).

This cumulative taxpayer and ratepayer investment is substantial. The DOE has spent about $19 billion, in 1996 dollars, since its inception on electric conservation ($8–9 billion) and nonhydro renewables ($10.7 billion). State demand-side management programs add approximately $16 billion more. Adding in tax preferences and above-market pricing for renewables, the annual benefit in 1994 alone was estimated as high as $5 billion.

A rough estimate of electric subsidies for renewables and conservation over the last 20 years is between $30 billion and $50 billion, which does not include the substantial private costs associated with building and appliance energy-efficiency standards. This represents the largest governmental peacetime energy expenditure in U.S. history, outranking the Strategic Petroleum Reserve program to date, as well as the spending on the 1974–1988 synthetic fuels program.

After the problems caused by the 1973–1974 Arab oil embargo the Strategic Petroleum Reserve program was set up to reduce vulnerability to the economic, national security, and foreign policy consequences of petroleum supply interruptions.

Eco-energy planning is confronting three major challenges in the move to a more competitive electric industry:

- Renewable-energy options [i.e., hydroelectricity and wind power] have [intractable] environmental drawbacks.
- Renewable-energy subsidies and mandatory conservation are proving to be incompatible with a competitive restructuring of the electric industry because of unfavorable economics and surplus existing capacity.
- Economic and environmental advances in the fossil fuels industry, particularly natural gas in electric generation and reformulated gasoline in transportation, have reduced the environmental costs of fossil fuel consumption that are necessary to justify subsidized alternatives.

In contrast to eco-energy planning, market-based energy environmentalism relies on private property, tort redress, and market incentives to address environmental degradation. In sum, eco-energy planning is predicated on the idea that energy markets are so riddled with imperfections that major interventions are necessary to manage society's energy choices. Market-based energy environmentalism rejects the idea that the energy economy is rife with "market failures" and questions the idea that government regulators can improve on the private choices of economic agents in the free market. Market-based energy environmentalists maintain that the best way to ensure the efficient use of economic and environmental resources is to rely on undistorted price data and government protection of private property rights.

Bradley's suggestion, that the influence of the market will ensure efficiency of energy supply, echoes classical free-market economic theory.

Summary

J. Richard Mayer's article "Can the world meet future energy needs using wind and solar energy?" explains the energy crisis that is afflicting California and other parts of the United States. Instead of looking to coal, natural gas, and nuclear power—which pollute the Earth—wind and solar power should be considered. Only a small portion of the solar energy reaching the Earth would need to be utilized to meet the world's energy needs. With worldwide programs to increase solar panels on buildings the cost of solar energy will decrease. High-tech wind turbines can create energy at a cost comparable to traditional electric costs. In the Midwest there is more than enough wind power to meet the needs of the entire United States. Using wind and solar power to meet energy needs would help prevent global warming, air pollution, and water quality degradation.

Robert L. Bradley Jr. in "Renewable energy—why renewable energy is not cheap and not green" discusses the available renewable energy methods. He finds problems with each type of renewable energy production. Hydropower damages stream habitats. Solar power takes up a lot of land and is expensive. Geothermal energy can be depleted, and biomass energy production produces air emissions. Wind power, which is the most likely renewable energy source, has some problems as well. It is uneconomic, and it damages the environment by killing birds, taking up a lot of land, and causing noise pollution. Due to advances in fossil fuel industries their environmental impacts have been lessened, making them better alternatives than renewable sources. Natural gas, for example, is a good choice for future energy production since it is cleaner burning and much less expensive.

FURTHER INFORMATION:

Books:

Patel, Mukund R., *Wind and Solar Power Systems*. New York: CRC Press, 1999.

Useful websites:

www.epa.gov

Site of United States Environmental Protection Agency.

www.greenpeace.org

Site of environmental campaigning group, Greenpeace.

eelink.net

Environmental education on the Internet.

www.epa.gov/globalwarming/links/fed_links.html

List of federal agencies in U.S. dealing with energy.

www.seen.org

Sustainable Energy and Economy Network, a nonprofit organization studying lending for fossil fuel energy use.

The following debates in the Pro/Con series may also be of interest:

In this volume:

Topic 1 Does global warming threaten humankind?

Topic 9 Will hydrogen replace oil as our main primary source?

Topic 11 Do the benefits of nuclear power outweigh the risks?

CAN WIND AND SOLAR RESOURCES MEET OUR ENERGY NEEDS?

YES: Today's high-tech wind turbines generate electricity at a price competitive with any other electric power source

YES: The transition to renewable energy will be costly, but because fossil fuels are nonrenewable, their costs will inevitably rise

NO: Eco-energy planning relies on taxpayer subsidies

COST
Are renewable energy sources as cost effective as traditional power resources?

NO: Not all renewable energy sources are created equal: some are more economically viable than others

CAN WIND AND SOLAR RESOURCES MEET OUR ENERGY NEEDS?

KEY POINTS

YES: Almost 80 percent of the world's solar power is generated today in California's Mojave Desert

YES: There is more than enough wind power in the Midwest to meet all of the current electrical needs of the United States

MEETING DEMAND
Can wind and solar resources meet the energy needs of the United States?

NO: Solar and wind power are highly uneconomic, land-intensive, and fringe electric power sources for the forseeable future

ENVIRONMENTAL EFFECTS
Is renewable energy less harmful for the environment?

YES: Renewable energy is environmentally benign and ecologically sustainable, while fossil fuels aggravate pollution and global warming

NO: Wind farms are noisy, land-intensive, unsightly, and hazardous to birds, including endangered species

Topic 9
WILL HYDROGEN REPLACE OIL AS OUR PRIMARY ENERGY SOURCE?

YES
"HYDROGEN: THE FUEL FOR THE FUTURE"
U.S. DEPARTMENT OF ENERGY, 1995

NO
"FUELING THE CELLS"
MECHANICAL ENGINEERING, DECEMBER 1999
PAUL SHARKE

INTRODUCTION

During the Industrial Revolution (about 1750-1830) humankind discovered that fossil fuels could be used as a source of energy. With the start of mass production society's dependence on fossil fuels—coal, petroleum, and natural gas—grew substantially.

In the 20th century humankind became concerned with caring for the environment and the planet. Experts have now started to look for alternative energy sources to fossil fuels, which are limited resources and also produce gases harmful to the environment. Carbon dioxide is a greenhouse gas and has contributed to global warming (see pages 70-71). Sulfur dioxide and nitrogen oxides combine with water in clouds to produce sulfuric and nitric acids, which then fall on the land as acid rain.

It is thus inevitable that hydrogen (from the Greek *hydro* and *genes* meaning "water generator"), the most abundant element in the world, should be considered a viable energy source.

Indeed, since its discovery in the 18th century scientists have experimented with hydrogen, not least because it can be burned as a fuel similar to gasoline and natural gas. The main difference is that burning hydrogen produces only water as a waste product. That is because the combination of hydrogen and oxygen produces water (H_2O). Hydrogen can also be used in fuel cells that generate electricity by combining hydrogen with oxygen. This reaction gives off a current of electricity as well as heat; the only by-product is water.

There are numerous potential advantages to using hydrogen as a fuel source. Hydrogen gas can be used in vehicles and to heat offices and homes. Fuel cells can be used in place of batteries in anything from laptops and cell phones to automobiles. Hydrogen can be produced safely and cleanly. It represents a sustainable source of energy that could help the world decrease its dependence on fossil fuels. The performance of hydrogen-fueled cars is two to three times more efficient than gasoline powered internal combustion engines. Fuel cells last 20 times longer than traditional batteries. Since the only by-product of using hydrogen is water, there is no threat of increasing greenhouse emissions—primarily carbon dioxide— leading to global warming.

> *"Energy production and environmental protection are not competing priorities. They are dual aspects of a single purpose, to live well and wisely upon the Earth."*
> —PRESIDENT GEORGE W. BUSH

Despite all of these advantages, hydrogen power is still not widely accepted as an energy source since there are still many obstacles to using it cheaply and efficiently.

Cost is one of the main obstacles. Generation of hydrogen and production of fuel cells are expensive. In order to have hydrogen fuel, the hydrogen must first be separated from other materials.

Steam reforming of natural gas, electrolysis (splitting of water into hydrogen and oxygen using electricity), and photoelectrolysis (splitting of water using sunlight) are all possible production methods. Scientists are even conducting research into the possibility of using bacteria and algae since they both produce hydrogen during photosynthesis.

Storage of hydrogen represents another problem. Liquid hydrogen must be kept at temperatures below −250 °C (−418 °F).

As a gas the hydrogen needed to travel an equivalent distance requires more space than gasoline. This means that fuel tanks on cars would have to be enlarged, or people would have to stop for refueling more frequently. Hydrogen can be stored as metal hydrides—combinations of hydrogen and metal—or it can be absorbed onto activated charcoal; but that requires separating the hydrogen before it can be used.

Distribution of hydrogen creates another problem. The most efficient method of transporting hydrogen is through pipelines similar to those used for natural gas. However, hydrogen embrittlement can cause deterioration of pipes, and the small size of hydrogen molecules enables them to leak easily.

Despite these obstacles, hydrogen is currently used in several areas. Buses are able to use hydrogen for fuel because they have fixed routes on which travel distance between fill-ups is not a big issue.

NASA (the National Aeronautics and Space Administration) also uses fuel cells to provide spacecrafts with water, electricity, and heat. NASA received a lot of attention and criticism for using them after the explosion of the *Challenger* rocket in 1986, which killed all its crew, including some civilians. The explosion was reputed to have been caused by a hydrogen leak.

In the following articles the U.S. Department of Energy and Paul Sharke discuss the advantages and disadvantages of using hydrogen as a fuel source.

HYDROGEN:
THE FUEL FOR THE FUTURE
U.S. Department of Energy

See spaceflight. nasa.com, and find a recent space mission that has used hydrogen fuel.

See www.usitc.gov —the site of the United States International Trade Commission— and find out how much the United States spent on foreign oil products last year. How does this compare to other countries?

See page 114 for methods of production.

YES

With a roar of the engines amid clouds of smoke and steam, the launch of the space shuttle has almost become a commonplace scene for Americans. The liftoff is so precisely timed that we don't think of how much energy it takes to send the mission skyward, or what kind of fuel it takes to operate the space shuttle while in orbit. And very few of us pause to ask how much energy it takes to reenter the Earth's atmosphere. The fuel of choice for all the space shuttle missions is hydrogen—not a readily available fuel for consumers now, but a viable alternative fuel for the future.

Hydrogen is the simplest, naturally occurring element that can be found in numerous materials—natural gas, methanol, coal, biomass, and water. As an abundantly available fuel that can be produced domestically, it could help the United States decrease its dependence on foreign oil imports.

Hydrogen as an energy source
Hydrogen, an energy carrier, is anticipated to join electricity as the foundation for a globally sustainable energy system using renewable energy. Hydrogen can be made safely, is environmentally friendly, and versatile, and has many potential energy uses, including powering non-polluting vehicles, heating homes and offices, and fueling aircraft.

Interest has been spurred by a growing awareness of burgeoning environmental threats to which hydrogen produced by solar-generated electricity seems the near-perfect solution. The theoretical combination of the two is appealing: electricity generated from the limitless supply of solar energy, then used to produce a flexible, transportable, and easily stored fuel which is virtually non-polluting. Cost remains the largest single obstacle, although there are formidable engineering challenges as well.

An energy carrier, not a source, hydrogen must be manufactured, principally by either splitting water or by extracting it from natural gas through steam reforming. The major markets for hydrogen are in the petrochemical and fertilizer industries. The National Aeronautics and Space

Administration (NASA), in addition to using hydrogen to propel the space shuttle, uses hydrogen to provide all of the shuttles' electric power from on-board fuel cells. Fuel cells combine hydrogen and oxygen to generate electricity; the fuel cells' exhaust—pure water—is used for drinking water by the crew.

Advantages and opportunities

There are advantages and opportunities to using hydrogen as an alternative fuel:

- The production of hydrogen from renewable electricity and from biomass could reduce our dependence on imported petroleum. If the U.S. Department of Energy (DOE) reaches its goal of hydrogen energy providing 10 percent of total U.S. energy consumption by 2025, our dependence on oil imports could be reduced by half.

See www.eren.doe. gov/RE/hydrogen. html for U.S. Department of Energy policy on hydrogen.

- Hydrogen can be combined with gasoline, ethanol, methanol, or natural gas; just adding 5 percent hydrogen to the gasoline/air mixture in an internal combustion engine could reduce nitrogen oxide emissions by 30 to 40 percent. An engine converted to burn pure hydrogen produces only water and minor amounts of nitrogen oxides as exhaust.

- California's new "zero-emission" standard for passenger cars—requiring 2 percent of new cars sold in the state be non-polluting as of 1998—could be met by electric vehicles powered by hydrogen fuel cells (a kind of battery that combines hydrogen and oxygen to produce an electric current), or hybrids powered by hydrogen fueled internal combustion engines and batteries or flywheels. Manufacturing fuel cells to meet the potential demand could add 70,000 new jobs to the state.

- Hydrogen can be produced from a variety of renewable sources and has many uses in our economy. Because of the versatility of production methods and end use, wide-spread hydrogen energy use will create significant benefits to the agricultural, manufacturing, transportation, and service sectors of the U.S. economy.

Technological and economic constraints

[The] technological and economic constraints include safety, the form of the fuel, production and storage, and economics. The nation's infrastructure is not geared to a hydrogen-based economy, and hydrogen's basic cost turns out to be higher than that of conventional fuels. [DOE] research address[es] these constraints by examining improved fuel cells and storage capabilities.

COMMENTARY: Hydrogen

Hydrogen from water

The most widely used method of splitting is *electrolysis*, in which an electric current is run through water, decomposing it into its component elements, hydrogen and oxygen. A variation on this is *steam electrolysis,* in which some of the energy needed to split the water is imparted as raw heat rather than electricity, thus making the process more efficient.

Other methods of generating hydrogen

- Thermochemical water splitting

Chemicals such as bromine, iodine, or iodine, assisted by heat, split the water molecule in several, usually three, steps.

- Photosynthesis

In this process the molecule is split by sunlight aided by catalysts in a way that mimics photosynthesis.

- Biological and photobiological (sunlight-assisted) water splitting

In this process organisms not only produce hydrogen, but clean up pollution as well.

- Thermal watersplitting

This radically different approach has been investigated in the United States, Japan, Canada, and France; it uses temperatures of up to 3,000 °C.

Storage

There are several different ways to store hydrogen:

- Compressed gas storage tanks

New materials have permitted storage tanks to be fabricated that can hold hydrogen at extremely high temperatures. At present the costs of producing the tanks and using compression are high.

- Liquid hydrogen

Condensing hydrogen gas into its more dense liquid form enables a larger quantity of hydrogen to be stored, but is very expensive.

- Chemical hydrides (high and low temperature)

Various pure or alloyed metals can combine with hydrogen, producing stable metal hydrides. They decompose when heated, releasing hydrogen. Hydrogen can be stored in the form of a hydride at higher densities than by simple compression. This is a safe and efficient storage system.

- Gas-on-solid adsorption

Adsorption of hydrogen molecules on carbon can approach the storage density of liquid hydrogen.

- Microspheres

Tiny glass spheres can hold pressurized hydrogen. The spheres are heated and filled with the gas, which can pass through the ultra-hot glass wall. When the glass cools, the gas can no longer pass through and is trapped.

Fleet vehicles well suited to hydrogen

Hydrogen is being blended with other alternative fuels and used in fleets of buses in a number of cities. In many cases, alternative fuel vehicles whose engines are properly maintained produce fewer polluting emissions than do vehicles using diesel fuel.

In general, bus fleets are well suited to alternative fuels. Buses are used on routes that require a known range per tank of fuel. Buses have well-defined space and weight requirements for accommodating passengers. And transit buses are maintained in a single maintenance facility that can conveniently service alternative fuel vehicles.

Problems

No single engine/fuel combination has yet proven to be the best for all transit applications. Local factors, such as the availability of the alternative fuel, the size of the particular bus fleet, and specific environmental requirements, often help local transit officials determine which clean-air technology is their best choice.

In addition, cost and budget factors, availability of refueling stations, maintenance needs, and engine performance must be considered before deciding which new engine/fuel combination is best for each locale.

Hydrogen as a source of power for public utilities

Hydrogen can supplement other sources of energy to produce electricity. Gaseous hydrogen can be stored like an industrial gas. [Theoretically] hydrogen could be shipped in modified natural gas pipelines, thus carrying energy over long distances more economically than high-voltage transmission lines. Some researchers have estimated that it is about one-fourth as expensive to pipe hydrogen across long distances as it is to transmit electricity the same distance.

Energy supply potential

Using hydrogen to displace other fuels in the nation's energy supply require[s] numerous changes in existing infrastructures for storage, distribution, and utilization. The journey to a practical system may be a long one. Many different photoconversion approaches are candidates for future hydrogen production processes, but only a few have been examined through research and development projects. Given the environmental considerations, hydrogen may be a good choice for the United States and other industrial countries.

What other renewable energy sources could be used instead of hydrogen? See www.eren.doe.gov.

FUELING THE CELLS
Paul Sharke

English economist
Thomas Malthus
(1766–1834)
argued that
population growth
would exceed
food supplies and
that wars,
famines, disease,
and drought
would occur. See
www.ac.wwu.edu/
~stephan/malthus/
malthus.0.html.

See Global
Warming,
pages 70–71.

NO

A hundred years ago, people predicting what life was going to be like in the 20th century warned of more wars, and droughts, and famines. Some expected that agricultural advances would help feed the world. Others awaited refrigerated foods and wireless telegraphy. Many even envisioned the car replacing the horse.

Few, it seems, foresaw the position that automobiles would come to occupy in the foreground of our landscape. No one predicted how the then-insignificant auto, by encouraging a thirst for mobility that could be quenched by fossil fuels, would be accused of helping to warm the globe.

There remain any number of technological hurdles to jump over before fuel cells replace the internal combustion engine as the prime mover for our cars. For one thing, though fuel cell prices have descended drastically from their space-age levels, they are still much higher per kilowatt than the price of internal combustion engines.

Yet, efficiency from mass production is expected to reduce fuel-cell costs even more. And fuel-cell cars are looming on the horizon: DaimlerChrysler, to cite but one example, has promised production fuel-cell vehicles by 2004.

The hydrogen debate

It is energy for the fuel cell that has opened the greatest debate. [Among the questions asked are:] Just where is this hydrogen supposed to come from? How is it going to be stored? How is it going to be transported? Delivered? How will the public perception of hydrogen's danger have to change for it to gain acceptance?

The promise of the fuel cell is a car with zero emissions. Hydrogen, nature's most abundant element, does not stay long in a pure state, but combines readily with other atoms. Before it can be used as a fuel, hydrogen must be separated from its chemical bonds. The energy needed to crack those bonds can come from any of four sources: Fossil, nuclear, solar, or geothermal.

Everyone, though, agrees that hydrogen is tough to store and low in energy density. It is also expensive to make and suffers from image problems related to safety and the public

For a fuel-cell
vehicle to be truly
emissions-free, the
hydrogen for the
fuel cell must itself
come from a source
that produces
no emissions.

memory of two powerfully graphic disasters: the *Hindenburg* (1938) and the *Challenger* (1986).

Stored as a gas, hydrogen requires more tank volume than do liquid fuels for the same amount of mileage. Stored as a liquid, hydrogen requires cryogenic systems to keep it cold. One of the reasons that so much demonstration work in hydrogen-powered vehicles has focused on buses is because they generally run fixed routes. An airport bus need not carry a tremendous volume of hydrogen to effectively deliver passengers within the confines of an airport circuit. Refueling stations for buses, located strategically along a fixed route, add only a few minutes for a stop that is easily incorporated into a bus's regular schedule. Buses that do travel long distances between fueling stops can carry larger tanks.

The Hindenburg *was a German zeppelin, filled with hydrogen gas that exploded over Lakeside Naval Base on May 6, 1938. Challenger was a space rocket launched on January 28, 1986. It exploded 74 seconds after takeoff, killing all of the people on board. Leaking hydrogen gas may have caused the explosion*

A need to reform

Hydrogen storage on an auto is more difficult. A car does not allow much room for hydrogen tanks. And a car needs a reasonable driving range between fill-ups. Hence, methanol and gasoline are attractive hydrogen carriers: Both are liquid at ambient temperatures. Gasoline is already carted around today in millions of cars; methanol, derived from natural gas, could be carried likewise.

These fuels, however, must be reformed into hydrogen before they can be consumed by a fuel cell. On-board methanol reforming seems to be closer to practical realization than gasoline reforming. Indeed, many automakers are planning to structure their first fuel-cell vehicles around methanol reformer technology.

On-board reformers have their own drawbacks. One objection to such devices is the cost and complexity they add to a vehicle. Another difficulty is the time lag that reformers introduce between a driver's demand for power and a vehicle's response. Troubling, too, is the warm-up period that reformers require, which could be as long as one minute every time the car is started. Critics say the public will never accept such performance restrictions.

Would you be prepared to wait a minute every time you got into a car?

Arguments against on-board reformers suggest the option of situating reformers at filling stations. There, they could operate continuously. Size restrictions and performance limitations would not be nearly as pressing as they are for on-board reformers. The whole debate, however, returns to the question of on-board storage.

Talk of stationary reformers brings into focus another segment of the fuel-cell discussion. Fixed reformers could make use of established delivery systems for gasoline.

Studies have shown that methanol distribution could be phased into the current gasoline infrastructure without prohibitive expense.

Such attributes render gasoline and methanol desirable transitional fuels until we can sidle up o a full hydrogen economy. One of gasoline's biggest advantages as a hydrogen carrier is its already mature infrastructure. The transportation, the codes for safe handling, and the public's familiarity with the fuel all make gasoline a good choice for transitional ease.

But looming large over this optimistic picture are two flaws. Gasoline's high ratio of carbon dioxide to hydrogen weakens its desirability as a source of fuel-cell hydrogen. And gasoline, as it is supplied today, may be too laden with additives to make a hydrogen pure enough so it would not poison a fuel cell. Gasoline, it turns out, might have to be reformulated anyway.

Hydrogen is not extracted from the ground. Instead, producers must divorce hydrogen from the chemical bonds that it forms with other elements. Today, the hydrogen industry makes its product for industrial customers chiefly through steam reforming of natural gas.

Such reforming could generate enough hydrogen to power fuel-cell vehicles for about 100 years, the estimated reserve of natural gas. Natural gas has a well-developed infrastructure. Indeed, before the sudden interest in fuel cells, natural gas vehicles were touted as appropriate responses for the need to reduce emissions. They still have supporters who see natural gas vehicles as an immediately practical approach to reducing the carbon dioxide burden. Internal combustion engines, with little modification, run well using natural gas.

For more information on "hydrogen embrittlement" see www.corrosion source.com/learning center/hic.htm.

Buses, in an assortment of demonstration projects, have been burning natural gas for years. Some advocates of natural gas point out that the same pipelines used to move that product could eventually deliver hydrogen. That turns out to be only partly true, however. Newer pipelines that never carried hydrogen-rich "town gas" might fall victims to hydrogen embrittlement.

Icelandic New Energy Ltd. will investigate the possibility of replacing fossil fuels with hydrogen. It will first look at a hydrogen/fuel cell-powered bus.

A model hydrogen economy

Shell Hydrogen teamed up with DaimlerChrysler, Ballard, and Norske Hydro [in 1999] to experiment with a closed hydrogen economy in Iceland. Although the exact pattern of the experiment is awaiting definition, talk has centered around converting Iceland's large fishing boat fleet to hydrogen, and then powering its automotive and transit vehicles in the same manner. Iceland has vast geothermal energy sources, so using them to generate hydrogen makes good economic sense.

The systems required to deliver clean hydrogen fuel to a mass of hydrogen-powered vehicles will be enormous, and will require great sums of money to make them work.

The idea of a hydrogen economy is not new. In the early 1970s, as concern rose over limited supplies of fossil fuels, the American Gas Association commissioned the Institute of Gas Technology to study the feasibility of a system of hydrogen production, transmission, distribution, and use on a nationwide scale. At the time, the idea of global warming was still off in the future. The environment was not the motivation for looking into a hydrogen economy. Oil was.

"Geothermal energy" comes from the depths of the Earth and its interior heat source. It arises from a continual flow of heat energy toward the surface and manifests itself in the form of volcanoes, hot springs, and geysers, among other things.

The future of oil

Environmental issues aside, we simply may not have a 100-year supply of oil. Some experts are saying that world oil production could peak in the first or second decades of the [21st century]. After production peaks, oil's price will continue to rise unless demand slackens. The world's oil will never actually run dry; it will simply become more expensive to extract, until, eventually, it becomes too costly to burn.

This time around it is entirely possible that we will switch our economy over to a new fuel. With global warming a dominant issue, with oil supplies headed for extinction, and with fuel cells, renewable energies, and automobiles making great strides in efficiency, one might be tempted to take a guess at what life will be like in the next 100 years.

Summary

The article "Hydrogen: The Fuel for the Future" explains how hydrogen can be used as a nonpolluting fuel. Hydrogen is an abundant element and can be found in many different sources. It can be utilized as an energy carrier that is safe, environmentally benign, and versatile. Replacing oil with hydrogen would reduce greenhouse gas emissions, leading to a halt in global warming. It would also reduce our dependence on nonrenewable resources, such as oil and water, which have also been the cause of many wars. Solar energy can be used to separate hydrogen from water; the hydrogen can then be stored and used when needed. This represents a method of energy production that is sustainable. Improvements in fuel cells and storage of hydrogen will make hydrogen a viable fuel source in the future.

"Fueling the Cells" discusses the obstacles associated with using hydrogen as a fuel. While hydrogen would be an excellent fuel that would burn clean and not pollute the atmosphere, obtaining it would be a problem. Cost, storage, transportation, distribution, and potential danger are all blocks that need to be overcome before hydrogen will replace traditional fuels like oil. Energy is needed to separate hydrogen from its chemical bonds. It is expensive; and if fossil fuels are used, the process is no longer free of carbon-dioxide emissions. Also, changing the current system of gasoline use will be difficult. Cars will have to be altered along with refueling stations, costing consumers a lot of money. In order for hydrogen to compete with already existing fuels, its cost will have to come down.

FURTHER INFORMATION:

Books:
Cannon, J., *Harnessing Hydrogen*. New York: Inform, 1994.

Koppel, Tom, *Powering the Future*. New York: John Wiley & Sons, 1999.

Peavey, Michael A., *Fuel from Water: Energy Independence with Hydrogen*, 7th edition. New York: Merit Books, 1998.

Useful websites:
www.eren.doe.gov/RE/hydrogen.html

Hydrogen energy site of Energy Efficiency and Renewable Energy Network (EREN).

www.shell.com/hydrogen-en/content/0,6013,30718-56069,00.htm

Shell Hydrogen site—explains company's activities and also focuses on Icelandic hydrogen economy and Shell's attempts to help the environment.

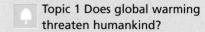

The following debates in the Pro/Con series may also be of interest:

In this volume:

Topic 1 Does global warming threaten humankind?

Topic 8 Can wind and solar resources meet our energy needs?

Global Warming, pages 70–71.

WILL HYDROGEN REPLACE OIL AS OUR PRIMARY ENERGY SOURCE?

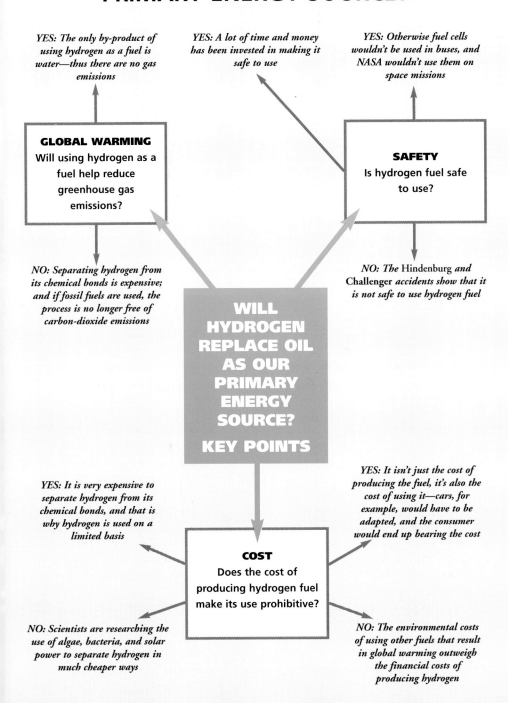

YES: The only by-product of using hydrogen as a fuel is water—thus there are no gas emissions

YES: A lot of time and money has been invested in making it safe to use

YES: Otherwise fuel cells wouldn't be used in buses, and NASA wouldn't use them on space missions

GLOBAL WARMING
Will using hydrogen as a fuel help reduce greenhouse gas emissions?

SAFETY
Is hydrogen fuel safe to use?

NO: Separating hydrogen from its chemical bonds is expensive; and if fossil fuels are used, the process is no longer free of carbon-dioxide emissions

NO: The Hindenburg and Challenger accidents show that it is not safe to use hydrogen fuel

WILL HYDROGEN REPLACE OIL AS OUR PRIMARY ENERGY SOURCE?

KEY POINTS

YES: It is very expensive to separate hydrogen from its chemical bonds, and that is why hydrogen is used on a limited basis

YES: It isn't just the cost of producing the fuel, it's also the cost of using it—cars, for example, would have to be adapted, and the consumer would end up bearing the cost

COST
Does the cost of producing hydrogen fuel make its use prohibitive?

NO: Scientists are researching the use of algae, bacteria, and solar power to separate hydrogen in much cheaper ways

NO: The environmental costs of using other fuels that result in global warming outweigh the financial costs of producing hydrogen

PART 3

ENVIRONMENTAL ETHICS

INTRODUCTION

People's attitudes toward the environment are highly complex. They are often conditioned by practical and economic factors. Practical objections to lumbering operations, for example, might be that they should be limited because they leave topsoil exposed and liable to be washed into rivers, which may then silt up. Another practical objection to deforestation is that because trees can absorb polluting carbon and release oxygen, it damages the atmosphere. Practical support for logging focuses on the economic benefit it brings to forest communities, the positive role played by thinning out mature trees, or programs that replace each tree felled with two new saplings.

When it comes to environmental issues, such practical considerations are sometimes combined with deep-seated ethical reactions toward the landscape. From an ethical point of view, for example, the argument against logging might be that humankind should respect other forms of life on Earth, and that it has no right to do otherwise. The argument in favor of lumbering, on the other hand, might focus on a moral obligation for humankind to use the resources of the planet to improve the lives of the whole human species.

Unavoidable impact

People's ethical attitudes toward the environment reflect how they perceive the position of humankind with relation to the rest of life on Earth. At the heart of the debate is the question of whether humans, as the most advanced species, have a moral duty to look after the rest of the planet—or a moral duty to look after humankind. The question is not clear-cut. It is, for example, possible for both moral obligations—to the planet and to humanity—to lead to the same conclusion. Many people argue that if humankind does not take more care of the planet, it will eventually destroy Earth's ability to sustain the population.

Not even radical environmentalists, meanwhile, argue that people can live without having some negative effect on the natural world. There are more than six billion people on Earth today. They need land to build houses, energy for heat, agriculture for food, and so on. They need fresh water, medicines, and clothes. All these have their roots in the natural world. Inevitably, such a large number of people produce wastes that pollute the land, the air, and the rivers and oceans. The issues at the heart of the environmental debate revolve less around whether human impact can be stopped and more on ways in which it might be limited.

Questions and answers

One of the most important areas to be addressed is the question of pollution. Humankind produces more waste than the planet can absorb. Who should clean it up? Topic 10, *Do corporations have a moral responsibility to nature?* considers the question of whether producers are obligated to care for the natural resources from which their profits ultimately derive.

Topic 11, *Do the benefits of nuclear power outweigh the risks?* touches on a typically complex ethical dilemma. Many of those who believe that it is

Animals and humankind

Many ethical dilemmas concern animals. Some people feel morally responsible for animals because animals cannot protect themselves. Other people argue that human dominance is the natural result of evolution and that, as throughout the animal kingdom, human behavior toward animals should not be classed as "right" or "wrong."

> *"[We stand] today poised on a pinnacle of wealth and power, yet we live in a land of vanishing beauty, of increasing ugliness, of shrinking open space and of an overall environment that is diminished daily by pollution, noise, and blight. This, in brief, is the quiet conservation crisis."*
> —STEWART L. UDALL, U.S. SECRETARY OF THE INTERIOR, 1960s

important to find cleaner ways of producing energy still object to nuclear power, even though it is cleaner than traditional fossil fuels, because of the potential danger of a nuclear accident. In the same vein, genetic modification may offer a way to improve crop yields without the use of fertilizers or the need to clear land for farming, both of which worry environmentalists; but species modified with untested technology might also upset the natural balance or make the food chain unsafe. The issue is discussed in Topic 12, *Is genetically modified food safe enough to feed the world's population?*

One lasting controversy surrounding animals is whether or not they should be kept in zoos. Topic 13, *Are zoos morally wrong?* considers the question. Some people feel that animals do not exist for human entertainment and should be left in their native habitats. Others argue that zoos teach people about animals, and that captive species released into the wild would not know how to fend for themselves. Similarly, they argue that zoos enable breeding of endangered species. Topic 14, *Should endangered species be cloned?* takes the dilemma a step further and examines the ethics of cloning.

Topic 10
DO CORPORATIONS HAVE A MORAL RESPONSIBILITY TO NATURE?

YES
"A ROAD MAP FOR NATURAL CAPITALISM"
HARVARD BUSINESS REVIEW, MAY/JUNE, 1999
AMORY B. LOVINS, L. HUNTER LOVINS, PAUL HAWKEN

NO
"BRINGING THE ENVIRONMENT DOWN TO EARTH"
HARVARD BUSINESS REVIEW, JULY/AUGUST, 1999
FOREST L. REINHARDT

INTRODUCTION

Consumers are increasingly pressured to buy sustainable produce and to conserve energy and natural resources. Everyone, from individuals to governments, has an important role to play in conserving the planet's remaining resources. But what does this mean for the business world?

Many of today's corporations transcend national boundaries and employ tens of thousands of people in numerous countries, in some cases creating more wealth than a number of small nations combined.

In those cases great power may be concentrated in the hands of a few. The role of the corporation constantly evolves in the face of changing societal pressures, but for the most part its existence is based on the maximization of profits for its shareholders. But at what cost is that role preserved? And also, who should be made to bear the burden of replenishing the natural

resources that have been used in the course of corporation's activities?

As late as the 19th century there appeared to be no limits on how much individuals could exploit nature in the pursuit of farming, lumbering, fishing, or mining. The advent of the 20th century, however, brought more organized and efficient ways to exploit these resources. Corporations were set up as a more efficient way to organize capital and human energy in order to provide goods and services and at the same time make investors a sizable return on their investment. In this drive for efficiency and return on investment some people argue that the values of conservation and sustainable yields have been neglected and eroded.

Direct overexploitation of resources is now a global issue. Fishing fleets in Europe's North Sea have been idled for strict periods to allow perilously low fish populations to recover. The Grand

Banks off Newfoundland are also almost fished out. In Amazonia new highways take farmers and lumberjacks ever deeper into the rain forests, and the forests of Indonesia are disappearing under palm-oil plantations.

Some companies also lack responsible policies for waste management or energy conservation. Progress is being made (chlorofluorocarbons, or CFCs, are widely banned, for instance), but toxic effluents from some plants still pollute our waterways, and greenhouse gases amass in the atmosphere.

To some extent consumers collude in the destructive processes. Unrestricted use of the automobile helps sustain the market for gasoline and hence for oil-drilling operations in fragile ecosystems; the wasteful use of disposable diapers, hardwood furniture, chopsticks, or junk mail drives deforestation. Demand for cheap food encourages big agribusiness to develop more powerful chemicals and large-scale farming methods.

At the start of the 21st century, however, a growing number of corporations have recognized that their economic success is tied to the health of the natural world. Big companies have successfully minimized their impact on nature and in some cases have restored nature to its original state, while at the same time making an acceptable profit for shareholders. Some companies have begun to incorporate business models that emulate the cycles of nature, finding in them a blueprint for ecologically sound practice. Consumers, too, now demand "ecologically friendly" or so-called "green" products, which enable them to show off their environmental principles—in some cases, this is literally a case of shoppers wearing their conscience on their sleeves.

In the following two articles both sides of the argument on this issue are outlined. In "A Road Map for Natural Capitalism" Lovins, Lovins, and Hawken argue that companies have a responsibility to husband our natural capital but can enjoy a profit while doing so. They propose a holistic approach, termed "natural capitalism."

"The future will need people who understand that sustainable development is not merely about a series of technological fixes, about redesigning humanity or reengineering nature in a extension of globalized industrialization—but about reconnection with Nature and a profound understanding of the concepts of care that underpin long-term stewardship."
—HRH THE PRINCE OF WALES, BBC REITH LECTURE, 2000

In "Bringing the Environment Down to Earth" Reinhardt defends the right of corporations to maximize profit—the point of their existence. He argues that companies should confront each new solution to an environmental issue on a case-by-case basis.

A ROAD MAP FOR NATURAL SOCIALISM
Amory B. Lovins, L. Hunter Lovins, Paul Hawken

On September 16, 1991, a small group of scientists was sealed inside Biosphere II, a glittering 3.2-acre [1.3-ha.] glass and metal dome in Oracle, Arizona. Two years later, when the radical attempt to replicate the earth's main ecosystems in miniature ended, the engineered environment was dying. The gaunt researchers had survived only because fresh air had been pumped in. Despite $200 million worth of elaborate equipment, Biosphere II had failed to generate breathable air, drinkable water, and adequate food for just eight people. Yet Biosphere I, the planet we all inhabit, effortlessly performs those tasks every day for 6 billion of us.

Disturbingly, Biosphere I is now itself at risk. The earth's ability to sustain life, and therefore economic activity, is threatened by the way we extract, process, transport, and dispose of a vast flow of resources—some 220 billion tns. a year. With dangerously narrow focus, our industries look only at the exploitable resources of the earth's ecosystems—its oceans, forests, and plains—and not at the larger services that those systems provide for free. Resources and ecosystem services both come from the earth—even from the same biological systems—but they're two different things. Forests, for instance, not only produce the resource of wood fiber but also provide such ecosystem services as water storage, habitat, and regulation of the atmosphere and climate. Yet companies that earn income from harvesting the wood fiber resource often do so in ways that damage the forest's ability to carry out its other vital tasks.

Ignoring the essentials

The reason companies are so prodigal with ecosystem services is that the value of those services doesn't appear on the business balance sheet. But that's a staggering omission. The economy, after all, is embedded in the environment. Recent calculations published in the journal *Nature* conservatively estimate the value of all the earth's ecosystem services to be at least $33 trillion a year. That's close to the gross world product, and it implies a capitalized book value

The "biosphere' is the life-supporting stratum that surrounds the globe, extending from the ocean depths into the atmosphere. It contains all living things, plus the nutrient resources on which they depend.

Felling trees adds to the amount of carbon dioxide in the atmosphere.

The authors express the core of their argument in a single sentence.

on the order of half a quadrillion dollars. What's more, for most of these services, there is no known substitute at any price, and we can't live without them.

The natural capitalist approach

This article puts forward a new approach not only for protecting the biosphere but also for improving profits and competitiveness. Some very simple changes to the way we run our businesses, built on advanced techniques for making resources more productive, can yield startling benefits both for today's shareholders and for future generations. This approach is called natural capitalism because it's what capitalism might become if its largest category of capital— the "natural capital" of ecosystem services—were properly valued. The journey to natural capitalism involves four major shifts in business practices, all vitally interlinked:

- Dramatically increase the productivity of natural resources. Reducing the wasteful and destructive flow of resources from depletion to pollution represents a major business opportunity. Through fundamental changes in production design and technology, farsighted companies are developing ways to make natural resources—energy, minerals, water, forests—stretch 5, 10, even 100 times further than they do today. These major resource savings often yield higher profits than small resource savings do— or even saving no resources at all would—and not only pay for themselves over time but in many cases reduce initial capital investments.
- Shift to biologically inspired production models. Natural capitalism seeks not merely to reduce waste but to eliminate the very concept of waste. In closed-loop production systems, modeled on nature's designs, every output either is returned harmlessly to the ecosystem as a nutrient, like compost, or becomes an input for manufacturing another product. Such systems can often be designed to eliminate the use of toxic materials, which can hamper nature's ability to reprocess materials.
- Move to a solutions-based business model. The business model of traditional manufacturing rests on the sale of goods. In the new model, value is instead delivered as a flow of services—providing illumination, for example, rather than selling lightbulbs. This model entails a new perception of value, a move from the acquisition of goods as a measure of affluence to one where well-being is measured by the continuous satisfaction of changing

Is it really possible to place a monetary value on ecosystem services? How might you do it?

There are moves in industry to produce recyclable goods, from photocopiers to autos. German law, for example, makes many manufacturers permanently responsible for their products.

COMMENTARY: Leaner, greener paper use

Investigations into environmentally friendly practices that also save money have yielded many success stories. One example is in more economic use of paper products in order to reduce lumber consumption.

The easiest savings come from not using paper that is unwanted or unneeded. In an experiment at its Swiss headquarters Dow Europe cut office paper flow by about 30 percent in six weeks simply by discouraging unneeded information. For instance, mailing lists were eliminated, and senders of memos got back receipts indicating whether each recipient had wanted the information. Taking those and other small steps, Dow was also able to increase labor productivity by a similar proportion because people could focus on what they really needed to read. Similarly, Danish hearing-aid maker Oticon saved upward of 30 percent of its paper as a byproduct of redesigning its business processes to produce better decisions faster. Setting the default on office printers and copiers to double-sided reduced AT&T's paper costs by about 15 percent.

Further savings can come from using thinner but stronger and more opaque paper and from designing packaging more thoughtfully. In a 30-month effort at reducing such waste Johnson & Johnson saved 2,750 tons of packaging, 1,600 tons of paper, $2.8 million, and at least 330 acres of forest annually. Recycling paper and substituting alternative fibers such as wheat straw saves even more.

expectations for quality, utility, and performance. The new relationship aligns the interests of providers and customers in ways that reward them for implementing the first two innovations of natural capitalism: resource productivity and closed-loop manufacturing.

• Reinvest in natural capital. Ultimately, business must restore, sustain, and expand the planet's ecosystems so that they can produce their vital services and biological resources even more abundantly. Pressures to do so are mounting as human needs expand, the costs engendered by deteriorating ecosystems rise, and environmental awareness increases. Luckily, these pressures all create business value.

For example, a power producer can fund tree planting to offset the carbon emitted by its power plants.

Still the question arises—if large resource savings are available and profitable, why haven't they all been captured already? The answer is simple: scores of common practices in both the private and public sectors systematically reward companies for wasting natural resources and penalize them for boosting resource productivity.

If the road ahead is this clear, why are so many companies straying or falling by the wayside? We believe the reason is that the instruments companies use to set their targets, measure their performance, and hand out rewards are faulty. In other words, the markets are full of distortions and perverse incentives.

Focusing on the wrong resources

The real trouble with our economic compass is that it points in exactly the wrong direction. Most businesses are behaving as if people were still scarce and nature still abundant—the conditions that helped to fuel the first Industrial Revolution. At that time, people were relatively scarce compared with the present-day population.

The rapid mechanization of the textile industries caused explosive economic growth that created labor shortages in the factory and the field. The Industrial Revolution, responding to those shortages and mechanizing one industry after another, made people a hundred times more productive than they had ever been.

The logic of economizing on the scarcest resource, because it limits progress, remains correct. But the pattern of scarcity is shifting: now people aren't scarce but nature is. This shows up first in industries that depend directly on ecological health. Here, production is increasingly constrained by fish rather than by boats and nets, by forests rather than by chain saws, by fertile topsoil rather than by plows. Moreover, unlike the traditional factors of industrial production—capital and labor—the biological limiting factors cannot be substituted for one other. In the industrial system, we can easily exchange machinery for labor. But no technology or amount of money can substitute for a stable climate and a productive biosphere. Even proper pricing can't replace the priceless.

The Industrial Revolution, which started in England (around 1750–1830), marked the shift from an agrarian to an industrial economy. It was the dawn of labor-saving machinery.

Toward a new economy

Natural capitalism addresses those problems by reintegrating ecological with economic goals. Because it is both necessary and profitable, it will subsume traditional industrialism within a new economy and a new paradigm of production, just as industrialism previously subsumed agrarianism.

The companies that first make the changes we have described will have a competitive edge. Those that don't make that effort won't be a problem because ultimately they won't be around. In making that choice, as [American automobile engineer and industrialist] Henry Ford [1863-1947] said, "Whether you believe you can, or whether you believe you can't, you're absolutely right."

A good quote is a memorable way to end a case. What do you think this one adds here?

BRINGING THE ENVIRONMENT DOWN TO EARTH
Forest L. Reinhardt

NO

The author sets out his main point: that the relationship between the environment and business is not a clear-cut issue, but varies from case to case.

The structure of the argument is easy to follow. Reinhardt introduces five approaches and briefly defines them. Then he goes on to consider them in more depth in the same order.

The debate on business and the environment has been framed in simplistic yes-or-no terms: "Does it pay to be green?" Many business school academics and environmental leaders have answered yes. Yet businesspeople are skeptical—and rightly so, since they instinctively reject such all-or-nothing thinking in other contexts: the right policy depends on the circumstances confronting the company and the strategy it has chosen.

The environment as a business issue

Much of the writing about business and the environment ignores that basic point. The underlying assumption is that the earth is sick—and that therefore it *ought* to be profitable to find ways to help it return to good health. Promoting such causes and activities as recycling, solar energy, and small-scale agriculture should redound to business's benefit. But this is faulty reasoning. The truth is, environmental problems do not automatically create opportunities to make money. That's why managers should look at environmental problems as business issues.

I have identified five approaches that companies can take to integrate the environment into their business thinking. Some companies can distance themselves from their competitors by differentiating products and commanding higher prices for them. Others may be able to "manage" their competitors by imposing a set of private regulations or by helping to shape the rules written by government officials. Still others may be able to cut costs and help the environment simultaneously. Almost all of them can learn to improve their management of risk and thus reduce the outlays associated with accidents, lawsuits, and boycotts. And some companies may even be able to make systemic changes that will redefine competition in their markets.

The appeal of any of the five approaches will depend on the time horizon over which they are evaluated. As with other business problems, the environmental strategy that maximizes short-term cash flow is probably not the one that positions the company optimally for the long run. That's true of all business strategies in general, of course, but it especially applies to the environmental arena because benefits from environmental investments are often realized over long periods.

Differentiating products

The idea behind environmental product differentiation is straightforward: companies create products or employ processes that offer greater environmental benefits or impose smaller environmental costs than those of their competitors. Such efforts may raise the business's costs, but they may also enable it to command higher prices, to capture additional market share, or both.

> Unlike the authors of the previous article, Reinhardt talks about environmental approaches in traditional business terms of profit and market share.

Three conditions are required for success with environmental product differentiation. First, the company must identify customers who are willing to pay more for an environmentally friendly product. Second, it has to communicate its product's environmental benefits credibly. And third, it has to protect itself from imitators for long enough to profit on its investment. If any of those three conditions break down, the product differentiation approach will not work.

It would be easy to take a universally gloomy message about the prospects for environmental product differentiation in consumer markets. Environmental quality, after all, is a public good: everyone gets to enjoy it regardless of who pays for it. From the standpoint of economic self-interest, one might wonder why any individual would be willing to pay for a public good.

But that view is too narrow. People willingly pay for public goods all the time: sometimes in cash, when they contribute to charities, and often in time, when they give blood, clean up litter from parks and highways, or rinse their soda bottles for recycling. The trick for companies is to find the right public good—or to offer an imaginative bundle of public and private goods—that will appeal to a targeted market.

> For example, many consumers are willing to pay extra for organic food, which is environmentally friendly (public good) and may also be better for their health (private good).

Managing your competitors

Not all companies will be able to increase their profits through environmental product differentiation. But some may be able to derive environmental and business benefits by working to change the rules of the game so that the playing field tilts in their favor. A company may need to incur higher costs to respond to environmental pressure, but it can still come out ahead if it forces competitors to raise their costs

COMMENTARY: Working alongside regulation

In 1984 after toxic gas leaked from the plant of a Union Carbide subsidiary in Bhopal, India, and killed more than 2,000 people, the industry's image was tarnished (below), and it faced the threat of punitive government regulation. The industry recognized that it had to act. The leading companies in the Chemical Manufacturers Association created an initiative called Responsible Care and developed a set of private regulations, adopted in 1988. CMA members must comply with management codes covering such areas as process safety, pollution prevention, and emergency response. The initiative has lifted the CMA's reputation by yielding results. From 1988 to 1994, for example, U.S. chemical companies reduced environmental releases of toxins by almost 50 percent. Their example has inspired their foreign counterparts to follow suit.

Women place posters along the walls of the closed Union Carbide plant in Bhopal, India, on the anniversary of the accident, December 1, 1999.

Initiating private regulations is one way of forestalling government action that may be more restrictive (see box above).

Exxon Corp. was fined $100m after its Exxon Valdez tanker ran aground in Prince William Sound, Alaska, in March 1989 and leaked 40m liters of crude oil.

even more. How can that be done? By joining with similarly positioned companies within an industry to set private standards, or by convincing government to create regulations that favor your product.

A third approach to reconciling shareholder value with environmental management focuses not on competitors but on internal cost reductions. Some organizations can cut costs and improve environmental performance simultaneously.

Managing environmental risk

For many businesspeople, environmental management means risk management. Their objective is to avoid the costs that are associated with an industrial accident, a consumer boycott, or an environmental lawsuit. Fortunately, effective management of the business risk stemming from environmental problems can itself be a source of competitive advantage. Is the company buying the right risk policies? Is it retaining risk when the coverage is overpriced?

Redefining markets

Some companies are following several approaches at once. In the process, they are rewriting the competitive rules in their markets. [This approach] can entail significant market, regulatory, and scientific risks; [it's] not for every company— or even for every industry. The companies that appear to be succeeding are leaders in industries that face intensifying environmental pressure. Those companies have the research capabilities to develop new ways of delivering valuable services to their customers, the staying power to impose their vision of the future on their markets, and the resources to manage the inevitable risks. Moreover, by creating an appealing vision of a more profitable and environmentally responsible future, they may be better able to attract and retain the managers, scientists, and engineers who will enable them to build on their initial success.

> *The most progress is often made by companies that face pressure from environmentalists; many companies' operations bring them into direct contact with the environment.*

Beyond all-or-nothing

All-or-nothing arguments have dominated thinking about business and the environment. But it doesn't have to be that way. Consider how ideas about product quality have changed. At first, conventional wisdom held that improvements in quality had to be purchased at a cost of extra dollars and management attention. Then assertions were made that "quality is free": new savings would always pay for investments in improved quality. Now companies have arrived at a more nuanced view. They recognize that improving quality can sometimes lead to cost reductions, but they acknowledge that the right strategy depends on the company and its customers' requirements. It is time for business thinking on the environment to reach a similar middle ground.

> *The author repeats his claim for a case-by-case treatment of environmental issues that affect the business world.*

As we've seen, environmental problems are best analyzed as business problems. Whether companies are attempting to differentiate their products, tie their competitors' hands, reduce internal costs, manage risk, or even reinvent their industry, the basic tasks do not change when the word "environmental" is included in the proposition.

Does all this mean that questions of social responsibility can be safely ignored? Not at all—but they're only one part of the equation. Companies aren't in business to solve the world's problems, nor should they be. After all, they have shareholders who want to see a return on their investments. That's why managers need to bring the environment back into the fold of business problems and determine when it really pays to be green.

> *The author states that a corporation's moral obligation to the environment is second to its responsibility to shareholders.*

Summary

In this debate both authors indicate the potential savings to be gleaned from ideas such as ecoefficiency, life-cycle management, and resource conservation, but they differ starkly over the notion of how those savings should be measured and whose responsibility they should be.

Lovins et al. have introduced the notion that businesses need to treat nature as though managing their financial capital. This "natural capital" is the foundation on which all life on the planet rests and is thus essential to the long-term viability of any business. In essence, it is the ultimate in risk mitigation on behalf of the shareholder. The authors build on the idea by presenting five ways in which a business can incorporate their natural capitalist approach and make it work to its advantage.

Presenting the counterargument, Reinhardt argues that corporations are not in the business to solve the world's problems. They exist to make money. While some companies can profit from their concern for the environment, many others cannot, and they should not be compelled to think they have a moral obligation to do so. Reinhardt presents risk management exclusively as a profit motive, not as the investment in ecosystem services as proposed in the first article.

It is the very essence of this difference of opinion that will shape the fate of the environment over the long run. As corporations take on more of a global dimension, and they have a more global impact in their manufacturing, market penetration, and resource utilization, their moral obligation to the husbandry of nature will increasingly be called into question. If many of the most powerful companies on earth absolve themselves of moral responsibility, then on whom does the burden rest? It is important for we the consumers—the beneficiaries, and occasionally victims, of corporate hunger—to identify who picks up the tab.

FURTHER INFORMATION:

Articles:

Power, Mary, "The Planetary Piggybank." *Nature*, August 7, 1997.

Useful websites:

www.oilspill.state.ak.us/

A case study on the 1989 *Exxon Valdez* oil spill in Alaska.

www.hrw.org/hrw/reports/1999/nigeria/

A case study by the group Human Rights Watch on oil extraction, pollution, and human rights abuses in Nigeria.

www.bsr.org/

Business for Social Responsibility is an organization for ethically and environmentally aware companies.

The following debates in the Pro/Con series may also be of interest:

In this volume:

Topic 6 Should corporations pay the full environmental costs of producing their goods?

Topic 7 Can a "pay-to-pollute" system significantly reduce air pollution?

DO CORPORATIONS HAVE A MORAL RESPONSIBILITY TO NATURE?

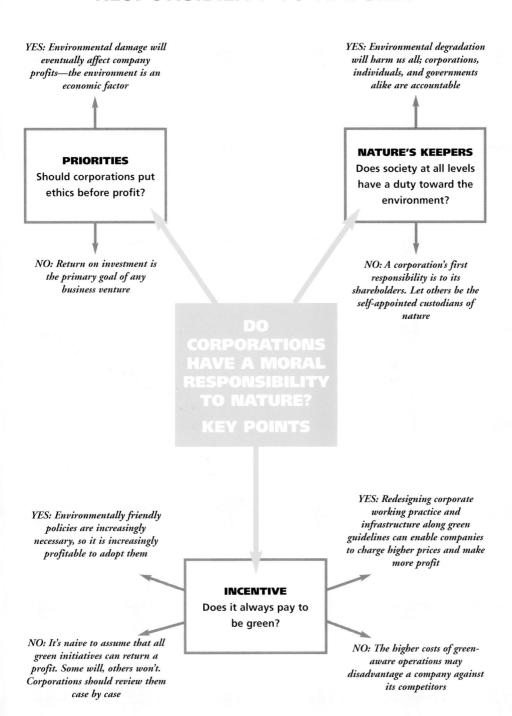

YES: Environmental damage will eventually affect company profits—the environment is an economic factor

PRIORITIES
Should corporations put ethics before profit?

NO: Return on investment is the primary goal of any business venture

YES: Environmental degradation will harm us all; corporations, individuals, and governments alike are accountable

NATURE'S KEEPERS
Does society at all levels have a duty toward the environment?

NO: A corporation's first responsibility is to its shareholders. Let others be the self-appointed custodians of nature

DO CORPORATIONS HAVE A MORAL RESPONSIBILITY TO NATURE?
KEY POINTS

YES: Environmentally friendly policies are increasingly necessary, so it is increasingly profitable to adopt them

YES: Redesigning corporate working practice and infrastructure along green guidelines can enable companies to charge higher prices and make more profit

INCENTIVE
Does it always pay to be green?

NO: It's naive to assume that all green initiatives can return a profit. Some will, others won't. Corporations should review them case by case

NO: The higher costs of green-aware operations may disadvantage a company against its competitors

Topic 11
DO THE BENEFITS OF NUCLEAR POWER OUTWEIGH THE RISKS?

YES
"THE NUCLEAR POWER ADVANTAGE"
BERNARD L. COHEN

NO
"STATEMENT OF LINDA GUNTER"
SAFE ENERGY COMMUNICATION COUNCIL, 2001
LINDA GUNTER, COMMUNICATIONS DIRECTOR

INTRODUCTION

The idea of nuclear fission was first investigated in 1895. When elements were bombarded with neutrons, artificial radionuclides were formed. In 1939 Lise Meitner and Otto Frisch, working under Niels Bohr, found that when a neutron was captured by the nucleus, it caused severe vibrations. They resulted in the fission (splitting) of the nucleus into two smaller, unequal nuclei. Meitner and Frisch concluded that the missing mass had been converted into energy—a theory described by Albert Einstein in the equation $E = mc^2$. From 1939 to 1945 fission research was centered on production of the atomic bomb. After World War II research turned to harnessing the energy for naval propulsion and electricity production.

In a nuclear power plant energy is created by the fission of uranium atoms. Fission releases a lot of heat energy, gamma rays, and spare neutrons, which then split more atoms,

and so the process continues in a chain reaction. The released heat is used to convert water into steam, which turns a turbine generator, creating electricity.

The first commercial nuclear power plant opened in 1956 in England, and the United States soon followed. Many industrialized nations, including France and the former Soviet Union, began to use this technology soon after.

The attraction of nuclear energy is that from a relatively small amount of fuel a much greater amount of energy is released than in a chemical reaction, promising more abundant and therefore cheaper electricity. No fuel is burned, and therefore air pollutants, such as carbon dioxide (CO_2), nitrogen oxides (NO_x), and sulfur dioxide (SO_2), are not released into the atmosphere. CO_2 is associated with global warming, NO_x causes ground-level ozone, and SO_2 contributes to acid rain.

Water drawn into a nuclear plant for cooling is regulated under the Clean

Water Act as well as the National Pollutant Discharge Elimination System (NPDES). To obtain a NPDES permit, the plant must ensure that rereleased water contains no harmful pollutants and is at a temperature benign to aquatic life.

"Nuclear waste is a heavy burden to lay on our children and their children and their children's children and their children's children's children and their children's children's children's children ..."

—RUFINA M. LAWS,
FOUNDER OF HUMANS AGAINST NUCLEAR WASTE DUMPS

Waste from a nuclear plant is used uranium fuel, which is radioactive and dangerous. It is stored at the plant in steel-lined concrete vaults filled with water or in steel containers. It is later moved to a long-term storage area, such as Yucca Mountain in Nevada. Waste regulations limit dosage to the maximally exposed individual to 15 millirem per year. In comparison, the average U.S. citizen receives 300 millirem per year from natural radiation, including indoor radon.

Storage of nuclear waste is a key concern. Campaigners worry about long-term storage areas and fight to keep them away from cities. The nuclear industry asserts that waste is produced in smaller quantities than in other forms of power production. It also insists that the radioactivity of the waste decreases through decay.

There are other environmental threats from nuclear power. Strip mining of uranium disturbs huge areas. Waste created by milling the uranium, called mill tailings, is often left untreated, endangering nearby crops, animals, and humans. The removal of water for cooling purposes and its rerelease harm aquatic life. Most people fear that the use of nuclear power will lead to the production of nuclear weapons.

An accident at the nuclear power plant on the Susquehanna River on March 28, 1979, brought Pennsylvania's Three Mile Island into the limelight. It has since become a symbol in the national argument over the safety of nuclear energy—although the nuclear power industry argues that the accident showed that its safety systems worked.

There have been other notable accidents at power plants around the world since then, including a fire at Chernobyl in Ukraine in April 1986 that resulted in widespread radioactive fallout, deaths, and pollution in a large part of Europe. It takes only one such incident to cause immense damage.

In 2001 there were more than 400 commercial nuclear reactors in around 30 countries. Combined, they supply 16 percent of the world's electricity, and nearly one-third of this figure comes from the United States. In addition, there are more than 270 research reactors in operation. The prohibitive cost of nuclear plants has led most western nations to phase out existing nuclear power plants. But, the need for energy remains pressing.

The following two articles examine whether or not the benefits of nuclear power outweigh the risks.

THE NUCLEAR POWER ADVANTAGE
Bernard L. Cohen

YES

One important advantage of nuclear power is that it avoids the wide variety of environmental problems arising from burning fossil fuels—coal, oil, and gas. These environmental problems probably exceed those of any other human activity. The ones that have received the most publicity have been "global warming," which is changing the earth's climate; acid rain, which is destroying forests and killing fish; air pollution, which is killing tens of thousands of Americans every year, while degrading our quality of life in many ways; the destructive effects of massive mining for coal; and oil spills, which do great harm to ecological systems.

The author's use of quotation marks indicates the fact that the existence of global warming is still disputed by many scientists, who claim instead that the earth's temperature cycles occur naturally.

Global warming

Burning fossil fuels produces vast quantities of carbon dioxide [CO_2]—for example 3.7 tons for each ton of coal burned, and CO_2 in the atmosphere traps heat, increasing the temperature. Estimates of the rate of the temperature rise and of the consequences vary, but eventually the effects are bound to be important. Agriculture is very sensitive to climate and hence will be heavily affected, requiring shifts in crops that cannot be grown in different areas. Eventually the melting glaciers will cause sea levels to rise—this floods valuable land, escalates the frequency and severity of disasters from hurricanes, allows inland penetration of salt water, which heavily impacts aquatic life (e.g. oyster harvests), and leads to loss of urban water supplies and contamination of groundwater. Effects of changing storm tracks, rainfall, and wind patterns are bound to be important.

Crop production will also be hindered by the unpredictability of the climate.

Acid rain

Burning fossil fuels releases large quantities of sulfur dioxide and nitrogen oxide gases, which combine with moisture in the air to produce acids that fall with rain. The effects are complicated and conclusions about them are controversial, but there is strong evidence that, in some cases, acid rain is making lakes unlivable for fish and is badly damaging forests. The emissions from coal burning power plants in the midwestern United States are the cause of acid rain in

More than 20 percent of Sweden's 85,000 larger lakes have been damaged by acid rain.

Eastern Canada, and this has been a top priority political issue in Canada. The situation is similar in Europe, where coal-burning emissions from Britain are damaging lakes and forests in Scandinavia and Germany.

Air pollution

While global warming causes only economic disruption, and acid rain kills only fish and trees, air pollution kills people and causes human suffering through illness. Vast amounts of research have gone into understanding the processes involved and tying down the responsible components, but successes have been limited. There are well recognized health effects from many of the components, sulfur dioxide, nitrogen oxides, carbon monoxide, fine particulates, hydrocarbons, ozone, volatile organic compounds, and toxic metals, but probably the health effects result from combinations of several of these.

The problem is complicated by the fact that effects build up slowly over many years or decades, causing illness and weakening constitutions to the point where death eventually results but is not obviously tied to air pollution. The epidemiological evidence, however, seems fairly clear in indicating that something like 30,000 deaths per year in the United States result from air pollution due to emissions from fossil fuel-burning power plants.

The life expectancy of the average U.S. citizen is shortened by 80 days by air pollution; that of a coal miner is less than the average by 1,100 days.

Shifting from fossil fuel to nuclear power would avert these deaths, and if electricity becomes much more widely used for transportation (e.g. with electric cars), the life saving would be much larger. Human discomfort [from] ill health is an important part of the price we pay for burning fossil fuels. Economic losses from worker absence and/or reduced efficiency due to illness are also substantial.

Coal mining

Sixty percent of U.S. coal is obtained by strip mining, which involves removing up to 200 feet [60 m] of topsoil. There are laws and good faith efforts to reclaim the land, but these have had only limited success, and the land is often left badly scarred. The remaining 40 percent of coal comes from underground mines, and this percentage is increasing. Acid drainage from these mines gets into streams, killing fish and leaving the water unfit for drinking, swimming, or industrial applications. About one-fourth of the 8 million acres of U.S. land about coal mines has subsided, causing buildings on the surface to crack or be destroyed, and often changing drainage patterns so as to make land unfit for farming.

Oil spills

The [*Exxon Valdez*] 40,000-ton oil spill off the coast of Alaska in 1989, even after 10 years of clean-up costing several billion dollars, has still left substantial long-term damage to the ecology of the region.

[T]here have [however,] been much larger oil spills, including one of 305,000 tons off the coast of Tobago in 1979 and one of 237,000 tons that ruined many miles of French beaches in 1978.

At any given time, 100 million tons of oil is being transported by ships, so accidental spills are inevitable. Land-based accidents can also be important. A Mexican well spilled 700,000 tons of oil into the Gulf of Mexico in 1979, doing extensive damage to the aquatic life.

The accidental or negligent release of used petroleum products adds 3.9m–6.6m tons of oil to the world's waterways annually.

COMMENTARY: Death caused by wastes

This table shows the eventual number of human deaths caused by the wastes from generating 1000 MWe [megawatts electric].

Nuclear	
High-level waste	0.018
Radon emissions	−420*
Routine emissions (krypton, xenon, carbon-14, hydrogen-3)	0.3
Low-level waste	0.0004

Coal	
Air pollution	75
Radon emissions	30
Chemical carcinogens	70

Solar (photovoltaics)	
Coal for materials (steel, glass, aluminum)	3
Cadmium sulfide (if used)	80

* The negative number indicates deaths averted, rather than caused.

Waste disposal issues

We have been bombarded with propaganda about the potential dangers of long-lived radioactive waste from nuclear reactors. But these wastes … are very small in volume and can be easily contained … deep underground. The wastes from coal burning, including those that end up in the ground, are far more dangerous (see table). These include chemical carcinogens like beryllium, cadmium, arsenic, nickel, and chromium which, unlike the nuclear wastes, last forever. They also include uranium, which occurs as an impurity in coal, ends up in the top surfaces of the ground, and serves as a source for random emissions; nuclear power, in contrast, consumes uranium, thus averting future deaths from exposure to radon gas.

Having dealt at length with other forms of energy, Cohen turns to nuclear energy.

Radon's source, radium, is produced when uranium decays. Radon rises from underground rock and is now recognized as the main cause of lung cancer among U.S. nonsmokers.

Accident risks

[Public fears of reactor accidents] nearly always focus on the effects of the worst accident evaluated in some study, and never treat the probability of such an accident. In fact, it is often said that probability doesn't matter; the only important thing is the worst possible accident. To face the accident risk squarely, one must recognize that it is absolutely essential for probability to be considered because there is no such thing as the worst possible accident—any hypothetical accident can be made worse by extenuating circumstances, albeit with reduced probability.

For example, one of the innumerable gasoline tank trucks that roam our streets can have a collision, spilling the fuel, leading to a fire that could destroy a whole city, killing millions. It might require a lot of improbable circumstances combining together, like water lines being frozen to prevent effective fire fighting, traffic … limiting access to fire fighters, substandard gas pipes which the heat of the fire causes to leak, a high wind frequently shifting to spread the fire in all directions, a strong atmospheric temperature inversion after the whole city becomes engulfed in flame to keep the smoke close to the ground, bridges and tunnels closed for various reasons to eliminate escape routes, errors in advising the public, and so forth. Each of these situations is improbable, so a combination of many of them occurring in sequence is highly improbable, but not impossible. This is another important advantage for nuclear power—the probabilities have been determined and they are very small indeed. The risk to an average American of a very large U.S. nuclear power program is equivalent to the risk of a regular smoker smoking one extra cigarette every 15 years.

Loss of life expectancy (LLE) for an average U.S. smoker of one pack a day is 2,300 days. Exposure to all U.S. electricity nuclear accidents would generate an LLE of 0.012 days.

STATEMENT OF LINDA GUNTER
Linda Gunter

NO

[The following statement was presented by Linda Gunter of the Safe Energy Communications Council in Washington, D.C., on February 22, 2001.]

I'd like to open with a quote from our report *Licensed to Kill*. It is a [couplet] from James Russell Lowell's aptly titled *The Present Crisis*:

Once to every man and nation comes the moment
to decide
In the strife of Truth with Falsehood, for the good or
evil side.

The present crisis we face is the effort to roll back environmental laws to accommodate an unfettered power industry. The same industry that is manipulating the energy market and lobbying to lift these laws has already brought us the nuclear myths: "the peaceful atom," and "electricity too cheap to meter." This report debunks the nuclear power industry's wildlife myths: "Sea creatures and nuclear plants get along well," [and] "Nuclear energy peacefully coexists with the environment." We found that the industry significantly misrepresents the fate of sea creatures around reactors using the once-through cooling system, the technology that is the focus of this report.

Lethal cooling system

The once-through cooling system, through its intake and discharge of tremendous volumes of water, as much as a million gallons a minute, has four major impacts on the marine environment:

1) When drawing in water, the reactor also sucks in billions of fish, larvae, spawn and other essential marine organisms, destroying these creatures, a process called entrainment.

2) Larger animals such as endangered sea turtles, American crocodiles, and manatees … may become lodged or impinged on intake structures and drown.

3) As marine creatures pass through the reactor they are scalded and pulverized. When discharged, they create debris that can block light from reaching important undersea plants.

A poet and a diplomat, James Russell Lowell (1819–1891) pursued a lifelong interest in such ethical issues as the abolition of slavery.

Once-through cooling systems pick up cooling water directly from and then discharge it directly to a body of water. They use water at a much higher rate than do cooling towers, which dissipate heat energy into the atmosphere.

4) The force of the discharge water scours the surrounding environment to bare rock. The elevated temperature of the discharge water destroys or drives away indigenous marine populations, upsetting the balance of nature.

Bending the law

Furthermore, the Nuclear Regulatory Commission (NRC) and the National Marine Fisheries Service (NMFS), two of the federal agencies that monitor and regulate the nuclear industry, routinely succumb to the industry's financial and economic needs over those of marine wildlife and especially of endangered species. This laxity has resulted in the industry's ability to bend or break the law. For example:

The California utility Pacific Gas and Electric, currently much in the news, suppressed data for ten years that showed the true extent of thermal marine damage by its Diablo Canyon reactors, breaking the Clean Water Act. PG&E also presented data it knew was incomplete to the state Water Board but remained silent during this cover-up.

The Clean Air Act (1970) and Clean Water Act (1972) limit air pollution and wastewater discharge respectively.

The Seabrook Nuclear Station in New Hampshire drowned young seals in its intake pipe without a lethal take permit, a violation of the Marine Mammal Protection Act for which NMFS declined to penalize the utility.

The Millstone reactors in Connecticut massacre vast quantities of fish and lobsters with impunity, including the depletion of 50 percent of the winter flounder population in Niantic Bay, while fishermen are fined for illegal catches.

Southern California Edison has collected an estimated $100 million from ratepayers for mitigation of the marine damage at its San Onofre reactors identified by the 1989 Marine Review Committee study, whose recommendations Edison agreed to abide by. To date, the utility has spent just $2.7 million on a tiny experimental reef. San Onofre is already allowed to discharge water at 25 degrees hotter than ambient, even though Diablo Canyon's discharge at 22 degrees hotter has resulted in the near-complete destruction of marine habitat in the vicinity of the plant. Lack of enforcement and the further weakening of such discharge standards could sound the death knell for the Southern California marine ecosystem.

The maximum effluent discharge temperature of each nuclear utility is regulated by federal and state agencies.

Although NRC is liable for enforcement of these laws, in every case where endangered sea turtles were present around the reactors studied, NRC supported utility efforts to raise or even eliminate the take limits for these animals—take limits being the annual amount of sea turtles that can be legally killed or captured during reactor operation.

COMMENTARY: Nuclear accidents

Nuclear accidents are so infrequent that statistically you are more likely to die choking on food (a fate that befalls 300 people each year) than from radioactivity released by a nuclear power plant. However, if and when accidents do happen, they may have a potentially devastating effect.

On March 28, 1979, a chain of automated malfunctions and human errors took place at the Unit 2 reactor core of the Three Mile Island nuclear power plant near Harrisburg, Pennsylvania. They resulted in the release of a tiny volume of gas into the containment vessel of the reactor building. No lives were lost, and normal functioning was swiftly restored. However, the U.S. nuclear power industry was badly shaken. Similar reactors were shut down immediately (though temporarily), and contracts on new reactors were suspended. The accident consolidated public fears about the safety of nuclear power, fears that have not abated since.

However, the same level of concern did not take effect in the former Soviet Union. On April 26, 1986, the world's worst nuclear accident occurred when explosions rocked the Unit 4 reactor at the Chernobyl nuclear power plant in Ukraine. Clouds of radioactive gas were released over Belarus and eventually spread around the Northern Hemisphere. More than 4,000 of those who helped clean up have since died, and local cancer rates continue to be high. The power plant finally ceased operation in December 2000, but the total shutdown is expected to take decades. The effects of the Chernobyl disaster are currently being monitored.

Lax attitude to wildlife

Contrary to the industry's wildlife-friendly advertising campaign, nuclear utilities prefer to kill more animals rather than spend the money to protect them.
For example:

- A 1990 National Academy of Sciences study—"Decline of the Sea Turtles, Causes and Prevention"—and Florida Power and Light's own 1985 report showed that sea turtles are injured during transit through the St. Lucie intake pipe, an experience verified by scuba diver Bill Lamm, whose steel tanks were slashed when he was sucked through that pipe in 1989. However, Florida Power and Light has refused to acknowledge responsibility for injuring sea turtles through the pipe since that 1985 study and has rejected all potential deterrent structures, largely on the basis of cost.

- Thermal scalding at the Diablo Canyon reactors has destroyed 90 percent of the resident threatened black abalone population. Yet it is illegal for any of us to take a single black abalone along the California coast.

• When a flock of 103 scaup, a species of diving duck whose numbers are dropping at an alarming rate, were drowned in a single incident at the Nine Mile Point atomic reactor near Syracuse, New York, there was scant reporting and no suggestion of mitigation.

• Salem's offer to repair damage under a so-called estuary enhancement program has resulted in unacceptable environmental alterations with the deaths of countless numbers of horseshoe crab and herbicide spraying over thousands of acres around the New Jersey site.

Horseshoe or king crabs (Limulus polyphemus) spend most of their lives at sea. Each spring the adults gather on Atlantic beaches to breed and are then at their most vulnerable.

"I think when you look at health effects [with regard to] Three Mile Island nuclear power, you have to remember, we live in a country where the tobacco industry is still saying tobacco doesn't cause cancer."

—ERIC EPSTEIN, *THREE MILE ISLAND ALERT*

This report serves notice to NRC and NMFS that:

• NMFS must make public the science by which it arrives at kill quotas for endangered species.

• The public will no longer accept arbitrary and capricious decision making about kill and capture limits.

• We expect NRC to enforce the law rather than operate as an advocate on behalf of the industry pocketbook.

• Harm done to endangered species at coastal reactors must be measured as a cumulative effect, not assessed individually.

• Because the industry made an economic decision not to install cooling towers, the "best technology available" under the standards of the Clean Water Act, it, not the marine environment, should pay the price.

[W]e urge that existing ... laws be enforced, not worked around, ignored or rolled back. Trading off environmental quality while allowing the energy industry to arbitrarily operate outside the Clean Water Act, Endangered Species Act, and other essential standards is robbing present and future generations of a safe, clean, healthy environment. Negotiations behind closed doors that pander to expanding industry profit[s] over the survival of endangered species and the health of the oceans ... can no longer be tolerated.

Gunter has studied only one small element of nuclear energy production but suggests that the whole industry can be damaging to the environment.

Summary

The article "The Nuclear Power Advantage" presents a largely negative argument in explaining that fossil fuels are a less welcome option than nuclear power. Nuclear energy production does not contribute to global warming, air pollution, or acid rain. It does not contribute to oil spills that damage the ecosystem. There is enough uranium to supply the world with energy for centuries at least. Wastes from nuclear power production are smaller in volume and more easily disposed of than wastes created from burning coal. Although nuclear energy is viewed as being dangerous, calculated risks from nuclear accidents are extremely low. Using nuclear power instead of relying on fossil fuels would keep the United States from becoming involved in political battles over remaining oil reserves. Nuclear energy is the answer to future energy needs.

Linda Gunter points out that when nuclear plants draw coolant water from rivers, lakes, and coasts, they harm aquatic wildlife. This admittedly small issue illustrates the kind of problem that might easily occur on a larger scale. She accuses the nuclear regulatory agencies of turning a blind eye to violations of environmental laws and permits. In order for the power plants to continue operation, they must lessen their disturbance of the environment. Gunter's argument is restrained in that it does not call for the abolition of nuclear power. There are many who do want to see nuclear plants shut down in favor of alternatives such as wind and solar energy. From 1948 to 1998, U.S. federal spending focused primarily on nuclear power. The tide may now be changing.

FURTHER INFORMATION:

Books:

Cozic, Charles P., and Karin L. Swisher (editors), *Nuclear Proliferation: Opposing Viewpoints*. San Diego, CA: Greenhaven Press, Inc., 1992.

Galperin, Anne L., *Nuclear Energy/Nuclear Waste*. New York: Chelsea House Publications, 1992.

Nardo, Don, *Chernobyl*. San Diego: Lucent Books, 1990.

Rhodes, Richard, *Nuclear Renewal*. New York: Whittle Books, 1993.

Goldsteen, Raymond L., John K. Schorr, and James P. Lester, *Demanding Democracy after Three Mile Island*. Gainsville: University Press of Florida, 1991.

Useful websites:

www.rachel.org/home_eng.htm
Homepage of the Environmental Research Foundation.

www.home.acadia.net/cbm/
A site discussing human-made sources of radioactivity.

www.enn.com/enn-features-archive/2000/09/09012000/nuclearenergy_30538.asp
Environmental News Network (ENN).

The following debates in the Pro/Con series may also be of interest:

In this volume:

 Part 1: Economic Forces

Topic 8 Can wind and solar resources meet our energy needs?

Topic 9 Will hydrogen replace oil as our primary energy source?

DO THE BENEFITS OF NUCLEAR POWER OUTWEIGH THE RISKS?

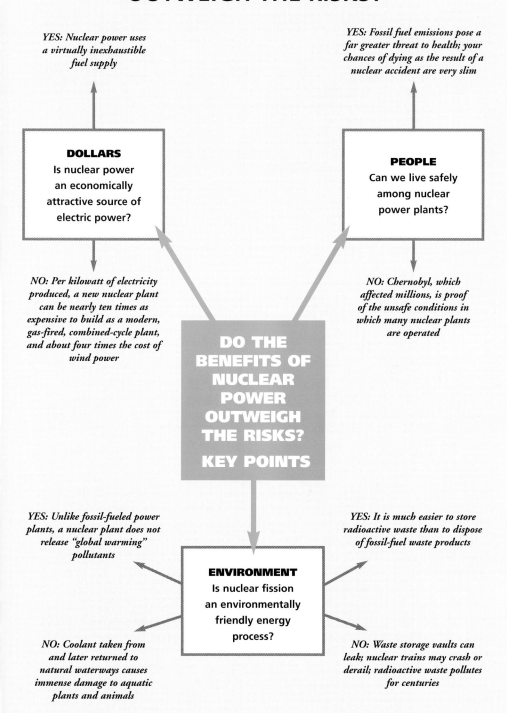

YES: Nuclear power uses a virtually inexhaustible fuel supply

YES: Fossil fuel emissions pose a far greater threat to health; your chances of dying as the result of a nuclear accident are very slim

DOLLARS
Is nuclear power an economically attractive source of electric power?

PEOPLE
Can we live safely among nuclear power plants?

NO: Per kilowatt of electricity produced, a new nuclear plant can be nearly ten times as expensive to build as a modern, gas-fired, combined-cycle plant, and about four times the cost of wind power

NO: Chernobyl, which affected millions, is proof of the unsafe conditions in which many nuclear plants are operated

DO THE BENEFITS OF NUCLEAR POWER OUTWEIGH THE RISKS?

KEY POINTS

YES: Unlike fossil-fueled power plants, a nuclear plant does not release "global warming" pollutants

YES: It is much easier to store radioactive waste than to dispose of fossil-fuel waste products

ENVIRONMENT
Is nuclear fission an environmentally friendly energy process?

NO: Coolant taken from and later returned to natural waterways causes immense damage to aquatic plants and animals

NO: Waste storage vaults can leak; nuclear trains may crash or derail; radioactive waste pollutes for centuries

Topic 12
IS GENETICALLY MODIFIED FOOD SAFE ENOUGH TO FEED THE WORLD'S POPULATION?

YES
"BIOTECHNOLOGY AND FOOD"
AMERICAN COUNCIL ON SCIENCE AND HEALTH, 2000
ALAN MCHUGHEN

NO
"BIOTECHNOLOGY AND THE ENVIRONMENT"
CONFERENCE PROCEEDINGS, BIOTECHNOLOGY: THE SCIENCE AND THE IMPACT
THE HAGUE, NETHERLANDS, 2000
JOSÉ SARUKHÁN

INTRODUCTION

As with any newly applied technology, there are risks and benefits associated with genetically modified (GM) crops and foodstuffs. The question is whether the benefits outweigh the risks. Benefits range from golden rice that combats vitamin-A deficiency in the developing world to a sweet potato that resists a virus on African potatoes and greatly increases production in an area that is high in malnutrition.

The risks include allergic responses to crops that have been crossed with foods containing allergens such as shellfish, nuts, and fish. There are those who say GM food needs to be labeled for this very reason. Other risks include threats to the environment, particularly to wildlife species on which GM crops may have unpredicted effects.

Sides have been drawn in this highly charged debate. Organizations that

appear to be pro-GM foods include the American Medical Association (AMA), the World Bank, and the biotechnology industry. Groups and organizations that appear to be anti-GM foods include Greenpeace, the Sierra Club, and Friends of the Earth.

In response to concerns the European Union has imposed a ban on the import of GM food, and concern is growing in the United States. Against the promise that GM food will help feed the world's growing population is a broad mistrust of the new technology.

Governments and industry have frequently stressed the need for decisions on GM food to be made in the light of "sound science." However, current GM research calls into question the extent of scientific knowledge, as well as the validity of the notion of what is sound science.

There are those who take a middle view: That genetically modified food is neither intrinsically safe or unsafe, and that certain GM products may be suited to specific needs that can no longer be

> *"Superstition and fear should not interfere with this technology. Unfounded concerns about hypothetical risks are far outweighed by the real benefits that will soon be realized, if … genetically modified agriculture is allowed to proceed unhindered."*
>
> —GILBERT ROSS,
> AMERICAN COUNCIL OF SCIENCE AND HEALTH, 2000

met by a traditional counterpart. They propose that certain guidelines should be followed. They include:

- Where there is public unease, respond decisively to that unease through discussion and deliberative techniques.
- Where unambiguous scientific proof of cause and effect is not available, it is necessary to act with care.

- Always listen to calls for a change of course, include representatives of such calls into stakeholder dialogues, and maintain transparency throughout.
- Where the benefits of early action are judged to be greater than the costs of delay, it is appropriate to inform the public why such action is being taken.
- Where there is the possibility of irreversible damage to natural life support functions, precautionary action should be taken.
- Never shy away from publicity, and never try to suppress information. In the age of the Internet someone is bound to find out if information is being distorted or hidden.

In the following two articles the arguments for and against the question of whether GM food is safe enough to feed the world's population are outlined clearly.

In his article "Biotechnology and Food" Alan McHughen argues that GM foods have no adverse side effects on humankind or the environment. The technology is simply expediting what occurs naturally in nature.

Conversely, José Sarukhán in "Biotechnology and the Environment" questions the effects on the ecosystems of the world through the introduction of GM plants. The author admits that traditional farming has helped damage the environment, but he advocates caution until society knows for certain what effect GM organisms will have on the environment.

BIOTECHNOLOGY AND FOOD
Alan McHughen

DNA, or deoxyribonucleic acid, is the complex molecule found in cells that codes genetic material and carries it from one generation to the next.

See Genetic Modification, pages 160–161.

Traditional biotechnology has given us almost all of our foods, from corn and beef to bread and wine. In the 1970s modern biotechnology (i.e. genetic modification, genetic engineering, recombinant DNA or rDNA, gene splicing, etc.) started giving us lifesaving drugs such as Humulin (human insulin). In the past several years the same technology has been applied to enhance agriculture and food production. Gene modification is a natural event. Many of our traditional foods are products of natural mutations or genetic recombinations. Nature is constantly mutating genes and even moving them from one species to another. With biotechnology, humans can direct genetic changes to benefit the quality and quantity of food, human and animal health, and the environment.

Biotechnology and the consumer

The precision attained by molecular plant breeding can provide, for example, greatly increased crop production and nutritional enhancements at little or no additional cost. Fruits and vegetables can be picked and delivered at the height of flavor and ripeness, thanks to carefully tailored improvements that reduce softening and bruising. For health-conscious consumers, cooking oils from GM corn, soy, or canola will provide lower saturated fat content. Leaner meats will be available from cattle and pigs improved both directly and through improved feeds. Sensitive new testing kits can detect tiny amounts of potentially harmful toxic contaminants in foods. New plant varieties that are biologically protected against insects and diseases are now on the market, just in time to help farmers hard-pressed to maintain efficient production with fewer chemical control agents.

The application of rDNA to medical problems was rapidly embraced by researchers and by the public. However, the same technology, applied to agriculture, is facing resistance from those who think it might be inherently hazardous. Misinformation and misunderstandings about biotechnology in the popular media make it difficult for consumers to make informed assessments. These circumstances give rise to needless anxiety and, at the same time, obscure any real

Do you think the media coverage of GM technology is fair and unbiased?

hazards that might exist as well as possible means of controlling them. A basic understanding of the techniques and goals of biotechnology research is important for deciding the merits of concerns and proposed solutions.

Methods in biotechnology

The first GM plants were produced in 1983, and food scientists lost no time in applying GM technology to crops. Biotechnology provides new tools for scientists working on long-standing agricultural problems in pest and disease management, animal and crop yield, and food quality. These tools complement and extend traditional selective-breeding techniques by providing the means for making selective, single-gene changes in plants and animals. In contrast, off-spring created through conventional breeding present a random combination of thousands of genes from each parent.

The traditional and modern methods differ primarily in precision, speed, and certainty. Moreover, because DNA is biochemically equivalent in all organisms, the modern techniques also enable scientists to take advantage of the full spectrum of genes present in nature—genes derived from microbes, plants and animals—in their efforts to improve agriculture. So, while the goals of traditional breeding and modern genetic engineering are similar, the new techniques greatly expand the realm of possible strategies by eliminating the interspecies barriers presented by sexual reproduction.

Modern biotechnology is well established in food processing—particularly in the genetic improvement of bacteria and yeast strains used in various fermentation systems including improved bread yeast and brewing yeast. Vegetarians might now enjoy cheese made with GM chymosin instead of animal source rennin. Some recent developments in agricultural biotechnology involve using plants and animals to make products not traditionally associated with agriculture—products such as medically important pharmaceuticals and industrial materials to replace petroleum-based oils and plastics.

Feed the world, the environment

The world population, currently six billion, is expected to reach about 10 billion by mid century. Much of the growth is occurring in developing countries, where local capacity for food production is seriously unstable because of poverty, political disruption, climatic stresses, soil erosion, pests, and disease. Biodiversity is at risk not from genetic modification, but from natural environments being converted to farmland

In 1986 the Department of Agriculture approved the sale of the first living GM organism: a virus to serve as a pseudorabies vaccine.

For example, bioluminescent genes from jellyfish can be spliced with those of potatoes or grasses to make plants that glow in the dark when ready for harvest.

COMMENTARY: The rise of Monsanto

"Biotechnology's been around almost since the beginning of time. It's cavemen saving seeds of a high-yielding plant. It's Gregor Mendel, the father of genetics, cross-pollinating his garden peas. It's a diabetic's insulin, and the enzymes in your yogurt...."

—U.S. AGRICULTURE SECRETARY DAN GLICKMAN

The 20th century witnessed the rise of the Monsanto Company, which has achieved preeminence in the field of biotechnology in spite of opposition from environmentalists.

The Monsanto Chemical Works was founded in St. Louis, Missouri, in 1901 by John F. Queeny, initially to make the artificial sweetener saccharin. Monsanto flourished during the first part of the century and diversified, producing styrene during World War II for the manufacture of synthetic rubbers. It was under Queeny's son, Edgar, who controlled Monsanto from 1928 to 1960, that the company grew into a giant, with a wide range of products from natural gas and phosphates to agricultural and industrial chemicals. During this period plastics, resins, and surface coatings made up a significant share of Monsanto products. Along the way the name changed to the Monsanto Chemical Company (1933) and later to Monsanto Company (1964).

In 1960 Monsanto's Agriculture Division was established. The fledgling division was strengthened by the success of the Lasso herbicide, launched in 1969. Spinoff products included Agent Orange, the powerful defoliant used during the Vietnam War. Meanwhile, the company was busy opening up trade in East Asia, South America, and Europe, and investing heavily in agrichemical research. Monsanto's Roundup herbicide, launched in Malaysia and Great Britain in 1974, contained a new active ingredient, a molecule called glyphosate, one of the most toxic herbicides, which some claim has been linked to cases of pesticide illness among agricultural laborers.

In 1982 Monsanto scientists were the first to genetically modify a plant cell. During the '80s the company was restructured, focusing on life sciences, pharmaceuticals, and food. In 1993 the first biotechnology product, a bovine somatropin (BST), was approved. In 2000 the company merged with Pharmacia & Upjohn, and the name Monsanto survived as the agricultural division of Pharmacia. By then its genetically modified crops were planted on more than 15 million acres in the U.S. alone. Monsanto continues to invest millions in crop technology and patents its own strains of cotton, soybean, corn, and crops that are resistant to pests and diseases.

to provide more food for the growing population. When more productive GM crops are grown, less wild land is destroyed to make farmland. Parks and refuge areas can be left for everyone to enjoy and for biodiversity to flourish.

The scientific view on safety

Most scientists knowledgeable about genetic engineering support this technology. They know that much of the negative information in the public debate is based on false assumptions, and they know that the tremendous potential benefits far outweigh the manageable hazards. But most importantly, they understand that risks are associated with particular products, not with the methods by which those products are made.

The author argues that genetic engineering itself is not a dangerous process, but that like any process, it can be turned to good or bad ends.

GM products are not inherently hazardous. Manufacturers have been using GM to make pharmaceuticals for a quarter century. In April 2000 the U.S. National Academy of Sciences released a report of its blue-ribbon group to study the matter and issued its own statement, which concluded, "The committee is not aware of any evidence that foods on the market are unsafe to eat as a result of genetic modification." Since GM foods have now been consumed by very large numbers of humans for several years, any inherent problems with genetic modification as a technology would almost certainly have been revealed by now. But not one problem has been documented.

McHughen quotes an authoritative body to support his case.

Conclusion

Modern biotechnology is being used in … food production to provide more, better, and safer products. The extent to which it will be fully utilized for the benefit of consumers depends on support for innovation and improvement in farming and food production, on the one hand, and on support for scientifically sound regulatory policies that protect against tangible food safety risks, on the other. This is a delicate balance. Medical and human health biotechnology, using similar genetic techniques, is accepted by the public and professional communities as a safe and effective means to [improve] treatments. Because agricultural biotechnology is younger and some critics remain wary, new food products will appear gradually in the marketplace over the next few years. [But] with the continuing accumulation of evidence of safety and efficiency, and the absence of any evidence of harm to the public or the environment, more and more consumers are becoming as comfortable with agricultural biotechnology as they are with medical biotechnology.

Why do you think consumers who happily use GM drugs might be more suspicious of GM food?

BIOTECHNOLOGY AND THE ENVIRONMENT
José Sarukhán

NO

The agricultural revolution has been, arguably, the most fundamental innovation in the history of the cultural and socioeconomic development of humankind. This was, from the beginning, a revolution with a definite environmental impact on biodiversity through the complete removal of natural ecosystems. Due to the expansion of the agricultural frontier through the centuries to provide food and goods for an ever-increasing human population, it has been repeatedly mentioned that agriculture has been a human activity intrinsically destructive of biological diversity.

It is not surprising that this argument has been used to palliate statements concerning the possible negative effects of the use of GMOs (genetically modified organisms) on the biological diversity of a region. This is particularly true when agriculture is practiced in a resource-inefficient way, or when it uses technologies not adapted to the environmental characteristics (soils, slopes, or climatic regimes) of an area. But it is not acceptable as a "blanket statement" to justify risks imposed by GMOs.

Assessing the effects of GMOs

GMOs have been released into the environment relatively recently, and their geographical expanse and ecological conditions are so far relatively constrained. Consequently, solid information about their actual effects on the environment and on biological diversity is still very sparse, and there is not yet an agreed measurement of the seriousness of their environmental harm.

Most of the released GMOs have traits that fall into the following four categories: 1) Herbicide resistance, allowing the use of broad-spectrum, short-lived herbicides, to which the GMO is resistant; 2) Resistance to viral, bacterial, and fungal infections, mostly through the introduction in the plant of genetic material of the viruses, in a technique similar to vaccination in humans; 3) Resistance to insect attacks, mostly through the introduction of the Bt gene from *Bacillus*

The agricultural revolution is the name historians give to the process by which humans learned to develop and grow crops, domesticate and raise livestock, and prepare land for farming. It began more than 9,000 years ago.

The author dismisses the claim, put forward by GM apologists, that farming practices have always affected the natural environment.

In cases of viral engineering those elements of the virus that may be destructive to a plant are deleted before the gene is added to the plant.

thuringiensis, a bacterium toxic to many insect species, especially moths and butterflies, and 4) Resistance to conditions of high salinity or toxic concentrations of certain metals such as aluminum in degraded tropical soils. These are traits difficult to obtain since numerous genes regulate them. Undoubtedly, to each beneficial aspect it is possible to also define a possible harmful effect. There will always be risks inherent in any technological intervention with nature.

A few instances of specific environmental harm related to GMOs have been reported in the literature. A well known and publicized example is the one referring to the effect of pollen of Bt maize on larvae of monarch butterflies. John E. Losey and collaborators reported that caterpillars of the butterfly fed with milkweed leaves dusted with Bt-engineered maize pollen showed 46 percent mortality. They conclude that given the projected increase of acreage of Bt maize in the United States, "It is imperative to gather data necessary to evaluate the risks associated with this new agrotechnology and to compare these risks with those posed by pesticides and other pest-control tactics."

Concern has also been expressed about the effects of GM crops on honeybees—on their health and on the possible GM content of their honey.

The need for solid evidence

The paucity of reliable data on the effects of GMOs on biodiversity does not make acceptable the argument stating that "the lack of evidence of harmful effects is evidence of lack of harmful effects." Adopting a precautionary approach when releasing a GMO into the environment is clearly and scientifically sustained by the theoretical and empirical knowledge provided by evolutionary ecology. It is extremely dangerous to generalize about the ecological properties of a species. There is no meaningful way in which a study made of one sample from a species can be said to represent that species, until the range of variation within and between its populations can be established.

Nevertheless, arguments have been advanced by eager GMO promoters saying that: a) there is no reason to apply such principle now, because it was never applied before in deciding which agricultural technologies are acceptable in relation to their effects to the environment or, b) the principle constitutes a hindrance to further research and development of new technologies.

These arguments make little sense. The precautionary principle should be interpreted as a vigorous promoter of more research to understand better the possible implications of these new agricultural technologies for the environment, and not as an obstacle to innovative research. There is need

A protester against "Frankenfoods" at a Friends of the Earth rally in England. FoE, along with Greenpeace, has been a vocal opponent of GM crop tests.

to monitor the cumulative effects of modified crops, since it is this impact that may become unacceptable, rather than the individual cases.

Meeting local requirements

One reason for the failures of the Green Revolution of the 1960s is that new crops and chemicals created in the laboratory were unsuited to conditions in the countries where they were expected to have an effect.

The aptitude to evaluate and manage the potential risks of GMOs is directly related to the capacity to produce and/or use them in a safe and efficient manner. This is an important issue. Both the potential benefits and risks of releasing GMOs into the environment are site, region, and country dependent. This implies that national, regional, and local aptitudes are key components to make decisions regarding the release of GMOs. These aptitudes involve not only a country's scientific skills; they are also related to regional or national agricultural policies, as well as socioeconomic and cultural traits.

Such traits and skills are fundamental in determining whether the use of the new GMO technologies may be a true alleviator of environmental stresses posed by present-day agriculture, or if they will become one more deleterious addition to already existing conventional technologies which negatively impact the biological diversity of the world.

Progress by compromise

Three premises must be observed in order to reduce the negative impacts of using GMOs. The first is that we have a limited knowledge of how ecological systems operate and react to different impacts of human activities; consequently, particular care should be taken in the assessment of the environmental effects of GMOs on impact assessments by establishing truly efficient and long-running monitoring mechanisms. The second is that, globally speaking, no single agricultural technology is the answer to an ecologically sustainable and economically successful agriculture. If we want to preserve as much as possible the biodiversity of an area, we must adopt diversified agricultural systems that maximize such diversity, developing multistrategy technologies, based in the best available agricultural practices that are environmentally "friendly." These may include anything from the so-called traditional or indigenous agricultural practices to the use of GMOs. And finally, the third is that it is technically feasible to design GMO crops which avoid the potential risks that some of the present generation of GMOs have.

Far from being opposed to the principle of GM foods, the author predicts a bright future for them, so long as they are developed, tested, and deployed within strict guidelines.

Environment first

In order to achieve in the following decades the enormous potential that genetic engineering has for securing food production and their possible role for ecological restoration, the development, introduction, and adoption of GMOs cannot be based in regarding the environmental damage as an externality in the economic considerations of both genetic engineering companies and nations alike.

A final conclusion is that science must be placed at the center of any discussions or controversies about the potential benefits or harms that GMOs [may visit on] the environment. And the well-being of mankind should be the aim of those discussions, considering humans as a species totally dependent on the ecological systems which contain the world's biological diversity and provide the ecological services essential for sustaining life on earth as we now know it.

Summary

In support of biotechnology, McHughen argues that many people would not be alive today were it not for drugs produced through gene modification. The process is, he says, used all the time by nature. Scientists are merely harnessing the natural processes for the good of humankind. Healthier oils, leaner meats, disease-proof crops—these are just some GM-derived benefits. But public mistrust, fueled by the media, is holding scientists back. This mistrust, claims McHughen, is misplaced. In reality, genetically modified goods will be better for humans and better for the environment, partly because they produce a higher yield per acre, reducing the need to clear more wilderness. And genetic modification is safe—according to the National Academy of Sciences. In time, when public fears are laid to rest, the industry will flourish.

Sarukhán argues for caution. Though he admits that traditional agriculture has had an irreversible effect on the environment, he denies that this gives agribusinesses free rein to deploy genetic modification and risk unknown harm. First, they must stringently test any new crops, conducting these tests in realistic conditions and with the full cooperation of the local people to whom they will be marketed. Only when the full implications of genetic modification are understood should it be given a niche within the framework of agricultural technology, with each use tailored to the end user.

FURTHER INFORMATION:

Books:

Grace, E. S., *Biotechnology Unzipped: Promises and Realities*. Washington, D.C.: Joseph Henry Press, 1997. McHughen, A., *Pandora's Picnic Basket: Potential and Hazards of Genetically-Modified Foods*. New York: Oxford University Press, 2000.

Articles:

Couglan, A., "Filling the Bowl: For Billions Worldwide, a Modified Grain Could End the Lean Times." *New Scientist*, April 1, 2000.
Potrykus, L., R. J. Bilang, C. Futterer, M. Sautter, M. Schrott, and G. Spangenberg, "Genetic Engineering of Crop Plants," in *Agricultural Biotechnology* edited by A. Altman, New York: Marcel Dekker, 1998.

Useful websites:

www.epa.gov/opptintr/biotech/
US Environmental Protection Agency site.
www.agbioworld.org/articles/21century.html
Agriculture in the 21st Century 2000 report.

www.newscientist.co.uk/news/news_223230.html
"GM Foods: Opportunities to Improve Human Health," OECD Conference report, Edinburgh, Scotland, March 2000.
www.explorezone.com/news/
Has new stories on environment, including GMO.s
www.special.northernlight.com/gmfoods/#over
Site with many links to GM-related sites.

The following debates in the Pro/Con series may also be of interest:

In this volume:

Topic 3 Are famine and hunger avoidable?

Genetic Modification, pages 160–161.

IS GENETICALLY MODIFIED FOOD SAFE ENOUGH TO FEED THE WORLD'S POPULATION?

YES: Public fears surrounding GM food have been whipped up unnecessarily by the media

YES: Pest- and disease-resistant crops obviate the need for polluting chemicals

PUBLIC OPINION
Can government and the private sector override public concerns?

ENVIRONMENT
Is GM food safe for the environment?

NO: People have a right to know what food contains and to make an informed choice about what they eat

NO: GM crops may affect ecological systems and harm animal life, especially fish, amphibians, and pollinating insects, such as bees; they may also spread uncontrollably to contaminate other foods

IS GENETICALLY MODIFIED FOOD SAFE ENOUGH TO FEED THE WORLD'S POPULATION?

KEY POINTS

YES: Biologists can produce improved foods, such as potato chips with enhanced starch content to absorb less frying fat

YES: They can support a rising population, providing healthier, cheaper, and more abundant food

HUMAN HEALTH
Are GM crops good for us?

NO: They may have a risk of infection. For example, genes in GM cattle feed may travel up the food chain and reach humans through rare meat

NO: GM foods are not always suitable for growing in the parts of the world where people need food the most

GENETIC MODIFICATION

History

The scientists James Watson and Francis Crick identified the double-helix structure of DNA (deoxyribonucleic acid) in 1953. DNA carries the genetic information of any living organism. In 1973 Stanley Cohen and Herbert Boyer removed a gene from one organism and successfully transplanted it into another. This process became known as transgenics. Genetic modification can now be carried out that allows crossbreeding between organisms that would not occur under "natural" circumstances. For example, it is now possible to grow a tomato containing genes taken from arctic salmon, allowing the plant to survive in extreme weather conditions.

In 1983 the first transgenic tobacco plant was created, and by 1994 brand new foodstuffs began to appear, such as the FlavrSavr tomato and potatoes genetically modified to produce a protein toxic to insects. In 1997 almost two million hectares of land had been given over to the production of GM crops in the Western Hemisphere. In 1998, 44 percent of soybeans and 36 percent of corn grown in the United States were genetically modified.

The debate

At the beginning of the 21st century the debate about the safety and benefits of GM foodstuffs is intensifying. Those in favor frequently cite the case of world hunger and other food-related problems in developing countries as a reason for having genetically modified organisms (GMOs). Products such as "golden rice" have higher vitamin content and could help ease current food problems.

Those opposed to GMOs fear that the scientists responsible are irreversibly altering nature. Products such as tomatoes created from arctic salmon are unnatural, and this outweighs any gain in them being resistant to cold weather. It also raises issues for vegetarians and vegans who may not be comfortable eating vegetables and fruit that contain fish and animal genes.

As well as the ethical reasons for opposition to GM foods there are some potential risks that need to be taken into account. It is possible for GMOs to grow outside of the areas allocated for them into the wild and therefore enter and affect the food chain. Pests could also evolve resistance to GM food; therefore superfoods would simply result in superbugs. Genes taken from products that people are allergic to such as shellfish and peanuts can also find their way into other products, providing potential fatal risks to the consumer.

Europe and the United States

Since 1998 the European Union has not allowed the development of new GM crops. It also introduced new labeling procedures for food that contained GM products. This effective ban on GM crops in Europe has helped the cause of

THE CASE OF THE MONARCH BUTTERFLY

In 1999 a case study by John Losey, from Cornell University, New York, claimed that genetically modified pollen could harm the larvae (caterpillars) of the monarch butterfly. Losey took a sample of both modified and unmodified corn pollen and dusted milkweed leaves with the pollen. Monarch caterpillars were then allowed to feed on the leaves for four days under laboratory conditions. After four days Losey discovered that only 56 percent of the caterpillars that ate modified pollen survived, as opposed to a 100 percent survival rate for the caterpillars that digested '"regular" pollen. He further found that the survivors were of a smaller size than would be considered normal. Losey's findings, which were published in *Nature* magazine, led to an outcry among those opposed to genetic modification in farming and food, and the monarch butterfly became a symbol for their cause. The threat to monarch butterflies was seen as a real one for the following reasons:

• Monarch butterflies prefer to lay their eggs on milkweed plants. The caterpillars then feed on the leaves they hatch onto.
• Genetically modified corn that grows in the Midwest is invariably planted next to milkweed, and therefore monarch larvae suffer.
• Pollen from genetically modified corn can drift onto the adjacent milkweed and therefore onto the monarch larvae.

Supporters of GM crops point out that the pollen has been modified to reduce the use of pesticides. Pesticides generally are lethal to many insects, and in the long-term even monarchs would benefit from the continued use of GM crops. Similarly, they argue that heavy modified-pollen only has a range of 8 feet when drifting, and thus only those monarchs that live on the outskirts of milkweed patches would be affected.

Anti-GM protesters assert that the main reason for using modified corn pollen is to produce a higher crop yield and therefore maximize profit. They believe that scientists are pursuing those profits at the expense of the natural world. More studies on the effect of GM pollen on the monarch butterfly are being carried out; and although it appears from the initial evidence that monarchs are being affected, no conclusive evidence has appeared. Hence, the debate continues.

environmental organizations such as Greenpeace and Friends of the Earth, who see any GM product as biological pollution. It is not unusual for protesters in Europe to take direct action and physically destroy genetically modified crops. The GM debate is gaining importance in the United States, and there has been a growth in anti-GM support, as seen in the protests against GM products outside the World Trade Organization (WTO) meeting in Seattle in late 1999 and the IMF/World Bank meetings in Washington D.C. in April 2000.

Topic 13
ARE ZOOS MORALLY WRONG?

YES
"AGAINST ZOOS"
NATIONAL ASSOCIATION FOR BIOMEDICAL RESEARCH
DALE JAMIESON

NO
FROM *ZOOS AND ANIMAL RIGHTS: THE ETHICS OF KEEPING ANIMALS*
STEPHEN ST. C. BOSTOCK

INTRODUCTION

The question of whether zoos are morally wrong or not is one is one that has caused great debate. Advocates argue that zoos, or places where domestic or wild animals are housed and exhibited in captivity, are necessary in order to protect endangered species and aid breeding programs, among other things. Critics argue that zoos are cruel and unsanitary places, rather like prisons.

It is hard to estimate when the first zoos were established. Certainly, in what is now Iraq, there is evidence that pigeons were kept in captivity as early as 4500 B.C. Some 2,000 years later semidomesticated elephants were kept at the royal courts in India. The biblical king Solomon was reputed to be a farmer-zookeeper in around 1000 B.C.

Later in Europe Philip VI of France kept a menagerie in 1333, and the Spanish explorer Hernán Cortés discovered a huge and impressive zoo in Mexico in 1519.

Modern zookeeping most probably dates to the establishment of Schönbrun Palace in Vienna in 1752,

which exhibited animals. After this the Royal Park in Madrid opened in 1775, and 18 years later the Jardin des Plantes opened to the public in Paris. In 1828 the London Zoological Society was established in Regents Park (where London Zoo is).

The term "zoo" came into popular language in the 1800s and stems from "zoological garden" or "zoological park." No matter what its origin, a zoo currently represents an area where people can go to view animals. The United States first built zoos in the 1870s. Today there are hundreds of zoos across the country that serve millions of visitors from around the world.

Zoo supporters assert that zoos provide many valuable services to society and to wildlife itself. The most important function of zoos is to keep endangered species from extinction. Rare species are researched, and their eggs and sperm are stored in "frozen zoos" in hopes of keeping the species alive. Breeding strategies have been designed to minimize inbreeding while producing a diverse population of animals that can be released into the wild when their habitats are restored, and after threats to their survival are removed.

We live in a world in which every minute 13 species become extinct. Therefore the ability of zoos to reproduce endangered species is invaluable, say apologists for zoos.

"To achieve and promote the worldwide conservation of animals and their habitats."

—MISSION STATEMENT, ZOOLOGICAL SOCIETY OF LONDON, 2000

A good example of a successful breeding program took place at the San Diego Zoo with the giant pandas Bai Yun and Shi Shi. They gave birth to baby Hua Mei in August of 1999.

Zoos also educate the public about animals they would not normally see or be aware of. When people discover and understand animals, they become appreciative of the need to preserve and protect remaining species. Visitors to zoos often donate money so that more animals can be saved.

Animal activists accuse zoos of being cruel. However, zoo animals live without fear of predation or famine, they have fewer diseases and parasites, and they live longer lives than their wild counterparts.

Animal rights activists also argue that zoos do very little for society. Only a small percentage of zoos devote space to endangered species. Most species that become extinct are insects or other

"unglamorous" creatures, yet zoos cater mostly to large African mammals, such as elephants and giraffes, that are not endangered—and moreover are ill suited to such confinement. Successful breeding of captive endangered species is uncommon, and successful return of animals to the wild is even more rare.

Zoo critics argue that a better way to protect endangered species is through preservation of their natural habitat. If money used to keep zoos running was instead directed toward protecting habitats, and if wider public opinion could be convinced of the greater merits of such a strategy, there would be no need for zoos to preserve species. They also argue that zoos do not educate the public. The average visitor spends a minimal amount of time viewing each animal. They will pause to watch animals only if they are playing, and they leave the zoo with uninformed stereotypes about species still in place.

Visitors upset some animals' natural sleep patterns, and animals that are normally reclusive are kept out in the open for everyone to see. This can lead to psychological problems. Many zoo animals, most notably large mammals such as bears or elephants, exhibit signs of mental ill-health—pacing, swaying, and self-mutilation. Also, displaying animals as captive, bored, cramped, and lonely sends out the wrong message.

Some zoos try to give their animals adequate habitat, but they can never come close to the space, freedom, and interactivity animals require to stay mentally and physically healthy.

The following two articles discuss whether zoos are morally wrong. The key map at the end of this topic illustrates the main points in the issue.

AGAINST ZOOS
Dale Jamieson

We can start with a rough-and-ready definition of zoos: they are public parks which display animals, primarily for the purposes of recreation or education. Although large collections of animals were maintained in antiquity, they were not zoos in this sense. Typically these ancient collections were not exhibited in public parks, or they were maintained for purposes other than recreation or education.

The Romans, for example, kept animals in order to have living fodder for the games ... even the first tigers brought to Rome, gifts to Caesar Augustus from an Indian ruler, wound up in the arena. The emperor Trajan staged 123 consecutive days of games in order to celebrate his conquest of Dacia. Eleven thousand animals were slaughtered, including lions, tigers, elephants, rhinoceroses, hippopotami, giraffes, bulls, stags, crocodiles, and serpents. The games were popular in all parts of the Empire. Nearly every city had an arena and a collection of animals to stock it. In fifth-century France there were twenty-six such arenas, and they continued to thrive until at least the eighth century.

In antiquity rulers also kept large collections of animals as a sign of their power, which they would demonstrate on occasion by destroying their entire collections. This happened as late as 1719 when Elector Augustus II of Dresden personally slaughtered his entire menagerie, which included tigers, lions, bulls, bears and boars.

> According to Hernán Cortés, who visited Mexico in 1519, Montezuma's menagerie was so large it was tended by 300 keepers. Its jaguars and ocelots were fed the human remains of Aztec sacrifices.

The modern zoo

The first modern zoos were founded in Vienna, Madrid and Paris in the eighteenth century and in London and Berlin in the nineteenth. The first American zoos were established in Philadelphia and Cincinnati in the 1870s. Today in the United States alone there are hundreds of zoos, and they are visited by millions of people every year. They range from roadside menageries run by hucksters to elaborate zoological parks staffed by trained scientists.

The Roman games no longer exist, though bullfights and rodeos follow in their tradition. Nowadays the power of our leaders is amply demonstrated by their command of nuclear weapons. Yet we still have zoos. Why?

> The keeping of performing animals in circuses, now a controversial issue, dates from France and the United States in the 1830s.

A moral judgment

Before we consider the reasons that are usually given for the survival of zoos, we should see that there is a moral presumption against keeping wild animals in captivity. What this involves, after all, is taking animals out of their native habitats, transporting them great distances and keeping them in alien environments in which their liberty is severely restricted. It is surely true that in being taken from the wild and confined in zoos, animals are deprived of a great many goods. For the most part they are prevented from gathering their own food, developing their own social orders and generally behaving in ways that are natural to them. These activities all require significantly more liberty than most animals are permitted in zoos.

The author presents the arguments for and against zoos in the form of a moral debate.

If we are justified in keeping animals in zoos, it must be because there are some important benefits that can be obtained only by doing so.

This conclusion is not the property of some particular moral theory; it follows from most reasonable moral theories. Either we have duties to animals or we do not. If we do have duties to animals, surely they include respecting those interests which are most important to them, so long as this does not conflict with other, more stringent duties that we may have. Since an interest in not being taken from the wild and kept confined is very important for most animals, it follows that if everything else is equal, we should respect this interest.

"It is important that the visitor goes back with a positive image of the zoo, as otherwise he is going to be totally distracted by the negative experiences and not really be bothered to learn about conservation."

—RAVI CHELLAM,

WILDLIFE INSTITUTE OF INDIA

Suppose, on the other hand, that we do not have duties to animals. There are two further possibilities: either we have duties to people that sometimes concern animals, or what we do to animals is utterly without moral import. The latter view is quite implausible, and I shall not consider it further. People who have held the former view, that we have duties to people that concern animals, have sometimes thought that such duties arise because we can "judge the heart of a man by his treatment of animals," as Kant remarked in "Duties to Animals." It is for this reason that he condemns the man who shoots a faithful dog who has become too old to serve.

The German philosopher Immanuel Kant (1724–1804) held that there is an absolute moral law that we must obey.

If we accept Kant's premise, it is surely plausible to say that someone who, for no good reason, removes wild animals from their natural habitats and denies them liberty is someone whose heart deserves to be judged harshly. If this is so, then even if we believe that we do not have duties to animals but only duties concerning them, we may still hold that there is a presumption against keeping wild animals in captivity. If this presumption is to be overcome, it must be shown that there are important benefits that can be obtained only by keeping animals in zoos.

The author has tried to eliminate, piece by piece, any moral justification for ill-treating animals (eg., by denying them liberty).

But different reasons provide support for different kinds of zoo. Preservation and perhaps research are better carried out in large-scale animal preserves, but these provide few opportunities for amusement and education. Amusement and perhaps education are better provided in urban zoos, but they offer few opportunities for research and preservation. Moreover, whatever benefits are obtained from any kind of zoo must confront the moral presumption against keeping wild animals in captivity. Which way do the scales tip? There are two further considerations which, in my view, tip the scales against zoos.

Unjustifiable suffering

First, captivity does not just deny animals liberty but is often detrimental to them in other respects as well. The history of chimpanzees in the zoos of Europe and America is a good example.

Jamieson focuses on one specific example to make his general point.

Chimpanzees first entered the zoo world in about 1640 when a Dutch prince, Frederick Henry of Nassau, obtained one for his castle menagerie. The chimpanzee didn't last very long. In 1835 the London Zoo obtained its first chimpanzee; he died immediately. Another was obtained in 1845; she lived six months. All through the nineteenth and early twentieth centuries zoos obtained chimpanzees who promptly died within nine months. It wasn't until the 1930s that it was discovered that chimpanzees are extremely vulnerable to human respiratory diseases, and that special steps must be taken to protect them. But for nearly a century zoos removed them from the wild and subjected them to almost certain

There is less than 2 percent variance between chimpanzee and human genomes.

death. Problems remain today. When chimpanzees are taken from the wild the usual procedure is to shoot the mother and kidnap the child. The rule of thumb among trappers is that ten chimpanzees die for every one that is delivered alive to the United States or Europe. On arrival many of these animals are confined under abysmal conditions.

Do you think that zoo visitors should be made aware of such statistics?

Chimpanzees are not the only animals to suffer in zoos. In 1974 Peter Batten, former director of the San Jose Zoological Gardens, undertook an exhaustive study of two hundred American zoos. In his book *Living Trophies* he documented large numbers of neurotic, overweight animals kept in cramped, cold cells and fed unpalatable synthetic food. Many had deformed feet and appendages caused by unsuitable floor surfaces. Almost every zoo studied had excessive mortality rates, resulting from preventable factors ranging from vandalism to inadequate husbandry practices. Battan's conclusion was: "The majority of American zoos are badly run, their direction incompetent, and animal husbandry inept and in some cases nonexistent."

A necropsy is undertaken to determine the cause of an animal's death or to study the extent of the disease from which it died.

Many of these same conditions and others are documented in *Pathology of Zoo Animals*, a review of necropsies conducted by Lynn Griner over the last fourteen years at the San Diego Zoo. This zoo may well be the best in the country, and its staff is clearly well-trained and well-intentioned. Yet this study documents widespread malnutrition among zoo animals; high mortality rates from the use of anaesthetics and tranquillizers; serious injuries and deaths sustained in transport; and frequent occurrences of cannibalism, infanticide, and fighting almost certainly caused by overcrowded conditions. Although the zoo has learned from its mistakes, it is still unable to keep many wild animals in captivity without killing or injuring them, directly or indirectly. If this is true of the San Diego Zoo, it is certainly true, to an even greater extent, at most other zoos.

Our place in nature

The second consideration is more difficult to articulate but is even more important. Zoos teach us a false sense of our place in the natural order. The means of confinement mark a difference between humans and animals. They are there at our pleasure, to be used for our purposes. Morality and perhaps our very survival require that we learn to live as one species among many rather than as one species over many. To do this, we must forget what we learn at zoos. Because what zoos teach us is false and dangerous, both humans and animals will be better off when they are abolished.

167

ZOOS AND ANIMAL RIGHTS: THE ETHICS OF KEEPING ANIMALS
Stephen St. C. Bostock

This document is the concluding section from the author's book Zoos and Animal Rights.

We have seen that various relatively wild animals can be kept in zoos in what may reasonably be regarded as a state of well-being, and I have discussed various criteria by which to judge the suitability of their conditions. No doubt much zoo-keeping today is still, by those criteria, falling short of what our responsibility to the animals concerned requires. And humans are fallible, sometimes even cruel, so the continuing of some substandard zoo-keeping is hardly surprising. It may be even virtually certain so long as zoos continue at all. So ought we just to abolish them? Is this the right moral solution, whether or not it is practical?

I don't think so, for such reasons as these:

The world's most important zoos now embrace a central role in conservation rather than merely in providing us with entertainment.

1) Certain zoos are of a very high standard, in the way their animals' needs are catered for, and in their conservational aims and achievements.

2) New ethological research is showing us, and is likely to do so more and more, how we can keep various relatively wild animals fully satisfactorily.

3) Only the coming years may reveal how short-sighted zoos' abolition could be. They may have an enormously important role to play in safeguarding many large vertebrate species in a world overrun by one dominant primate species.

4) One conservational role arises from a very important educational role, that of encouraging empathy with and appreciation of other living beings in zoo visitors, adults and children. Even if this is a clearer achievement of zoos than their instructional role, it is a very important one (indeed more so than academic instruction, though the two should go hand in hand).

Attacking the zoo

Critics of zoos (they include many of course who work in them!) should be listened to, and their criticisms complied with where they cannot be shown to be mistaken. But some opponents of zoos let their respect for truth be blunted by their reforming zeal. They use any effective weapon, even dishonesty, in the fight against—as they see them— remorseless exploiters of animals. An example would be the kind of article which implies that zoos regard their conservational captive breeding as the only significant kind of conservation. Of course zoos see their role as no more than a supplement—but still a very important supplement—to the protection of animals' natural habitats.

Sometimes those running zoos can be hypocritical, not least in their readiness to claim all zoo-keeping as genuinely conservational in aim or achievement. But some opponents of zoos can also be hypocritical or muddled, not least in their espousal of the probable need for conservational breeding centers essentially distinct from existing zoos. [The British writer and conservationist] Sir Christopher Lever … defines such a center as necessarily specialist, scientific, and conservational, and explicitly denies that any zoo fulfills those expectations. But it should stare him in the face that, to take one obvious example, the Jersey Wildlife Preservation Trust is specialist, scientific, and conservational—and Lever has himself praised its management! What is the point of criticising (say) British zoos, perhaps justifiably in many respects, while determinedly refusing to pay credit to the work of zoos like Jersey?

The "right" kind of zoo

There is in some critics a reluctance, also, to recognize that some zoos, despite their failings, are capable of evolving, and likely to evolve, into the right kind of zoo or conservational breeding center. Institutions, which of course include zoos, themselves tend to evolve, and we are much more likely to arrive at a fully satisfactory zoo by improving a less satisfactory one than by trying to start a fully satisfactory zoo from scratch. In any case, even if this were the best course in some ways, it is unlikely to be the best course with institutions that keep animals. For if we close zoos down, and then set about starting "proper" conservational breeding centers, where on earth are the animals to come from? Surely not (in most cases) from the wild, for even today's imperfect zoos recognize the moral objections (apart from the legal ones) to taking endangered animals from there.

I haven't defined zoos at any point, and perhaps there isn't much need—after all, the term only came into general use thanks to a music-hall artist!—but perhaps I ought to have done in view of some zoo opponents' tendency to define "zoo" in such a way that "zoos are bad" becomes a necessary

Bostock makes an effective point against critics of zoos.

In place of zoos Lever favors nature films as a valid means of studying wildlife.

The Jersey Zoo runs a number of captive-breeding programs, helping save animals such as the St. Lucia parrot and the golden lion tamarin.

Bostock effectively weaves practical points into what is also a moral argument.

COMMENTARY: A zoo success story

Today the golden lion tamarin enjoys a future in Brazilian wildlife reserves thanks to captive-breeding programs in zoos.

A tiny, squirrel-sized monkey, the golden lion tamarin (*Leontopithecus rosalia*) is native to the Atlantic Coastal Forest of Mato Grosso, Brazil. It lives in the trees in close family groups that defend a communal territory. The name derives from its lustrous mane of brilliant gold hairs.

The Atlantic coastal rain forests of the tamarin's native range are today surrounded by some of the most densely populated parts of Brazil. The result has been near-total clear felling of the forests to make room for human activities.

In the early 1970s, when the species' plight became publicized, a global captive-breeding program was initiated as a joint venture between the U.S. National Zoological Park and Smithsonian Institution, the Instituto Brasileiro Desenvolvimiento Florestal, and the Centro de Primatologia do Rio de Janeiro, Brazil.

Today the Golden Lion Tamarin Conservation Program enlists further help from the University of Maryland and the World Wide Fund for Nature. In all, more than 120 zoos take part in rearing lion tamarins and helping release them into the wild in special protected Brazilian reserves, in particular the Poço das Antas Biological Reserve, a mere two hours' drive from Rio de Janeiro. Before their release the captive-bred monkeys are taken to so-called gateway zoos that serve as "boot camps." There the monkeys learn to walk on trees, find food, and establish social skills with others. From the gateway zoos they are taken to Brazil. Several American zoos participate in the gateway program, including those in Atlanta, Los Angeles, and Milwaukee, as well as the National Zoo and the Metro Washington Park Zoo.

The released monkeys have shown themselves to be capable of adjusting to the wild and breeding, and by the start of the century scientists could report a 65 percent survival rate among wild-raised offspring. The success of the venture has depended not only on a concerted captive-breeding program, but also on strict preservation of what remains of the wild habitat. Without both of them the golden lion tamarin would not be here today.

truth. That is, they immediately exclude any example one offers of a good zoo, if they admire it also, from being a zoo. This of course is partly playing with terms.

In any debate it is important to clarify definitions.

The diversity of zoos' origins should assist us in directing (so far as we can) the ways in which they develop in the future…. In some respects deerparks should be regarded as the best zoos of past centuries. After all, why shouldn't the extremely large enclosures of a zoo such as Whipsnade be regarded as being evolved from deerparks as much as from menageries? One pioneer of conservational captive breeding was, of course, the 11th Duke of Bedford, whose deerpark can have had few rivals throughout history. Modern "deerparks," or large animal parks, may be in many cases the best zoos (or whatever we choose to call them) for captive breeding of ungulates and perhaps some carnivores. But there is a role, too, for zoos of smaller area near cities, provided they can keep their animals, and select which animals they keep, by the kind of criteria I have outlined. Where it can be shown that the animals in such zoos are thriving … then those zoos are desirable because of the enormous possibilities they provide for human enrichment, not just recreation or entertainment, but biological, emotional, moral, even spiritual enrichment.

In the 1890s the 11th duke obtained the last surviving Asian Père David's deer (Elaphurus davidianus) from European zoos to form a successful breeding herd. His original deerpark, at Woburn Abbey in England, is today a wild animal park.

Animal apartheid?

There are those who favor (were it possible) a complete separation of animals and humans. They would like our species to have no contact with other species, not even domestic animals, still less wild ones. Marthe Kiley-Worthington has labeled this approach or policy "animal apartheid." The long history of zoos and animal keeping has shown us how deep in humans must lie the desire for contact with other species. However misguided much of past (and even recent) zoo-keeping has been, it testifies to a great desire for close involvement with other animals.

Kiley-Worthington, an expert in animal behavior, was commissioned by the British RSPCA (Royal Society for the Prevention of Cruelty to Animals) to undertake a scientific study of animals in captivity.

Perhaps I can leave the last word on the value of being close to animals to [writer] C. S. Lewis. In April 1962, George Sayer was driving Lewis back to Cambridge from a period in hospital. They stopped briefly by the Duke of Bedford's great estates at Woburn, wandered along a little path (marked Private!), and were suddenly "in a glade surrounded by a number of miniature deer. Jack [C. S. Lewis] was entranced. 'You know, while I was writing the Narnia books I never imagined anything as lovely as this,' he said." They tried on another occasion to find the deer again, but failed. "'Well,' said Jack, 'as I found once before, you can't expect the same miracle twice.'"

Summary

The article "Against Zoos" examines the history of keeping animals. In the past animals were kept for reasons other than recreation and education. They were used to show power or as combatants in the Roman games. Today zoos are often cited as providing amusement, education, opportunities for scientific research, and preservation of species. However, they rarely provide all of these services, and they are often harmful to animals. Amusement seems to be the main reason for the existence of zoos, which is clearly not a good enough reason to keep animals imprisoned. Zoos also disrupt public perceptions of how animals should be treated, creating a generation of people who see nothing wrong with putting animals on display for our benefit. Through reasoned moral debate the author concludes that the benefits of keeping animals in zoos do not outweigh the moral principle of keeping them free.

In the article "Zoos and Animal Rights" Bostock explains the reasons for keeping animals in zoos. Conservation of species is high on the list. Another role of zoos lies in educating the public and encouraging them to support species conservation. Critics of zoos are reluctant to admit that zoos can change and evolve, but many zoos provide high-quality habitat for their animals. Research is improving our knowledge of animals' needs so that their living conditions can be made closer to those encountered in the wild. Zoos play a necessary part in the future of some animals, and we cannot predict the consequences of destroying zoos, so it would be disastrous to get rid of them at this time. Improving existing zoos so that they provide suitable conditions for animals, the author admits, is necessary.

FURTHER INFORMATION:

 Books:

Bostock, Stephen St. C., *Zoos and Animal Rights*. New York: Routledge, 1993.

Croke, Vicki, *Modern Ark*. New York: Scribner Pub., 1997.

Hancocks, David, *A Different Nature*. Berkeley: University of California Press, 2001.

Jordan, Bill, and Stefan Ormrod, *The Last Great Wild Beast Show*. London: Constable Publishers, 1978.

Kiley-Worthington, Marthe, *Animals in Circuses and Zoos—Chiron's World?* Basildon, UK: Little Eco Farms Publishing, 1990.

McKenna, Virginia, William Travers, and Jonathan Wray (editors), *Beyond the Bars*. Wellingborough, UK: Thorsons Publishers, 1987.

Shepherdson, David J., *Second Nature: Environment Enrichment for Captive Animals*. Washington, D.C.: Smithsonian Institution Press, 1999.

 Useful websites:

www.aza.org
The American Zoo and Aquarium Association.

www.bornfree.org.uk
Homepage of the Born Free Foundation.

The following debates in the Pro/Con series may also be of interest:

In this volume:

ARE ZOOS MORALLY WRONG?

YES: It is demeaning to animals to keep them caged for our entertainment; society has moved on from the days when menageries were playthings

YES: We get a far more realistic idea of animal behavior from watching modern nature documentaries shot in the wild

ENTERTAINMENT
Is it wrong to expect zoos to entertain us?

EDUCATION
Is it wrong to use the zoo as a human schoolroom?

NO: Providing the animal is respected, entertainment can be invaluable in giving humans a taste of the natural world

NO: An appreciation for, and empathy with, zoo animals can encourage people to take an active role in conservation

ARE ZOOS MORALLY WRONG?
KEY POINTS

YES: A scientific conservation establishment is incompatible with the traditional zoo

YES: Captives suffer terrible deprivations, physical maladies, and mental torture

CONSERVATION
Should conservation programs be conducted solely in the field?

CRUELTY
Is it cruel to keep animals in captivity?

NO: Many zoos help raise funds for conservation or use their expertise to run successful captive-breeding programs

NO: Big enclosures run on modern guidelines are adequate; zoos now phase out species that do not take to captivity at all

Topic 14

SHOULD ENDANGERED SPECIES BE CLONED?

YES
"REPRODUCING THE ARK"
BEN HOARE

NO
"NOAH'S NEW ARK"
TIME MAGAZINE, VOL. 157, JANUARY 8, 2001
MARYANN BIRD

INTRODUCTION

Since the successful cloning of Dolly the sheep in Scotland in 1997 the possibilities of future cloning projects have been endless. The significant thing about Dolly was that she was a mammal and that she was produced from a common cell—not from reproductive tissue.

This discovery has lead to the possibility of cloning human beings. Scientists talked of cloning geniuses, and medical groups discussed cloning humans for organ donation. Recently, the focus has turned to the cloning of endangered species.

A clone is an individual that is produced from the cells of another individual. Unlike sexual reproduction, it does not involve the combination of two sets of genes. It results in an individual having the exact same DNA (deoxyribonucleic acid, the basic genetic "blueprint" of an individual) as the original. The process of cloning is accomplished by removing the nucleus from an egg using a needle. Another

needle is then used to inject a whole cell under the egg's outer layer. An electric pulse is used to fuse the cell to the egg. The cell will then respond like a normal fertilized egg, dividing itself and growing into a baby. Once the egg is large enough, it is implanted into a surrogate mother to come to term.

In 1973 the Endangered Species Act was established by Congress to "conserve the ecosystems upon which endangered species depend and to conserve and recover listed species." Since the act's establishment some animals have become extinct, and some have recovered enough to be removed from the list. Cloning represents a possible way to recover endangered species. Whether cloning is a practical solution, and whether cloning animals will keep animals from extinction, still remains to be determined.

Human beings have always had an effect on the environment. Our actions have consequences that affect the ecosystems in which we live. A good example of this can be seen in our agricultural practices. Fields are cleared of all vegetation, thus displacing all the animals that were originally living there. If these animals cannot find other suitable habitat, they will die. If the animals happen to be the last population of a species, that species will become extinct.

"The sheep in Scotland and the monkeys in Oregon represent first steps down what is a very long road. They show cloning is possible but they do not prove it is practical. The techniques used are not only not safe to try in humans, they are still not very effective or efficient for use in animals."

—ARTHUR CAPLAN, UNIVERSITY OF PENNSYLVANIA

Rachel Carson's book *Silent Spring* (1962) called the public to take responsibility for their actions and to prevent the extinction of plants and animals. But even with public awareness species continue to become extinct.

The goal of scientists intent on cloning endangered species is to bring species that are close to extinction back from the brink. Scientists have already successfully cloned the gaur (see page 180), an endangered animal from Southeast Asia that is similar to an ox. Plans are in place to clone the bucardo mountain goat, a species that became extinct in 2000. It is believed that cloning could greatly benefit many species, especially those that do not reproduce easily in captivity, such as the giant panda, chimpanzee, tiger, and most kinds of reptiles.

Opponents state that cloning animals when there is no habitat left for them to live in does not solve the problem. They believe that cloning animals will send the wrong message to the public, a message that the threat to animal species could be ignored. Instead, the public should be educated on ways to save valuable habitat. If animals are provided with the proper habitat and living conditions they need, they will reproduce naturally.

People are also worried that cloning may lead to a "genetic bottleneck" in which the gene pool of a species dwindles, and all the survivors end up with the same genetic material. Such populations could be wiped out in a single disease outbreak. Other people are deeply troubled by what they see as an ethical issue in which scientists are playing at being God. There are questions, too, about whether it is worth struggling with a process that can cause much suffering to the surrogate animals.

No one wants to see species become extinct. Future generations should be able to enjoy the same diverse species that inhabit the earth today. Whether or not cloning will eventually be used to save endangered species remains to be decided. The following two articles examine the issues surrounding this question.

REPRODUCING THE ARK
Ben Hoare

Conservationists regularly appear on TV news bulletins to talk about "Earth's intensifying mass extinction crisis." Some people are still skeptical about such claims, but it is not as easy as it once was to dismiss these reports as alarmist scare stories. Scientists generally agree that rates of extinction are now 1,000–10,000 times higher than the average level that would be expected under entirely natural conditions (that is, without the influence of the human species) due to the massive habitat destruction occurring worldwide. The World Wildlife Fund (WWF) estimates that at present rates of extinction as many as one-third of the world's species could be gone in the next 20 years.

These figures sound impressive, but does the author explain their significance?

Desperate times call for desperate measures, and cloning is the latest weapon to be adopted by beleaguered conservationists. The cloning of vertebrates is a fledgling branch of science with many critics, and it is unlikely to become a viable conservation technique for the forseeable future. Nevertheless in the battle against extinction the stakes are now so high that it would be unwise to rule out any new method of artificially increasing the populations of endangered species before it has had a chance to prove itself.

The power of cloning
Cloning is particularly suited to animals that breed infrequently in zoos, such as the chimpanzee, giant panda, and the majority of reptiles, and it could be the only available tool to breed animals like whales. The giant panda is a prime candidate for cloning because it occurs at very low population densities (therefore requiring large expanses of habitat), reproduces slowly, and has proved resistant to all other captive-breeding techniques. In fact, relatively few species reproduce well in captivity. Cloning therefore has the potential to be useful for a large number of species. Cloned animals would be kept in captivity until such a time as their habitats were sufficiently well preserved or restored for them to be released into the wild.

Why might reproduction be difficult for many species in captive conditions?

The beauty of cloning is that it offers scientists the prospect of maintaining the gene pool of an endangered species. A major problem faced by conservationists trying to save animals with tiny remnant populations—and hence weakened gene pools—is that the surviving animals are vulnerable to sudden changes in their environment, such as disease. For example, the critically endangered black-footed ferret of the North American prairies was almost driven to extinction by an outbreak of canine distemper in the mid-1980s; the virus reduced the ferret's entire global population from around 130 to fewer than 30 animals. There are countless similar tales involving other endangered species. "When you get down to a few dozen members of a species you're really talking about very serious problems," says Dr. Robert Lanza of Advanced Cell Technology, the biotech company involved in the recent project to clone a gaur, an endangered oxlike species native to Southeast Asia.

The author uses a specific example to make a more general point.

One way of maintaining an endangered species' gene pool is to collect semen and eggs from the animals in the wild and then store the gametes (sex cells) by a technique known as cryopreservation. However, few zoos currently have cryopreservation facilities, and eggs are both difficult to extract and damaged by freezing. The cloning technique, on the other hand, requires only common body cells from nonreproductive tissue, which are more straightforward to collect and store.

Early days

As with many scientific techniques in their infancy, cloning has produced only modest successes to date. The great drawbacks of cloning are that live cells are needed, and the fact that once DNA from a species' body cell has been merged into an egg cell stripped of its own DNA, the resulting composite must then be implanted into an adult female for gestation. Given that the females of an endangered species are by definition in short supply, this is a real problem. Researchers are trying to get round this stumbling block by using closely related, nonthreatened species as surrogate mothers.

Scientists argue that cloning technology is still relatively primitive. Do you think that the press accurately reflects its current status?

Frozen zoos

A small but vocal band of scientists has advocated the establishment of a worldwide network of repositories to hold frozen tissue from all the individuals of an endangered species from which it is possible to collect samples. This frozen material would serve as a "genetic trust" for restoring populations of a particular species. The cost of maintaining such "frozen zoos" would compare favorably with that of keeping animals in zoos, which is in fact an extremely

COMMENTARY: Dolly the sheep

The Roslin Institute in Edinburgh, Scotland, produced the world's most famous sheep by taking the ovum of a Scottish blackface ewe and replacing its contents with the nucleus of a mammary-gland cell from a six-year-old Finn Dorset ewe. The modified ovum was replaced within the blackface, who served as Dolly's surrogate mother.

The birth of Dolly on July 5, 1996, caused excitement because she was the first mammal ever cloned from an adult cell, rather than an embryo cell. The two differ crucially in that an embryo cell is totipotent: It has the potential to grow into an embryo in its own right. But at a certain point in development these cells lose their totipotency and become adult cells, each of which then permanently adopts a sole function: for example, as a skin cell or muscle cell. The Roslin team discovered that by arresting an adult cell's development, they could induce it to regain its totipotency.

If the technology can be applied to other rare species, Roslin's discovery has important consequences. Now that scientists can take cells from any adult, using swabs, skin samples, or hair follicles, they can sample a wider selection of genetic material than before. The success of a captive-breeding program depends on maintaining genetic diversity, so cloning—or nuclear transfer (NT), as it is also known—may be a vital weapon in the fight to save rare species. But there are drawbacks. First, Roslin started with 277 NT eggs. Of them only 29 seemed to develop normally to blastocyst (preembryo), and of this batch Dolly was the only successful birth. Second, cloning does not work with all animals. Since Dolly's birth scientists have cloned cattle, mice, goats, and pigs, but failed with rabbits, monkeys, or rats. Third, clones can be defective. As Roslin's Harry Griffin explained, "A clone will also inherit ... mutations from the donor and this in turn may lead to premature aging or a higher incidence of cancer later in life."

Later cloning work at Roslin has involved the creation of sheep that carry human genes. Their milk can be made to produce, cheaply and plentifully, drugs to treat hemophilia and other grave human diseases.

Dolly the cloned sheep with her first lamb, Bonnie, in 1998.

expensive way of saving populations of endangered species. Today two frozen zoos are at the forefront of cloning research: the Center for Reproduction of Endangered Species at San Diego Zoo and the Audubon Institute Center for Research into Endangered Species in New Orleans.

The concept of the frozen zoo should not be dismissed as something that belongs in the realms of science fiction. At the Royal Botanic Gardens in Kew, England, a multi-million dollar project to collect, catalog, and store the seeds of 10 percent of the world's flowering plants (more than 24,000 species) is already well underway. The Millennium Seed Bank, as the ambitious scheme is called, will prove an invaluable resource for future generations of researchers. Seeds are generally far easier to handle than live animal cells, and can be preserved in larger quantities, but although frozen zoos cannot hope to preserve the DNA of more than a handful of species, the guiding principle is the same in both cases: to safeguard as much genetic material as possible.

Do you think that preserving cells by freezing would be acceptable if applied to human beings?

Race against time

Cloning should be seen as a kind of insurance policy against habitat loss. Habitat destruction—the main cause of approximately 90 percent of all species extinctions—is taking place on such a scale that conservationists are running out of time. While funds are raised and often complex habitat-protection programs are devised and implemented, populations of threatened species continue to decline. The relentless growth of human populations and the resultant pressure on natural habitats from agriculture, industry, and urbanization will make it impossible to save enough habitat to save all (or even most) endangered species. Moreover, the regions that have borne the brunt of species extinctions over the last 200 years, and which harbor the largest number of endangered species, are also those that are least able to halt and reverse the process. Current extinction "hotspots" include Indonesia, the Philippines, India, China, Brazil, and Colombia, all nations that for economic or cultural reasons historically have been unable to devote sufficient resources to habitat protection.

Habitat preservation should remain the holy grail of conservationists. However, the pressures on Earth's wild places are now so great that, when all else fails, cloning may be the only chance of survival for species such as the Vancouver Island marmot (1998 population: fewer than 100), Javan rhino (2000 population: 70), and northern hairy-nosed wombat (1998 population: 65).

The author places habitat preservation above cloning. Do you agree with his priorities?

NOAH'S NEW ARK
Maryann Bird

NO

This analogy makes for a memorable argument.

Noah's Ark has set sail again, crossing stormy scientific waters and buffeted by winds of controversy. Unlike the Old Testament vessel, however, today's metaphorical ark is not carrying threatened animals two by two to safety. Rather, if it lives up to its billing, it could produce potentially unlimited numbers of endangered creatures.

In its wild state the gaur is threatened by hunting, habitat alternation, and diseases from domestic cattle.

In the updated story, though, Noah is not the skipper of the rescue project. Instead, it's the name given in advance to the clone of a dead gaur, an endangered wild ox found in India, Bangladesh and Southeast Asia. The new Noah is expected to be born any day now to Bessie, a cow living on a farm near Sioux City, Iowa. Cows have given birth to gaurs before, but this is the first time that one animal species is acting as surrogate mother to a clone—an exact genetic duplicate—of a different species.

Noah arrived safely in January 2001, but died two days later of dysentery.

If Bessie's little gaur is delivered safely, the birth will come as a boost to many biologists in the United States and Europe who are engaged in a range of "assisted reproduction" conservation strategies. These include artificial insemination and in vitro fertilization. In particular, though, Noah's arrival will hearten the scientists at ACT [Advanced Cell Technologies], who recently signed a deal with Spanish officials to attempt to clone the bucardo, an extinct mountain goat native to the Pyrenees. The last bucardo died a year ago, struck by a falling tree in its final habitat, northern Spain's Ordesa National Park. Scientists had already preserved a quantity of its cells, and ACT hopes to transfer them into other goats' eggs, perhaps later this year.

The wrong way to save animals?

As scientists await the clone's birth, other wildlife researchers express doubts about the project's conservation claims and think the wrong message is being sent. "We do not believe that cloning has any relevance to the routine management and conservation of endangered species," says David Wildt, a senior scientist at the Smithsonian Institution's Conservation and Research Center in Front Royal, Virginia. Instead, Wildt favors low-tech methods, like the artificial insemination used to breed the endangered black-footed ferret, which is now being reintroduced to the American West. "Our laboratory works all over the world with the rarest of species," he says, "and not once have I ever heard a real wildlife manager or wildlife scientist say, 'Gee, we must attempt to save this species using cloning.'"

The use of the word "real" subtly implies that critics are not real experts.

To William Holt, a research fellow at the Institute of Zoology in London, the best approach is to learn more about species' reproductive systems and the social conditions that can make animals want to breed naturally. "If you know those things, you can improve success rates a lot without doing anything invasive." Where cloning technology may be useful, Holt allows, is "where the species is down to 50 or so. You could sample cells from all of them. You could recreate all of these 50 individuals. You've still got the genetic variability that is important." Failing to do so, he suggests, could result in populations that lack the genetic diversity to fight off disease, setting the creatures up for a second extinction. Suitable habitats are also necessary. "You've got to ask, Are we helping these animals into the future?"

Limited gene pools do not always weaken a species. All of the world's pet golden hamsters are derived from a single female caught in the Middle East during the 1930s.

"[About] the tone of the response [to the announcement of the successful cloning of Dolly], I've been slightly disappointed in the public's rather limited concentration on science-fiction applications. If there were more interest in the potential beneficial applications, I would be more comfortable."
—IAN WILMUT, ROSLIN INSTITUTE, EDINBURGH

Helping animals into the future is a priority for the world's wildlife researchers as a growing number of species become imperiled each year. Oliver Ryder, a geneticist at the San Diego Zoo's Center for Reproduction of Endangered Species, is the driving force behind a 25-year effort to assemble a bank of frozen DNA, eggs, and sperm from endangered species. Under his direction, the frozen zoo now has living cells from 5,400 animals spanning more than 400 species and subspecies, cultured and frozen in liquid nitrogen.

COMMENTARY: The alternatives to cloning

Ethical objections to cloning have much to do with public fears about how the technology might be applied to humans in the field of eugenics—the deliberate selection of biological traits from a number of people to create "superhumans." Others fear that someone may one day try to create a clone of a famous historical figure. But there are more practical reasons why cloning has yet to become commonplace: It is prohibitively costly and complex, with too high a failure rate. Thankfully, in the race to conserve critically endangered animal species biologists can rely on less controversial methods of manipulating the genetic stocks at their disposal.

The time-honored method is unassisted captive breeding. Few wild animals breed freely in captivity, however. Peter Bryant, author of *Biodiversity and Conservation*, points out that "only 26 of 274 species of rare mammals in captivity are self-sustaining," and that a mere 10 percent or so of reptile species in zoos have bred. A zoo may ship a prize specimen, such as a giant panda or tiger, many miles to another zoo, only to find that the operation so distresses the animal that a successful mating is impossible, or that the two suitors are simply ill-matched and refuse to couple.

Assisted breeding

Some of the problems associated with captive breeding are smoothed out with the use of artificial insemination, in which sperm is combined with the egg in vitro (in the laboratory) and the fertilized egg then placed in the female's womb. In March 2000 at the Indianapolis Zoo a 24-year-old African elephant cow named Kubwa gave birth to a healthy calf, the first of its species ever to have been conceived by artificial insemination. To maximize the chance of success in such an operation, zoo biologists spend several weeks monitoring the level of the hormone progesterone in the cow elephant's blood, looking for traces of luteinizing hormones, which predict the start of ovulation. On the due date for the operation semen is taken from the bull, who will have been selected from a list of available donors. A successful operation will result 22 months later in the birth of a calf.

Artificial insemination does, however, have its drawbacks, such as the difficulties of storing sperm. In Kubwa's case fresh sperm was used, but in many instances the sperm sample must be frozen, either for long-distance travel or for long-term storage. Not all samples freeze well, with variation even across individuals. (Here genetic engineering can help biologists, who analyze samples for gene markers that will in future identify "good" or "bad" sperm.) Another problem with artificial insemination is that eggs of endangered species, such as giant pandas, are inevitably in short supply. If an artificial insemination operation fails for whatever reason—and many do—the eggs used on that occasion are permanently lost. With cloning from adult cells this is not a problem.

One missing creature is often on Ryder's mind. "Could you take a cell from a Morro Bay kangaroo rat and bring it back, and would it be the same?" he asks. "There are a lot of questions, but we don't have that option now because nobody saved the cells" while lab work was being conducted on the rodent in the 1970s. "The future will want to know about these species, and the lingua franca of biology is increasingly going to be genomic information. If nobody saves the DNA of these samples, it's going to be a very fragmented picture." There is also a present-day, practical side. By providing vital clues to the mingling of subspecies and the types of environment they require, genetic data can help zoologists care for endangered animals in captivity.

"Lingua franca" is a Latin phrase meaning common language.

Exploring our options

At Austria's Salzburg Zoo, scientists are developing a recipe they hope will lead to the first production of white rhinos through artificial insemination. Franz Schwarzenberger of Vienna's University of Veterinary Medicine believes success with the tricky technique could help save even more endangered rhino species, such as the northern white. "It may be possible to collect semen in the wild and inseminate animals in captivity," he says. "This kind of assisted reproduction offers us a chance to improve the gene pool of the captive population without taking resources from the wild."

After years of watching one species after another become extinct, researchers are sounding optimistic. "We don't have the right to do nothing," says Mauget, who predicts that interzoo exchanges of sperm, oocytes, and embryos will develop rapidly. "Instead of shipping our animals from one zoo to another, we'll be sending sperm to the four corners of the earth." Meanwhile, in a corner of Iowa, another kind of delivery is awaited.

The oocyte is the cell that forms the ovum, or egg.

Summary

The article "Reproducing the Ark" describes how endangered species can be cloned to increase their dwindling numbers. This form of "assisted reproduction" will keep endangered species from becoming extinct, but will not bring back extinct species such as dinosaurs. The cloning technique is likely to be most useful for increasing the populations of endangered species that do not breed easily in captivity. Zoos do not have the space or technology to preserve great quantities of eggs and semen for use in artificial reproduction, but preserving body cells for use in cloning is a realistic possibility because it takes very little room and energy. Cloning technology is still being perfected. It will be a while before enough species can be cloned to remove them from the endangered species list. The author emphasizes that every effort should be made to preserve wild habitat and induce natural reproduction, but asserts that cloning can produce results when all other conservation methods have failed.

In the article "Noah's New Ark" Maryann Bird states that cloning is a labor-intensive procedure with a low success rate. Some scientists believe that cloning is not a viable method for conservation of endangered species, and that there are better methods. They believe that studying reproductive systems and mating habits will improve success rates for natural breeding. They admit that using cloning to increase the number of individuals could be important for keeping genetic variability, but argue that low-tech methods such as artificial insemination and in vitro fertilization are better alternatives to the complex and costly method of cloning.

FURTHER INFORMATION:

Articles:

Wilson, E. O., "Vanishing Before Our Eyes," in *Time* (special report on Earth Day 2000), April–May 2000.

Useful websites:

www.roslin.ac.uk/public/cloning.html
Pages from the website of the Roslin Institute, Edinburgh, covering many issues on cloning, from technicalities to the moral debate.
www.anth.org/ifgene/
Ifgene, the International Forum for Genetic Engineering, is a useful public awareness site and forum for discussion.
www.newscientist.com/nsplus/insight/clone/clone.html
A *New Scientist* report on cloning.
www.nal.usda.gov/bic/
A general U.S. government information site on biotechnology.

www.synapses.co.uk/science/clone.html
Simplified explanation of cloning of Dolly the sheep.

The following debates in the Pro/Con series may also be of interest:

In this volume:

Topic 13 Are zoos morally wrong?

Topic 12 Is genetically modified food safe enough to feed the world's population?

SHOULD ENDANGERED SPECIES BE CLONED?

YES: Cloned animals can be created as and when suitable habitat is restored or created

YES: By taking adult cells, scientists can sample a much wider pool of animals than by sampling eggs and sperm alone

HABITAT
Can cloning work alongside habitat preservation?

GENETIC DIVERSITY
Will cloning improve the genetic diversity of endangered species?

NO: Cloning, a costly and high-profile technology, will overshadow conservation in the field and take money from habitat preservation

NO: Cloning by its nature merely replicates the genes of one animal; it does not blend them with those of another (as in sexual reproduction) to create a new and unique individual

SHOULD ENDANGERED SPECIES BE CLONED? KEY POINTS

YES: It's our duty to conserve endangered animals by any means in our power

YES: Bringing dinosaurs back is impossible—but there will be many extinctions in the years to come. A gene bank may help bring them back

MORAL PURPOSE
Do we have a moral duty to clone animals?

JURASSIC PARK
Can we resurrect extinct species?

NO: It's morally wrong for scientists to adulterate natural processes and play at being God

NO: In most cases the DNA of extinct animals is so degraded by age as to be unusable

HOW TO WRITE AN ESSAY

While you are preparing to write your essay, you should always keep the following four points in mind:

PURPOSE   What is the point?
CONTENT   What am I writing about?
STRUCTURE What's the best way to put my argument across?
STYLE   Am I using the correct language and grammar?

1. UNDERSTANDING YOUR TOPIC

If you misunderstand the question you're answering, you immediately start at a disadvantage. Look up anything you don't understand, or ask someone else.

2. COLLECTING THE INFORMATION YOU NEED

It is important to organize your research time well.
See *Government*:   *Research Skills*,
                       pages 58–59

3. EFFECTIVE THINKING

Once you have finished your research, sit down in a clear work space and organize your information. Look through your notes, and make a mind map or key map, similar to the one found, for example, on page 21.

STRUCTURING YOUR ESSAY

Essays need an introduction, body, and conclusion. The introduction tells the reader what you will tell them in your argument. The body explains your argument. And the conclusion reminds the reader of the argument you have just presented. Essays should state the following:

Introduction

- What you understand by the title
- What your objectives are
- What aspects of the topic you're going to deal with, i.e., themes and approach
- What you're going to explain or argue

Body

- Build up and expand on the ideas outlined in your introduction
- Support your key ideas with examples, case studies, statistics, and anecdotes.

Conclusion

- Sum up your argument, and echo or reiterate the title of your essay
- Make the reader aware of the main points of your essay
- Show how you have fulfilled the goals laid out in the introduction

Write down a list of main points for your argument, and see how they link together. Once you have done this, you can start to construct your essay.

4. HOW TO ARGUE

DO
- Define any odd terms
- Clarify your points
- Remove misconceptions
- Reason clearly and calmly

See *Science* Critical Thinking, *Critical Thinking*, pages 60-61

DON'T
- Be biased in your views
- Become emotional
- Use generalizations
- Use cliches or non sequiturs
- Use language incorrectly

5. GIVE YOUR WORK CREDIBILITY
- Use stories and anecdotes
- Describe key words and terms
- Use technical terms correctly
- Back up your arguments with facts and statistics
- Use quotations from famous people to lend weight to your arguments

6. STYLE AND CONTENT

Language
- Use simple, concise, and accurate language
- Don't misuse words or spell the names of well-known people incorrectly
- Avoid overlong sentences
- Use the active rather than passive voice

Edit/rewrite
- Once you have a first draft, read the essay through in full:
- Get rid of any sentences or paragraphs that are not essential. Ask yourself: "Why have I included this?" or "Does this answer the question?"
- Correct incorrect language and spelling
- Add examples if you need to strengthen your argument
- Clarify anything that is unclear
- Restructure your essay if it doesn't make sense

Examine the content
Ask yourself: Have my objectives been met?

Have I answered the question?

Is my argument convincing?

If you follow all of the above steps, they should help you write a clear and well-structured essay.

PART 4

ENVIRONMENTAL LAW AND REGULATION

INTRODUCTION

Since environmental protection became an important global issue in the early 1960s, environmentalists and governments have backed laws and regulations as an important way to control human behavior toward the natural world. In 1970, for example, the United States created the Environmental Protection Agency (EPA) to introduce federal laws to safeguard the environment. Its purpose is to "protect human health and to safeguard the natural environment—air, water, and land—upon which life depends."

For a number of reasons, however, environmental laws have not always been an effective way to influence people's actions. One is the difficulty of drafting the legislation in the first place. Governments have a duty to the environment, but they also have a stake in the human activity that sometimes damages it. While it is common to penalize a factory that pollutes a river, for example, most governments remain reluctant to impose regulations that might make it more difficult for domestic industry to compete in international marketplaces. Some businesspeople, meanwhile, protest that any kind of environmental consideration threatens to make their business uncompetitive.

The international nature of the problem further complicates the search for a solution. Regulation often operates at only a local level. Strict safety standards exist at nuclear power plants in Scandinavia, for example. But when there was a serious accident at the Chernobyl nuclear reactor in Ukraine in 1986, radioactive clouds drifted throughout northern Europe, damaging wildlife and forests throughout the Scandinavian countries.

International problems

Countries disagree about the level of regulation required. The Rio and Kyoto Earth Summits in 1992 and 1997 respectively, where all the major governments of the world gathered, showed that the international community was happy to agree in principle that the environment should be protected. Achieving workable regulations on environmental issues, however, is far more difficult. Four years after the Kyoto Protocol was created to help control the pollution that leads to global warming, the signatory nations are still squabbling about the details.

Another problem with regulation lies in the differences between developed and developing countries. Developed countries often have demanding antipollution laws, for example. But developing countries argue that they cannot afford the costs of adopting similar standards.

Even when it is possible to put environmental legislation in place, does it work? Fines or imprisonment may discourage persistent intentional polluting, but they have little effect when it comes to accidents like that at Chernobyl. Similarly, when the oil tanker *Exxon Valdez* ran aground in Alaska's Prince William Sound in 1989, the ship's owners, Exxon Oil, suffered regulating pollutant by pollutant or crisis by crisis. It aims to change corporate and individual behavior to reduce environmental degradation.

Although much U.S. environmental legislation operates at a federal level, states also play an important role. They can enact environmental laws as long as they are as strict as or stricter than federal laws. State agencies like

---

"I look forward to an America which will ... protect the beauty of our natural environment ... and which will build handsome and balanced cities for our future."
—JOHN F. KENNEDY, U.S. PRESIDENT

---

one of the largest fines ever imposed: $25 million, plus $100 million toward restoration of the site. But the damage had already been done. Fish, mammals, and birds had died along some 350 miles of coastline. Regulation did not protect the environment—but it did pay for the cleanup afterward.

The U.S. experience

Although environmental protection legislation has limits, its proponents argue that it has achieved much. The EPA in the United States has a full program of research, monitoring, standard setting, and enforcement. Some of the EPA's biggest successes have been the banning of carcinogenic chemicals, the establishment of sewage treatment networks, the banning of leaded gasoline, the regulation of industrial pollutants, the establishment of curbside recycling programs, and the protection of children from lead paint.

Lately the EPA has been exploring an initiative that moves away from

departments of environmental quality (DEQ), departments of ecology (DOE), and departments of natural resources (DNR) assist with environmental impact assessments, the cleanup of pollution, regulating air and water quality, and education. Other state work includes granting permits: allowing a certain amount of pollution, for example, or a certain amount of human access to wilderness. If a state does not enforce environmental laws strictly enough, the federal government can charge it with noncompliance.

Environmental laws protect human health as well as the environment. The use of cars creates pollution and congestion, which affect both the environment and health. Topic 15 examines whether the government should encourage the use of public transportation through financial subsidy or regulation. Topic 16 discusses whether regulations should make corporations responsible for their impact on the environment.

Topic 15

SHOULD GOVERNMENT ENCOURAGE THE USE OF PUBLIC TRANSPORTATION THROUGH SUBSIDIES?

YES

"OPTIMIZING PUBLIC TRANSIT BENEFITS"
TEXAS TRANSPORTATION PLANNING CONFERENCE, 1998
WWW.VTPI.ORG/OPTRANBE.HTM
TODD LITMAN

NO

"HOW TO 'BUILD OUR WAY OUT OF CONGESTION'"
WWW.RPPI.ORG/PS250.HTML
PETER SAMUEL

INTRODUCTION

At the start of the 20th century the first gasoline automobiles were being produced, but no one predicted what kind of an effect the automobile would have on society. Today people have become reliant on automobiles. They need their cars to get to and from work, to get to the grocery store, and some even to get to their mailboxes.

Cars offer people a sense of status and freedom, but they also bring problems: Burning gasoline releases carbon dioxide. Carbon dioxide is a greenhouse gas and contributes to global warming.

Many people believe that public transportation is the way to release Americans from their ties to automobiles. In theory, it offers a stress-free, efficient, and environmentally friendly way to get to and from destinations. Users are freed from traffic and can relax with a book or enjoy the scenery. Instead of being stuck in traffic experiencing road rage, riders are moved along at a constant speed and ensured that they will arrive at their destination on time.

There is also less chance that they will be involved in an accident. Public transportation is much cheaper than driving a car. Since they are not driving their cars, paying for parking and finding a parking spot are no longer a problem. No insurance is needed. Also, riders do not have to worry about rising gas prices. The environmental advantage of public transportation is that more people are carried by fewer vehicles. Thus public transportation lessens the amount of carbon dioxide being emitted into the atmosphere. This slows the greenhouse effect and the threat of global warming.

Opposition to public transportation is strong. People do not want to leave the comfort and convenience of their cars. Drivers have the flexibility to drop off children at daycare and school and run errands while on their way to work. They do not have to arrange their day around train and bus schedules. With increased fuel efficiency in vehicles drivers are able to travel longer distances without worrying about fuel prices. Gas prices adjusted for current inflation rates are actually lower now than they were in the 1960s.

> *"No other manmade device since the shields and lances of the knights quite fulfills a man's ego like an automobile."*
> —WILLIAM ROOTES, INDUSTRIALIST

Another of the big deterrents to public transportation are the negative connotations associated with it. Most car drivers feel that they are either above riding public transportation, or they are too scared to. Public transportation is often the only means of transportation available to students, disabled, elderly, and poor people. Some people use their cars as status symbols. Driving a Mercedes or a Lexus says something about who they are. If they ride the bus or the train, they have no way of showing off.

Public transportation is also associated in people's minds with crime and violence. Some individuals fear that gangs or muggers will attack them while they are on the train.

In order to increase usage, public transportation needs to be made a more attractive alternative than the automobile. To accomplish this, experts—the actual riders and potential riders of public transportation—suggest offering high-quality service. By this they mean reliable service that is safe and comfortable. Clean trains and buses with courteous staff are needed. Convenient and comfortable waiting areas should be standard. Security and lighting in waiting areas and on trains should be increased and made plainly visible so that riders feel safe.

Also, car drivers need to be shown the hidden costs that driving incurs. Educate them about the prices of congestion, car accidents, parking, and insurance that they do not normally think about. The average American is not going to easily give up the convenience of his or her automobile unless public transportation offers a better deal.

The following two articles examine the varying advantages and disadvantages of using public transportation in the United States.

OPTIMIZING PUBLIC TRANSIT BENEFITS
Todd Litman

YES

There are several misconceptions that can lead to under-investment in transit. They not only hurt transit riders, but also drivers who could benefit from reduced traffic and parking congestion, and society as a whole due to a variety of potential economic and environmental benefits.

One common criticism of transit is that it is irrelevant; that we are now too automobile-dependent for public transit to make a difference. In most communities, only a small and declining percentage of total personal travel is now made by transit (although use of higher-quality rail transit and other premium services is increasing).

Are automobiles the answer?

In response to the tendency to dismiss transit, I ask: Is our current transportation system satisfactory? If not, is the answer to our mobility problems simply more of the same—more highways, more parking, and more per capita automobile mileage?

I think not. An automobile-dependent transportation system is good at some things but bad at others. There is a practical limit to the number of people automobiles can deliver to one place at one time, such as large commercial, educational, or recreation centers. Attempts to approach this limit incur huge highway and parking facility costs, plus congestion, delay, and frustration to users. These costs impose a burden on the economy that can reduce economic development.

An automobile-dependent transportation system contradicts many environmental and livability objectives. It leads to low-density land use patterns that are not only environmentally damaging, but economically inefficient as well. It fails to provide mobility for some people. It is unaffordable to many households.

Our highway system has expanded about as much as justified in many situations, even with rather favorable assumptions. There will be few new urban freeways built, few increases in parking requirements, few additional subsidies for petroleum producers, or automobile manufactures. It is unlikely that people want to spend even more time driving. We've been there, done that.

The author begins with the central point of his argument: That public transit, or transportation, is underfunded.

Litman lists the pitfalls of an automobile-dependent transportation system.

The author says that it is unlikely people want to spend more time driving. Is he correct in his assumption?

Further development of our transportation system requires giving consumers more choices by improving other modes, including transit, ridesharing, bicycling, walking, and telecommuting. None of these will individually "solve" our mobility problems, but each has a niche in an efficient transportation system.

Subsidizing transportation

Another criticism is that transit is overly subsidized, and as a result has become inefficient. But there are even larger subsidies of driving. Research by [the Victoria Transport Policy Institute] indicates that, in fact, automobile subsidies are about equal to transit subsidies when measured per passenger mile, but are far greater per user, since drivers tend to travel more than transit riders. A typical automobile user receives three to five times as much transportation subsidy overall than a typical transit user.

The difference is that transit subsidies are an explicit government expenditure, while most automobile subsidies are indirect. For example, zoning laws that require generous parking are economically little different than a property tax to build government-owned parking facilities. Similarly, failing to charge automobile users for costs they impose on society, including roadway expenditures, traffic congestion, accident risk imposed on others, and environmental impacts represent "hidden" subsidies. Because these subsidies are more difficult to measure, they tend to receive less scrutiny and criticism than tax expenditures. Yet they are equally distortive.

There is another important distortion that underprices driving. Most user costs of owning a car are fixed; vehicle owners must pay them regardless of how much they drive. Once paid, these fixed costs encourage consumers to drive, even when other travel modes are available.

These various types of underpricing lead to economically inefficient travel. In a recent study by our institute (Socially Optimal Transport Pricing and Markets), we estimate that an "optimal" transportation market, in which consumers had unbiased transportation choices, would result in 30–50 percent less driving, more use of alternative travel modes, and more efficient land use than what currently exists.

What does all this theory mean? It means that we must recognize that both driving and public transit can be efficient or inefficient, depending on conditions. Transport policy must strive to use each mode for what it does best. It means that we must make a solid business case for public transit, and plan public transit to be an effective component of our

"Telecommuting" means working from home. In 1999 there were thought to be 11.5 million telecommuters in the United States.

The crucial point of Litman's argument is that automobile users receive more subsidies than public-transit users.

Many countries are considering the introduction of charges for car drivers. Do you think they would discourage you from driving?

Asking rhetorical questions is often a good way to orient your argument.

A row of buses in Oakland, California, sits empty because of a bus drivers' strike. Disruption due to industrial action can be another reason for people not using public transportation.

transportation system. It also means that we must challenge biased policies and investment practices that inappropriately favor automobiles over transit.

Maximizing efficiency

There are many ways that public transit can become more effective and efficient at servicing communities, including better planning, more diversified and flexible service, public-private partnerships, and integration with other modes, to name a few important strategies. Transit is most efficient:

- providing mobility to non-drivers
- providing high-quality mobility along dense, congested corridors
- integrated with other modes
- with transit-supportive land use patterns
- when there are positive incentives to use transit when it is the best option

I would like to elaborate on this final point. Efficient transit requires more than just the right hardware. Transit service efficiency has as much to do with the incentives people face as with the operation of buses or trains. It is essential that people have a reason to use transit when it is most economically efficient from society's perspective. Transit agencies must work with employers to develop voucher and parking cash out programs. They must evaluate fare policies, payment systems, information, and marketing in terms of how users will respond. It is essential that transit agencies identify and remove barriers facing potential riders.

Do you think the kind of incentives Litman describes will encourage people to use public transportation?

As a mobility provider, rather than just a bus or train company, transit agencies should help develop transportation management associations, rideshare programs, commute trip reduction programs, parking management, pedestrian and bicycle friendly street environments, transportation efficient land use, and other TDM programs. Although these strategies require changes in the way we solve problems and organize institutions, they are worthwhile because they lead to a more efficient transportation system.

HOW TO "BUILD OUR WAY OUT OF CONGESTION"
Peter Samuel

Growing congestion on our cities' highways is being portrayed by government officials and transportation planners as inevitable. Plans for our major metro areas show projections for the year 2020, even after planned road improvements are made, in which average speeds on major arteries continue to decline, in rush hours that are extended to much of the working day.

For example in the Los Angeles area in its latest draft Regional Transportation Plan, the Southern California Association of Governments (SCAG) says that daily commute times will "double" by 2020 and what it calls "unbearable" present conditions on the freeways will become "even worse." At another point the plan says that "the future transportation system clearly will be overwhelmed." The report says that 3 percent of the current freeway network is "extremely congested" (by which they mean average speeds in the 10 to 16 mph range), but those kinds of conditions are expected to apply to 70 percent of the freeway network by 2020. Drivers currently spend 56 percent of their time in stop-and-go and are expected to spend 70 percent of their driving time like that in 2020. Some metro planning agencies are not quite as strong or candid in their language as those in Los Angeles, but a review of transportation plans around the nation's 30 or 40 largest cities will turn up similar predictions that traffic is going to get worse, many saying much worse. Almost none sees improvement.

Samuel presents a bleak picture of the growing congestion of U.S. highways. How might this help his argument?

The congestion lobby

Unfortunately, one school of thought positively favors defeatism about traffic congestion. They believe that the prospect of ever-worsening and insoluble congestion is the one way to break the "grip" of the automobile on the American consumer and to persuade people to carpool or take transit. Predictions of gloom and doom on the roads are seen by an associated pro-transit movement as the most powerful argument to get legislators to vote substantial tax monies to transit.

The author believes the protransit lobby uses pessimism about traffic congestion to get more subsidies. Do you think this works?

Most levels of government have programs in place to suppress single-occupant car usage in cities and to encourage carpooling with favored service (such as uncrowded High Occupant Vehicle [HOV] lanes and HOV bypass of ramp meters). Cities heavily subsidize transit trips and make large investments in transit infrastructure without any expectation of financial return on the investment. Growing congestion on the roads is seen by many planners as their most powerful tool to pry people from their cars and get them into the multiple-occupant vehicles that planners favor. Transit agencies and ride-share publicists advertise their modes as a hassle-free way to fly past the congestion of single-occupant vehicles on congested lanes.

So there is, in effect, a Congestion Lobby. But the major problem is the rigidity of the thinking and the institutional structures that govern urban transportation policies—the ineffectiveness of the Mobility Lobby, if we can call it that, in bringing together the smartest ideas, expounding them, and working to gain support for the reforms they suggest.

Transit cannot substitute the car

Many opponents of highway construction suggest that transit is a substitute for the private car, that somehow people can be gotten out of their cars and onto buses or rail. The sorry record of the past half century, in which some $340 billion of taxpayer money has been poured into capital and operating subsidies of transit, suggests otherwise. Transit does have certain niche markets. It works well, indeed is indispensable, for certain kinds of trips—for example for commuters' suburb-central business district (CBD) trips to and from work in the older centralized cities like New York, Chicago, Boston, Washington, Philadelphia, and San Francisco. In these kinds of trips the cost or scarcity of parking almost rules out the use of cars for daily commuting. People who aren't able, or can't afford, to drive their own car are another natural market for transit. The trips of CBD-commuters and nondrivers constitute the great bulk of transit users. Unfortunately for transit, these represent a small and declining minority of the urban transportation task.

> Do you regularly use transit for any kind of trip? What are the major reasons if you do not?

Almost everything is stacked against transit as a competitor with automobiles:

• Population growth is in cities without a tradition of transit (Los Angeles, Houston, San Antonio, Dallas, Miami, Phoenix, Seattle, Charlotte, Orlando) while the transit cities (New York City, Chicago, Boston, Philadelphia, Pittsburgh) have stable or declining populations;

- Commuting trips where transit can be competitive are in decline relative to trips for personal business, shopping, social occasions, spare time pursuits, etc, for which the car has overwhelming advantages;
- Central business districts are static or declining in jobs, with virtually all new jobs being in the suburbs, dispersing commuting destinations in a way that makes transit uncompetitive for the overwhelming majority of people whose trips form a spider web plan over any metro area;
- With both husband and wife working in most households, many trips are now "chained," combining the hauling of kids and shopping with the commute, which virtually rules out anything but the use of a car;
- Investments in fixed-rail transit are high-cost/high-risk and require major continuing subsidies which limit service and coverage, whereas improved highways in urban areas, while expensive in capital cost, are low-risk investments with low operating costs;
- About 70 percent of transit service—notably that provided by buses—uses roads and is harmed by congestion along with cars, indeed may be harmed more, given that car drivers are able to organize more creature comforts in their car than on a bus;

What would the author of the first article argue in reaction to this statement?

- Work hours, work patterns, and work locations are becoming more flexible and less predictable, again favoring the flexible, go-almost-anywhere-anytime mode, the car.

The last 20 years have seen enormous effort to engineer higher vehicle occupancy through encouragement of carpooling and use of vans and buses. Recognizing that the objective is to "move people not vehicles" in the slogan of carpooling, the federal government has increasingly turned its urban highway enhancement funds toward HOV (high occupancy vehicle) lanes. But there is no sign this focus has stemmed the shift to solo driving either. Forming, operating, and holding together a carpool is tough to manage and adds to travel time, and takes from the participants the flexibility of a solo-driver car, with its ability to leave whenever the driver is ready and to drive directly to the destination.

Carpooling

Alan E. Pisarski, a leading authority on commuting statistics, writes bluntly that real carpooling "died" in the 1980s, but he suggests that those associated with the death are in a state of denial. Almost 80 percent of carpool trips are now HOV-2 (driver plus one passenger), with HOV-3+ (three occupants or more) having almost halved during the past decade. Over half of carpoolers now seem to be family members, most of whom would drive together whether there were government high-occupancy policies or not. Only a minority are organized carpoolers—strangers gotten together by an organized trip matching system.

In your opinion is this negative opinion of carpooling justified?

Pisarski concludes his research project on commuting in America with the statement that the transportation policymakers' decades-long assault on the single-occupant car has been "dramatically ineffective." At best it has simply been pointless exhortation—a waste of breath and of money. At worst it has been inequitable and counterproductive to planning aims. It has hurt "those on the margin of the (financial) ability to own and operate a vehicle," writes Pisarski. And rather than use transit, people have reacted to congestion and higher car costs by seeking savings in housing by moving to locations on the outskirts, increasing commute distances, and exacerbating "urban sprawl."

In summary, transit and carpooling have a role in small niche markets such as serving dense central business districts, but they are simply not competitive across the board with the automobile and roads for most city travel. The problems of the roads have to be tackled on the roads.

Do you agree that the problems of the roads have to be tackled on the roads?

This shift to the car is not peculiar to the United States, as is sometimes claimed. The car has "a near monopoly in most west European countries" on growing suburb-to-suburb travel outside the dense city centers, according to European transportation expert Christian Gerondeau who adds:

This is not in the least surprising. Densities for this kind of trip are far too low to justify (transit).... Inhabitants of suburban areas often think that if suitable modes of public (transit) existed they would be sure to use them. But on taking a closer look it is found that the term 'suitable' has a very specific meaning.... They actually want a mode (of transit) that would pick them up at their doorstep, would drop them off right at their destination, at any time of day or night, without any waiting or transfers ... a car.

Given the double- and even triple-digit annual rates of growth of car ownership and major construction of toll motorways in the developing areas of major Asian and Latin American cities, the mode shift to the single-occupant car is a worldwide accompaniment of economic development and prosperity.

Summary

The article "Optimizing Public Transit Benefits" discusses the misconceptions associated with public transit. Increasing investment in public transportation will help drivers by reducing traffic and will also help people in need of transportation. Problems with highway congestion, accidents, and limited parking spaces are only going to increase in the future. Obviously the current system of building more highways is not working. Public transportation, carpooling, bicycling, and walking offer real solutions to these problems. Subsidies to public transit are comparable, or possibly less than, subsidies to driving. Public transit should be expanded so that riders have more choices for mobility. Public transportation therefore needs to be supported as part of the transportation system.

The second article, "How to 'Build Our Way Out of Congestion,'" asserts that attempts to increase carpooling and use of public transit have failed. The number of people carpooling has decreased, and public transportation has a limited market. People like their cars, and no matter how bad traffic gets, they are not going to give them up. Especially in today's society, with more people living in suburbs and parents having to run errands and drop children off, the car is a necessity rather than a luxury. Congestion is going to continue getting worse in the future as more people become able to drive. In order to improve mobility, improvements to highways and roads must be made, which means investing money in the road system rather than transit schemes. The convenience of the car for modern society cannot be matched by other modes of transportation, so people are going to continue to drive their cars.

FURTHER INFORMATION:

Books:

Mees, Paul, *A Very Public Solution: Transport in the Dispersed City*. Melbourne, Australia: Melbourne University Press, 2000.

Richmond, Jonathan, *The Private Provision of Public Transport*. Cambridge, MA: Harvard University Taubman Center for State and Local Government, 2001.

Useful websites:

www.publicpurpose.com/ut-ussby.htm
Lists of estimated public transportation subsidies in the U.S. since 1960.
www.abc.se/~m10183/eflwa03.htm
Article on why the public transportation system is losing out to private cars.
www.eltis.org/en/concept6.htm
Article on financing urban and regional public transit.

www.psrf.org/Cox1.htm
Wendell Cox article "Riders and Taxpayers Held Hostage."

The following debates in the Pro/Con series may also be of interest:

In this volume:

Topic 6 Should corporations pay the full environmental costs of producing their goods?

Topic 7 Can a "pay-to-pollute" system significantly reduce air pollution?

SHOULD GOVERNMENT ENCOURAGE THE USE OF PUBLIC TRANSPORTATION THROUGH SUBSIDIES?

YES: The anticar lobby uses negative predictions about traffic congestion to get subsidies awarded to public transportation

INVESTMENT
Would government subsidies be better invested in roads?

YES: The convenience of the car for modern society cannot be matched by public transportation

NO: Automobile users already receive three to five times as much transportation subsidy overall than transit users

NO: Problems with highway congestion, accidents, and limited parking are only going to increase

SHOULD GOVERNMENT ENCOURAGE THE USE OF PUBLIC TRANSPORTATION THROUGH SUBSIDIES?
KEY POINTS

YES: Almost everything is stacked against public transportation as a competitor with cars

YES: The shift to the automobile is a worldwide trend and a sign of economic prosperity

YES: Public transportation can be more attractive if it is better planned, more diversified, and offers a flexible service for users

YES: Users need extra incentives to use transportation that is more economically efficient from the perspective of society

AUTOMOBILE DEPENDENCY
Would an automobile-dependent transportation system work better?

ATTRACTING USERS
Can public transportation attract users?

NO: It leads to low-density land use patterns that are not only environmentally damaging, but economically inefficient

NO: There is a practical limit to the number of people automobiles can deliver to one place at one time

NO: People like their cars and will use them no matter how bad traffic gets

NO: Public transportation is irrelevant—only a small, declining percentage of people use it

201

YES

"CORPORATE SOCIAL RESPONSIBILITY: A GUIDE TO BETTER BUSINESS PRACTICES"
BUSINESS FOR SOCIAL RESPONSIBILITY EDUCATION FUND
S. VOIEN

NO

"THE NEW MEANING OF CORPORATE SOCIAL RESPONSIBILITY"
CALIFORNIA MANAGEMENT REVIEW, VOL. 40, NO. 2. WINTER 1998
ROBERT B. REICH

INTRODUCTION

The idea of doing well by doing good is gathering momentum in boardrooms around the globe. Current concerns associated with globalization and foreign trade are based on the belief that social and environmental standards are being compromised, or that investment decisions are insensitive to local needs. Since business corporations operate in an increasingly globalized world, the growing expectation is that their activities must benefit society in a variety of ways to which they may not be accustomed. Society expects companies to be more clear and open about how they operate, and the challenge is how will companies meet these expectations.

Corporate social responsibility (CSR) is the continuing commitment by business to behave ethically and contribute to economic development, while improving the quality of life of the workforce as well as of the local community and society at large.

As companies move forward to become more socially responsible, they must insure that shareholder value is maintained and at the same time identify what their increasing set of stakeholders expect. One fundamental principle is the understanding that business and society are mutually interdependent.

A recent World Business Council report suggested that for many companies managing CSR well is no longer seen as an extra cost or burden on hard-pressed management. More and more CSR is viewed not only as making good business sense, but also adding to the long-term prosperity of companies and, ultimately, their survival. Being a good neighbor and showing that you care, on the one hand, and being a successful business, on the other, are two sides of the same coin.

Several themes have emerged as the main tenets of the CSR movement around the globe. They include: human rights, employee rights, environmental protection, community involvement, supplier relations, reporting and disclosure, principles and codes, consumer education, product usage, stewardship, corruption, and full and open communication.

> *"Let's choose to unite the powers of markets with the authority of universal ideals. Let us choose to reconcile the creative forces of private entrepreneurship with the needs of the disadvantaged and the requirements of the future generations."*
> —UN GLOBAL COMPACT 2000

There is a significant question that needs to be asked, and that is what will the role of government be as corporations take a larger and larger responsibility for supporting social needs, especially in the area of human rights, environmental protection, and in community building. Critics of corporate social responsibility claim that corporations are only engaging in these areas to gain more power, control, and profit. They point to corporate campaign contributions and the expectation that the rules will be shaped to meet their specific business interests, which are often diametrically opposed to the will of the majority.

In the following articles the arguments are outlined for and against the responsibility that corporations have toward society and the environment.

In the article "Corporate Social Responsibility: A Guide to Better Business Practices" Voien argues that companies have a responsibility to society. The doing-well-by-doing-good model adds to the overall performance of the company on many fronts, not least in the area of long-term return on investment for shareholders.

Robert Reich, in his article "The New Meaning of Corporate Social Responsibility," reports that some advocates of social responsibility argue that what is good for the company shareholders over a long period of time is also good for its other stakeholders, for example, employees and the local community, over the long term.

Reich also investigates the paradox that at a time when society is asking corporations to be more socially responsible, it is also common to hear a groundswell of social advocates calling for the reigning in of corporations from engaging in the political process through their political donations. Thus for all practical purposes they are being asked to stay out of politics.

CORPORATE SOCIAL RESPONSIBILITY: A GUIDE TO BETTER BUSINESS PRACTICES
S. Voien

"Empirical studies" are those based on observation or experiment.

Over the past decade, a growing number of companies have recognized the business benefits of corporate social responsibility (CSR) policies and practices. Their experiences are bolstered by a growing body of empirical studies, which demonstrate that CSR has a positive impact on business economic performance, and is not harmful to shareholder value. Companies also have been encouraged to adopt or expand CSR efforts as the result of pressures from customers, suppliers, employees, communities, investors, activist organizations, and other stakeholders. As a result, CSR has grown dramatically in recent years, with companies of all sizes and sectors developing innovative strategies.

Defining CSR

It is important to clearly define any special terms for your audience.

While there is no single, commonly accepted definition of corporate social responsibility (CSR), it generally refers to business decision-making linked to ethical values, compliance with legal requirements, and respect for people, communities, and the environment. For the purposes of this report, CSR is defined as operating a business in a manner that meets or exceeds the ethical, legal, commercial, and public expectations that society has of business. Leadership companies see CSR as more than a collection of discrete practices or occasional gestures, or initiatives motivated by marketing, public relations, or other business benefits. Rather, it is viewed as a comprehensive set of policies, practices, and programs that are integrated throughout business operations, and decision-making processes that are supported and rewarded by top management.

The value of corporate social responsibility can be measured in a variety of ways, based on both quantitative and qualitative data. Companies have experienced a range of bottom-line benefits, including the following:

Improved financial performance

Business and investment communities have long debated whether there is a real connection between socially responsible business practices and positive financial performance. Several studies have shown such a correlation.

Reduced operating costs

Some CSR initiatives, particularly environmentally-oriented and workplace initiatives, can reduce costs dramatically by cutting waste and inefficiencies or improving productivity. For example, many initiatives aimed at reducing emissions of gases that contribute to global climate change also increase energy efficiency, reducing utility bills. Many recycling initiatives also cut waste-disposal costs and generate income by selling recycled materials. In the human resources arena, work-life programs that result in reduced absenteeism and increased retention of employees often save companies money through increased productivity and by a reduction in hiring and training costs.

Would it help Voien's case if he presented some specific examples of the initiatives he mentions?

Enhanced brand image and reputation

Customers often are drawn to brands and companies considered to have good reputations in CSR-related areas. A company considered socially responsible can benefit both from its enhanced reputation with the public, as well as its reputation within the business community, increasing a company's ability to attract capital and trading partners. For example, a 1997 study by two Boston College management professors found that excellent employee, customer, and community relations are more important than strong shareholder returns in earning corporations a place on *Fortune* magazine's annual "Most Admired Companies" list.

Increased sales and customer loyalty

A number of studies have suggested a large market for the products and services of companies perceived to be socially responsible. While businesses must first satisfy customers' key buying criteria—such as price, quality, appearance, taste, availability and, safety—studies also show a growing desire to buy based on other values-based criteria, such as "sweatshop-free" and child-labor-free clothing, smaller environmental impact, and absence of genetically-modified ingredients.

A 1999 landmark study revealed that:
- 90 percent of people surveyed want companies to focus on more than profitability;
- 60 percent of respondents said that they form an impression of a company based on its social responsibility (this can be defined as regard for people, communities, and the environment);

Would it be useful if Voien gave some background to the study he refers to? For example, why was it a "landmark" study?

On what grounds might you judge a company as not being socially responsible?

- 40 percent responded negatively to, or said they talked negatively about, companies that they perceived as not being socially responsible;
- 17 percent of respondents reported that they had actually avoided the products of companies they perceived as not being socially responsible.

Increased productivity and quality

Company efforts that result in improved working conditions, lesser environmental impact, or greater employee involvement in decision-making often lead to increased productivity and reduced error rate. For example, companies that improve working conditions and labor practices among their offshore suppliers often experience a decrease in defective or unusable merchandise.

Ability to attract and retain employees

Companies perceived to have strong CSR commitments often find it easier to recruit employees, particularly in tight labor markets. Retention levels may be higher, too, resulting in a reduction in turnover and associated recruitment and training costs. Tight labor markets—as well as the trend toward multiple jobs for shorter periods of time—are challenging companies to develop ways to generate a return on the considerable resources invested in recruiting, hiring, and training talent.

Reduced regulatory oversight

Can you think of any other ways government can encourage socially responsible behavior among corporations?

Companies that demonstrate they are engaging in practices that satisfy and go beyond regulatory compliance requirements are being given less scrutiny and more free reign by both national and local government entities. In the U.S., for example, federal and state agencies overseeing environmental and workplace regulations have formal programs that recognize and reward companies that have taken proactive measures to reduce adverse environmental, health, and safety impacts.

Access to capital

Are the figures Voien quotes useful in making his point? Always use statistics judiciously.

In the U.S. in 1999, there was more than $2 trillion in assets under management in portfolios that use screens linked to ethics, the environment, and corporate social responsibility. The figure has grown from $639 billion in 1995, to $1.185 trillion in 1997, to $2.16 trillion in 1999. The 1999 portfolio amount accounts for nearly 13 percent of the $16.3 trillion in investment assets under professional management in the U.S.

Given these numbers, it is clear that companies addressing ethical, social, and environmental responsibilities have access to capital that might not otherwise have been available.

A growing concern

The growth of corporate social responsibility as an issue in modern society stems from a wide range of events and trends. Recent years have seen a growth in the breadth of topics considered under the "corporate social responsibility" umbrella. Included among these are corporate governance issues, such as how boards of directors are chosen and compensated; religious freedom in the workplace; "cyber ethics" issues of access to and privacy linked to information technology, both for consumers and employees; consumer concern over the use of genetically modified organisms in agriculture; and the new demands brought about by the increased interest in environmental sustainability.

Voien's case is not based on points about principles. It is more effective and practical in an argument about business to use business criteria—in this case, financial success.

THE NEW MEANING OF CORPORATE SOCIAL RESPONSIBILITY
Robert B. Reich

NO

See the first paragraph opposite for a definition of the stakeholders Reich refers to.

"Corporate social responsibility" is hardly a new refrain, but it now comes at an awkward moment. To an ever-larger extent, it seems, corporations are being called upon to respond to the needs of "stakeholders" other than investors.

Yet this renewed interest in corporate social responsibility comes, ironically, at a time when investors—many of them large institutions with the capacity and will to topple underperforming CEOs—are escalating their demand that corporations maximize shareholder returns. The movement for better and more responsive "corporate governance" seeks to ensure that managers act in the best interests of their shareholders. Compensation of top corporate officers is more tightly linked to share prices than ever before. The steady improvement in corporate profitability over the last few years is due, at least in part, to restructurings that have resulted either in layoffs or in diminished wages and benefits.

Are layoffs and poorer work conditions worth the price of corporate profitability?

The nation is now far more competitive—and, arguably, far more productive—than it was in the 1980s. This allows our society to achieve a whole range of social objectives that it otherwise could not achieve. Moreover, many companies have taken an active role in improving their communities and have given their employees a share in their new-found prosperity.

A question of responsibility

Asking a central question can crystallize the argument. Reich asks if corporate social responsibility is compatible with investors' demands for profitability.

The issue here is not whether companies should be responsible in some way to society, but rather how they should be responsible: Is there a new meaning for corporate social responsibility, consistent both with the greater need for corporate responsiveness to employees and communities and with the greater demands from investors for performance?

One way to begin is with the now conventional proposition that a company has only one responsibility, both morally and legally: to maximize the value of the shares of those who have invested in it. Corporate board members and executives are "fiduciaries" under the law—agents solely of those who have invested capital in the corporation. But in fulfilling their responsibility to their investors, according to this view, boards and executives also indirectly fulfill their core responsibility to the rest of society—to other "stakeholders" such as their employees, members of their community, and fellow citizens—because they help assure that society's productive assets are allocated to their most efficient uses.

Most companies are concerned about their public images because they sell their products directly or indirectly to the public; indeed, companies spend billions of dollars each year burnishing their public images. Anything that tarnishes that image may result in lost sales, and also may make it more difficult for the company to receive permits, subsidies, or other discretionary benefits from government.

Common interests

Some advocates of corporate "social responsibility" take a somewhat different tack. They argue that what's good for the company's shareholders over the long term is also good for its other stakeholders over the long term (and, presumably, what's bad for these broader interests is also bad for shareholders, eventually). That is, if one looks far enough in the future, all interests converge; all stakeholders are ultimately the same. All have an interest in a strong economy, well-paid employees, a healthy and clean environment, and a socially tranquil society.

Reich approaches the issue of CSR from the position of his opponent. This is a useful debating strategy.

Yet, the "long-term" argument doesn't offer much more practical guidance than does the calculus over public opinion. The criterion is simply too broad and ill-defined. Long-term profit-maximization could be made to seem compatible with almost any socially worthwhile thing—and incompatible with almost anything deemed socially questionable—for the simple reason that corporations are social creations whose very existence depends on the willingness of societies to endure and support them. On the other hand, profit-maximization also enhances growth and allocative efficiency, which over the long term make it possible for a society to achieve all sorts of social objectives.

Do you agree with Reich's view of what shareholders care about?

There's no reason to assume that any single company's investors would willingly forego returns for the sake of achieving some articulated social purpose. It's the classic free rider problem: Let the other guys take the responsibility, we're taking our profits.

Corporations are, after all, creations of law; they do not exist in a state of nature. Corporate officials are bound to two broad sets of laws, neither of which has greater moral or legal claim than the other. The first, embracing securities and

COMMENTARY: Nike and the labor issue

Since the late 1990s Nike, the world's leading sportswear producer, has been repeatedly criticized for its alleged abuse of workers, many of them young women and children, at the company's factories in Asia. After CBS News ran a program about Nike workers in Vietnam, the U.S.-based organization Vietnam Labor Watch (VLW) visited the factories at Nike's invitation in 1997.

A young worker embroiders the Nike logo on clothing at a factory in Laos, a country whose low wages and willing workforce attract manufacturers such as Nike.

The VLW reported that workers were not making a living wage, earning an average 20 cents per hour, or $1.60 a day. It was common for workers to faint from exhaustion, heat, fumes, and hunger during their shifts. Verbal abuse and sexual harassment were said to be frequent, and corporal punishment was often used. The VLW visited other non-Nike shoe factories in Vietnam, where working conditions were better and wages higher.

Many Nike factories are actually run by subcontractors. For example, in China the factories are operated by subcontractors from Korea or Taiwan. But does this make Nike any less responsible for the conditions under which their goods are produced?

If a corporation squeezes a subcontractor on price or timetable to produce a product, the subcontractor will inevitably squeeze the workers. Supporters argue that Nike is raising the standard of living and bringing many jobs to poor countries. In much of the underdeveloped world it is normal to view children as economic assets, and the economies of these countries could not sustain young people not bringing in an income. Even the UN opposes an outright ban on child labor.

Nike has responded to criticisms by denying the charges and suggesting that the reports were based on anecdotal evidence. However, in 1998 it announced that it would raise the minimum ages for workers in its Asian plants and improve working conditions. But the world's largest manufacturer of athletic sportswear, which has not made shoes in the U.S. since 1984, has no plans to abandon production in developing countries.

corporate law, requires that they place the interests of their shareholders above all others. The second, comprising all other laws and regulations—labor, the environment, and so on—establishes a boundary around the first set of obligations. Board members and executives must place the interests of shareholders above all other interests except as limited by all other laws and regulations. The two sets of laws—the first, establishing their fiduciary responsibility to investors, the second, their responsibility to other stakeholders in the rest of society—form an integrated system of corporate societal responsibility.

Refraining from politics

All political activities are questionable, because the latitude given corporations to pursue investor interests within the first set of laws implies a forbearance from pursuing them within the second. Companies have no independent moral or legal authority to use their resources to influence the creation of laws defining their responsibilities to stakeholders other than investors. Society has ceded to them only the responsibility for maximizing investor returns, on the premise that in doing so they will spur growth and improve allocative efficiency. Society has not ceded to the corporation the responsibility to advance or protect other social interests. The meta-social responsibility of the corporation, is to respect the political process by staying out of it.

Reich argues that if corporations try to influence social politics, that is nondemocratic.

It is not possible to have it both ways. Corporations cannot simultaneously claim, as a matter of public morality and public policy, that their only legitimate societal mission is to maximize shareholder returns, while at the same time actively seek to influence social policies intended to achieve all the other things a society may wish to do. It must respect the boundary between the two different sets of laws—the one governing its fiduciary responsibilities, the other reflecting political judgments about its social responsibilities.

The paradox of our time, of course, is that the opposite is occurring. Even as institutional investors impose ever-greater pressure on management to maximize returns, causing corporations to loudly eschew broader social responsibilities, corporations are becoming more openly and aggressively involved in the making of social policy. Unless stakeholders other than shareholders are allowed full expression within the political process, public pressure will grow to have these interests expressed within the system of corporate governance. Corporations must forbear from politics, or they are sure to invite the politicization of the corporation.

Would it strengthen Reich's argument if he suggested how it might be possible to prevent the politicization of corporations?

Summary

The question "Should corporations be socially responsible?" goes to the heart of debates and demonstrations that occur around the globe when world leaders and corporate chiefs meet to discuss the world economy, trade, and globalization. The issue is about how power is shared in the democratic process, and who has responsibility for the quality of life for all.

A recent millennium survey by Environics International found that only 11 percent of Americans think companies should focus only on making a profit, paying taxes, employing people, and obeying all laws. Three times as many (35 percent) think they should also work to exceed lawful requirements, set higher standards, and help build a better society for all. Most Americans (53 percent) think companies should operate somewhere between these points of view. Citizens of only two other countries (Australia and Canada) take a more aggressive stance on this issue.

Voien argues that corporations need to be involved in supporting society's needs, and by doing so the company will improve, the return to shareholders will improve, and society will benefit. This vision is similar to the New Deal program that President Franklin Roosevelt presented to the government in the 1930s, only then corporations were not given a central role.

Reich, however, argues that if you give corporations a central role in providing for society's needs, then they will also play a large role in the politics of society. We see this happening increasingly today, and many people do not like it. The real question is if we build an expectation that corporations will be socially responsible for their employees, their communities, and the natural world, then should they not be able to take an active role in the discourse over these issues that is the political process? So, how can we exclude them from contributing to and trying to shape that process?

FURTHER INFORMATION:

Books:

Schwartz, Peter, *When Good Companies Do Bad Things: Responsibility and Risk in an Age of Globalization.* New York: John Wiley & Sons, 1999.

Useful websites:

www.bsr.org
The Business Responsibility Resource Center, a worldwide information resource on corporate responsibility.
www.ziplink.net/~mikegree/career/social.htm
Article on CSR by Michael H. Green.
www.free-market.net/features/spotlight/9708.html
Article on CSR from *Policy Spotlight*, 1997.

www.humanrights.about.com
A website that monitors corporate activity throughout the world.

> **The following debates in the Pro/Con series may also be of interest:**
>
> In this volume:
>
> 🌱 Topic 10 Do corporations have a moral responsibility to nature?

SHOULD CORPORATIONS BE SOCIALLY RESPONSIBLE?

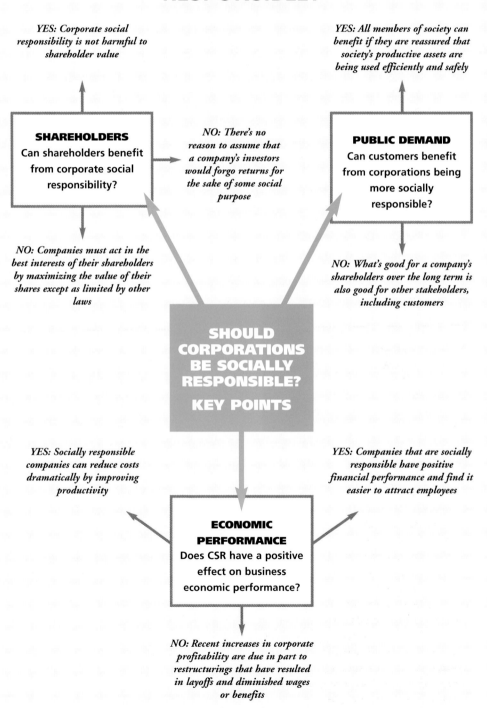

YES: Corporate social responsibility is not harmful to shareholder value

YES: All members of society can benefit if they are reassured that society's productive assets are being used efficiently and safely

SHAREHOLDERS
Can shareholders benefit from corporate social responsibility?

NO: There's no reason to assume that a company's investors would forgo returns for the sake of some social purpose

PUBLIC DEMAND
Can customers benefit from corporations being more socially responsible?

NO: Companies must act in the best interests of their shareholders by maximizing the value of their shares except as limited by other laws

NO: What's good for a company's shareholders over the long term is also good for other stakeholders, including customers

SHOULD CORPORATIONS BE SOCIALLY RESPONSIBLE?
KEY POINTS

YES: Socially responsible companies can reduce costs dramatically by improving productivity

YES: Companies that are socially responsible have positive financial performance and find it easier to attract employees

ECONOMIC PERFORMANCE
Does CSR have a positive effect on business economic performance?

NO: Recent increases in corporate profitability are due in part to restructurings that have resulted in layoffs and diminished wages or benefits

GLOSSARY

acid rain a term for rain containing sulfuric and nitric acids that damage plant life. It is believed to be caused when water in the atmosphere mixes with the fumes from, among other things, car exhausts and coal burning. *See also* pollution.

agribusiness the practice of intensive, large-scale commercial farming.

biodegradable a word that describes any material that can be broken down by living things, such as bacteria.

biotechnology the branch of science that makes use of the properties of living things to create products such as antibiotics or to carry out processes like sewage treatment.

carbon sink a feature of the landscape, such as a forest, which absorbs carbon, removing it from the atmosphere.

carbon trading a system that would allow countries or companies producing more than their permitted levels of carbon to buy quotas from countries or companies producing less than their permitted levels.

carcinogenic a term describing a substance that can cause cancer.

chlorofluorocarbons (CFCs) gases containing chlorine, fluorine, and carbon that were once widely used as aerosol propellants and dry-cleaning solvents, among other things. CFCs damage the ozone layer.

climate change a term for fluctuations in weather patterns that may be associated with increased levels of gases such as carbon dioxide in the atmosphere.

clone an individual animal or plant produced by genetic engineering that has exactly the same genetic code as its parent.

cloning a term for the production of clones. In the most advanced form of cloning scientists remove the nucleus of an adult cell taken from the animal or plant to be cloned and then substitute it with another nucleus from a different organism. Also known as genetic replication.

deforestation the process of clearing an area of trees, usually to enable agriculture or some other form of land use to take place.

developed country any one of the world's industrialized, wealthier countries, for example, Britain, Japan, or the U.S.

developing country any one of a range of countries that are primarily agricultural or partly industrialized or rely on a single product, such as oil. Most but not all are poor. Examples include Ethiopia and India.

DNA deoxyribonucleic acid; the acid located in the cell nucleus of an organism that is the molecular basis of heredity. The double-helix structure of DNA was discovered by a team of scientists in 1953.

Earth Summit a major meeting of world leaders held in Rio de Janeiro, Brazil, in 1992 to discuss ways of increasing wealth while also protecting the environment.

ecosystem a community of animals and plants, and their interrelated physical and chemical environment.

endangered species a type of plant or animal under serious threat of becoming extinct.

environmental impact assessment a study that analyzes how much environmental damage a planned project—building a new highway, for example—would cause.

Environmental Protection Agency (EPA) a U.S. government agency set up in 1970 that draws up and enforces national guidelines to limit the levels of harmful materials entering the environment.

evolution an ongoing process by which living things develop over generations into new forms to suit their environment.

extinction the disappearance of an entire type of plant or animal from Earth.

food chain a term for a group of interdependent animals and plants that live in the same habitat, in which each member is linked to the next by being its source of food. Also known as a food web.

fossil fuel a type of fuel derived from the mineral remains of once-living things, such as coal, oil, or gasoline.

genetic engineering the technique of modifying the basic building blocks (the genes) of a living thing to change or enhance its characteristics, for example, to produce vegetables with more flavor.

global warming a term for the gradual rise in temperatures around the world associated with higher levels of gases such as carbon dioxide in the atmosphere.

globalization the expansion worldwide of private corporations and of the culture of the countries they come from.

greenhouse effect the phenomenon in which the release of carbon dioxide and other gases caused by human activity traps the Sun's heat in the atmosphere, resulting in a rise in global temperatures.

gross national product (GNP) the total value of all goods produced and services provided by a country during one year, expressed as a cash figure.

habitat the type of place in which a plant or animal naturally lives.

ice age a term for any period in Earth's history during which much of the planet was covered with ice.

Industrial Revolution the rapid process of industrialization that started in Britain in the late 18th century and spread to western Europe and the U.S.

International Conference on Population and Development (ICPD) 1994 a major meeting organized by the United Nations (UN) and held in Cairo, Egypt, in 1994. It discussed issues connected with world population, and ways of increasing countries' wealth.

Kyoto Protocol an agreement drawn up at the 1997 Climate Change Conference in Kyoto, Japan. Under the protocol 39 industrialized nations were to reduce their production of gases such as carbon dioxide to an average of 5.2 percent (7 percent in the U.S.) below 1990 levels by 2012.

landfill the technique of burying garbage in pits as a means both of waste disposal and of filling in excavations.

nuclear fission a type of nuclear reaction in which a particle of nuclear fuel—uranium, for example—splits in two, releasing energy that can then be used to make electricity.

organic farming a method of agriculture that relies on animal or vegetable feeds and fertilizers and rejects the use of artificial growth aids and pest-control agents.

ozone layer a layer in Earth's atmosphere containing high levels of the gas ozone (O_3). It shields the planet's surface from much of the Sun's harmful radiation.

pesticide any agent that destroys insects or other forms of life that are harmful to crops or farm animals.

pollution a collective term for substances released by humans into the environment that are harmful to life found there. See also acid rain.

radioactive a word that describes material that gives off a type of energy—alpha and beta particles and gamma rays—that is dangerous to humans.

recycling the technique of processing used materials—for example, waste paper or empty bottles—so that they can be reused.

renewable energy a term for energy harnessed from sources that are not used up in the process, for example, wind, water, and solar power.

renewable resources materials that can be replaced by natural regeneration, for example, lumber from managed forests.

smog a haze caused by the concentration of car exhaust fumes or coal pollution in the air under certain atmospheric conditions. See also pollution.

sustainable development the process of increasing wealth around the world in a manner that does not outstrip the supply of natural resources.

urbanization the process of towns and cities expanding into the countryside.

Acknowledgments

Topic 1 Does Global Warming Threaten Humankind?

Yes: "Is Global Warming Harmful to Health"? by Tom Jackson. Copyright © 2001 by Tom Jackson. Used by permission. No: From "Warmer Days and Longer Lives" by Thomas Gale Moore, *World Climate Report*, Vol. 2, No. 4, October 28, 1996, published by Hoover Institution. Copyright © 1996 by Thomas Gale Moore. Used by permission.

Topic 2 Should the Human Population Be Stabilized?

Yes: From "A Special Moment in History" by Bill McKibben, *The Atlantic Monthly*, Vol. 281, No. 5, May 1998. Copyright © 1998 by Bill McKibben. Used by permission. No: From "The Fallacies and Hazards of Population 'Control'" by Rod N. Andreason, *Brigham Young University Law Review*, 1999. Copyright © 1999 by Brigham Young University Law Review, Provo, Wisconsin. Used by permission.

Topic 3 Are Famine and Hunger Avoidable?

Yes: From "Twelve Myths about Hunger." Copyright © 1999 by Share International (Jan.–Feb. 1999). Used by permission of Share International magazine, PO Box 971, N. Hollywood, CA 91603, United States (www.shareintl.org). No: From "Facing Reality at the World Food Summit" by Lester Brown. Copyright © 2000 by Worldwatch Institute (www.worldwatch.org). Used by permission.

Topic 4 Is Organic Food Better than Other Food?

Yes: From "Why Americans are Turning to Organic Foods" by Ronnie Cummins, Organic Consumers Association, 2000. Used by permission. No: From "The Folly of Organic Farming" by Dennis Avery, *Chemistry and Industry*, Issue 24, 1997. Copyright © 1997 by Chemistry and Industry. Reproduced with permission.

Topic 5 Do National Parks Preserve Wilderness?

Yes: "National Parks and Wilderness" by John C. Miles. Copyright © 2001 by John C. Miles. Used by permission. No: "Limits of National Park Protection of Wilderness" by Nathan Page. Copyright © 2001 by Nathan Page. Used by permission.

Topic 6 Should Corporations Pay the Full Environmental Costs of Producing Their Goods?

Yes: From "Justice and Financial Market Allocation of the Social Costs of Business" by Sandra L. Christensen and Brian Grinder, *Journal of Business Ethics*, Vol. 29, Issue 1/2, January 2001. Copyright © 2001 by Kluwer Academic Publishers, Dordrecht, The Netherlands. Used by kind permission of Kluwer Academic Publishers. No: From "A Consumer's Guide to Environmental Myths and Realities" by Lynn Scarlett, Reason Foundation, National Center for Policy Analysis, Policy Report No. 165, September 1991. Used by permission.

Topic 7 Can a "Pay-to-Pollute" System Significantly Reduce Air Pollution?

Yes: From "Greenhouse Gas Reduction Has Become a Seller's Market" by Dennis Blank. Copyright © 2001 by E/The Environment Magazine. Reprinted with permission of E/The Environmental Magazine (www.emagazine.com), Subscription Department (Subscriptions are $20/year): P.O. Box 2047, Marion, OH, 43306, USA. (815) 734-1212. No: Excerpt from "Smoke and Mirrors: Will Global Pollution Trading Save the Climate or Promote Injustice and Fraud"? by Michael Belliveau. Copyright © 1998 by Michael Belliveau and CorpWatch (www.corpwatch.org). Used by permission.

Topic 8 Can Wind and Solar Resources Meet Our Energy Needs?

Yes: "Can the World Meet Future Energy Needs Using Wind and Solar Energy" by J. Richard Mayer. Copyright © 2001 by J. Richard Mayer. Used by permission. No: From "Renewable Energy—Why Renewable Energy Is Not Cheap and Not Green" by Robert L. Bradley, Jr. Copyright © by National Center for Policy Analysis., Dallas, TX. Used by permission.

Topic 9 Will Hydrogen Replace Oil as Our Primary Energy Source?

Yes: From "Hydrogen: The Fuel for the Future," U.S. Department of Energy Hydrogen Program, 1995. Courtesy of the U.S. Department of Energy. No: From "Fueling the Cells" by Paul Sharke. Article courtesy of *Mechanical Engineering* magazine, Vol. 121/No. 12, December, 1999, pages 46–49; copyright © *Mechanical Engineering* (the American Society of Mechanical Engineers International). Used by permission.

Topic 10 Do Corporations Have a Moral Responsibility to Nature?

Yes: From "A Road Map for Natural Capitalism" by Amory B. Lovins, L. Hunter Lovins, and Paul Hawken in *Harvard Business Review*, May–June, 1999. Copyright © 1999 by the Harvard Business School Publishing Corporation; all rights reserved. Reprinted by permission.

No: From "Bringing the Environment Down to Earth" by Forest L. Reinhardt in *Harvard Business Review*, July-August, 1999. Copyright © 1999 by the Harvard Business School Publishing Corporation; all rights reserved. Reprinted by permission.

Topic 11 Do the Benefits of Nuclear Power Outweigh the Risks?

Yes: From "The Nuclear Power Advantage" by Bernard L. Cohen. Copyright © by Bernard L. Cohen. Used by permission.

No: From "Statement of Linda Gunter" by Linda Gunter, Communications Director, Safe Energy Communication Council. Copyright © 2001 by Safe Energy Communication Council. Used by permission.

Topic 12 Is Genetically Modified Food Safe Enough to Feed the World's Population?

Yes: This essay by Alan McHugen is from "Biotechnology and Food," a publication of the American Council of Science and Health, 1995 Broadway. 2nd Floor, New York, NY 10023-5800. It is reprinted with permission. To learn more about ACSH, visit ACSH online at www.acsh.org.

No: Excerpted from "Biotechnology and the Environment" by José Sarukhán, "Biotechnology: The Science and the Impact." Copyright © 2000 by *The Journal of Biolaw & Business* (www.biolawbusiness.com) Special Supplement, January 2000. Used by permission. For educational use only.

Topic 13 Are Zoos Morally Wrong?

Yes: From "Against Zoos" by Dale Jamieson, originally published in *Defense of Animals*, edited by P. Singer. Copyright © 1985 by Basil Blackwell, Oxford, UK. Used by permission.

No: From *Zoos and Animal Rights* by Stephen St. C. Bostock, Routledge Inc., New York. Copyright © 1993 by International Thomson Publishing Services. Used by permission.

Topic 14 Should Endangered Species Be Cloned?

Yes: "Reproducing the Ark" by Ben Hoare. Copyright © 2001 by Ben Hoare. Used by permission.

No: From "Noah's New Ark" by Maryann Bird, *Time* magazine. Copyright © 2001 by Time Inc. Reprinted by permission.

Topic 15 Should Government Encourage the Use of Public Transportation through Subsidies?

Yes: From "Optimizing Public Transit Benefits" by Todd Litman, Texas Transportation Planning Conference. Copyright © 1998 by Todd Litman. Used by permission.

No: From "How to 'Build our Way Out of Congestion'" by Peter Samuel. Reprinted with permission from Reason Public Policy Institute Study No. 250. Copyright © 2001 by Reason Foundation, 3415 S. Sepulveda Blvd, Suite 400, Los Angeles, CA 90034 (www.rppi.org).

Topic 16 Should Corporations Be Socially Responsible?

Yes: From "Corporate Social Responsibility: A Guide to Better Business Practices" by Steve Voien. Copyright © 2000 by Business for Social Responsibility (www.bsr.org/resourcecenter). Used by permission.

No: "The New Meaning of Corporate Social Responsibility" by Robert B. Reich. Copyright © 1998 by The Regents of the University of California. Reprinted from the *California Management Review*, Vol. 40, No. 2. Used by permission of The Regents.

Brown Partworks Limited has made every effort to contact and acknowledge the creators and copyright holders of all extracts reproduced in this volume. We apologize for any omissions. Any person who wishes to be credited in further volumes should contact Brown Partworks Limited in writing: Brown Partworks Limited, 8 Chapel Place, Rivington Street, London EC2A 3DQ, U.K.

Picture credits

Cover: Corbis; **Bruce Coleman Collection:** 66, 78; **Corbis:** Richard Cummins 160–161; Robert Holmes 49; Kevin Schafer 170; Ted Streshinsky 194; Ed Young 53; **Image Bank:** G & M David de Lossy 186–187; **NASA:** 70–71; **PA Photos:** Ben Curtis 156; EPA 26, 42, 132, 210; Roslin Institute 178; **Still Pictures:** Cyril Ruoso-Bios 14; Jorgen Schytte 102

SET INDEX

self-censorship **6**:129-30, 136
Chemical Manufacturers Association (CMA) **4**:132
Chernobyl **4**:137, 144
Child Online Protection Act (COPA; 1999) **6**:23
children
 advertising to **6**:86-87, 100-111
 gene manipulation in **5**:37, 38-39, 47
 right to medical care **5**:149
 see also cloning, human
Children's Internet Protection Act (2001) **6**:154-55
Children's Television Act (1990) **6**:102-3
Chile, privatization in **3**:43, 45
chimpanzees **4**:166-67
China
 communism **3**:8, 34, 35, 103
 economy **3**:168, 169
 and globalization **3**:188-89
 grain requirements **4**:41
 population control **4**:28, 30
 poverty **1**:11
Christian Scientists **5**:138-39, 140-47, 148
civic virtue **2**:76, 77
Civil Liberties Act (1988) **1**:177
civil rights **1**:23, 34-35
Civil Rights Acts **1**:84, 184; **6**:159
 of gay people **1**:71
 and obeying unjust laws **1**:98-99, 100-111
 and violent protest **1**:127, 128-31
 see also apartheid; protest; segregation
Clark, Tamara **5**:202
climate
 and food insecurity **4**:35
 see also global warming
Clinton, Bill **2**:62, 111, 188, 200-201, 203, 204-11; **6**:25
 and affirmative action **1**:85
 and the death penalty **1**:175
 and drug prices **5**:77
 and the environment **4**:25, 99
 and market economies **3**:27
 and the minimum wage **3**:91
 and social benefits **1**:18
 and the welfare system **3**:79
Clinton, Chelsea **6**:25, 26-28, 34
Clinton, Hillary **2**:*210*; **3**:67
cloning
 endangered species **4**:174-85; **5**:165, 170-72, 174
 human **5**:9, 22-33, 35
coal **4**:139
Cohen, Kissandra **5**:40
commercialization **3**:39
Communications Decency Act (CDA; 1996) **6**:161, 167
communism **3**:8, 34-35, 103
 see also socialism
companies *see* corporations/companies
competition
 free-market **3**:13-14, 21
 nonprice **3**:201
 perfect **3**:200-201

privatization and **3**:47
composting **4**:82-83
computers *see* information technology; Internet
Comstock Law **6**:16
Congress of Racial Equality (CORE) **1**:129
Congress, U.S. **2**:60, 79, 93
 and bureaucracy **2**:69, 71
 and the constitution **2**:118-19
 and executive privilege **2**:191, 192, 193, 194-96
Constitution, U.S. **2**:9, 10, 18, 36, 52-53, 130
 changing **2**:100
 and executive power **2**:174
 Framers **2**:46-47, 49, 52, 53, 54, 60, 76-77, 98, 167-68, 170, 190-91
 and government **2**:60, 74-75, 77, 98-99
 and impeachment/indictment of the president **2**:206, 207, 212
 see also Hamilton, Alexander; Madison, James, various amendments, e.g.: First Amendment
consumers
 awareness **3**:170
 environmental responsibility **4**:80-83, 84, 125
 and the Internet **6**:174-75
 protection **3**:171, 172-83
contracting out **3**:39
COP-3 **4**:90
copyright **6**:188-89
 and Napster **6**:178-87
corporate social responsibility (CSR) **4**:202-13
corporations/companies
 ethics **3**:171, 184-95
 and federal sentencing guidelines **3**:192
 monopolies and trusts **3**:172
 multinational **3**:196-97
 new economy firms **3**:48-49
 and patents **3**:21
 responsibility to nature **4**:124-35
 should be socially responsible? **4**:202-13
 should pay environmental costs? **4**:73, 74-85
cost-benefit analysis, environmental **4**:72
costs, production and selling **3**:201-2
"creative destruction" **3**:25
criminal justice, and racism **1**:33
critical thinking **5**:60-61
crops **5**:166-67
cryopreservation **4**:177
culture, globalization **3**:118; **6**:153, 166-77
cystic fibrosis **5**:37, 42-45

D

Darwinism, Social **3**:102-3

death
 televised **5**:137; **6**:29, 34
 see also euthanasia
death penalty **1**:162-75
debate **1**:112-13
debt, Third World **1**:11, 179-81; **3**:117, 152, 156-67; **4**:38, 39
 debt-for-equity swaps **3**:43-44
 territory-for-debt swaps **3**:163-65
democracy **2**:39, 46
 at odds with capitalism? **2**:9, 34-45
 and ballot initiatives **2**:123, 124, 125, 126
 direct **2**:10, 77, 124, 132
 and direct popular elections **2**:166-67, 171
 direct rule of the people v. representative democracy **2**:8-9, 10-21
 and equality **2**:9, 22-33
 globalization and **3**:125-26, 127, 128, 129
 is the U.S. truly democratic? **2**:46-57
 liberal **2**:126
 and political finance **2**:138-39
 procedural **2**:50-51
Democratic Party **2**:91, 93, 136, 145
Department of Agriculture, U.S. **4**:47, 49
Department of Energy, U.S. **4**:106, 113
deregulation **3**:106
desegregation **1**:23
developing countries/Third World
 antidumping actions **3**:136
 debt **3**:43-44, 117, 156-67
 drugs prices **5**:76-77
 energy demands **4**:100
 ethical corporate behavior in **3**:170, 185, 189, 197; **4**:210
 famine and hunger **4**:36-39
 and globalization **3**:129
 global warming and **4**:13
 political economies **3**:19
 poverty **1**:10-11
 WTO and **3**:144-55
Diana, Princess of Wales **6**:24-25, 76
Digital Library Initiative (DLI) **6**:206
disability **5**:47
discrimination **1**:8-9, 83
 economic **1**:75-77
 against homosexuals **1**:59
 linguistic **1**:9, 94
 positive *see* affirmative action
 racial *see* racism
 reverse **1**:81
 and violent protest **1**:137
 against women **1**:9, 47
diseases
 and cloning **4**:178
 and global warming **4**:10-11, 12, 13-15
 hereditary
 and gene manipulation **5**:42-45, 46, 47
 genetic testing for **5**:54
DNA **5**:8, *14*, 19, 34, 54